WITHDRAWN

W9-ABL-168

THE LIBRARY

OF

WALTER T. NAU

This book is from the Walter Theodore Nau Library
Given to the Carl A. Rudisill Library
Lenoir-Rhyne College, Hickory, NC
In memory of
**_The Reverend Dr. Henry and
Mrs. Helen Hempfling Nau_**
missionaries of the Lutheran
Church to India, Africa.
By
The Reverend Dr. Walter T. Nau.
Professor of French & German
B.A. of Theology (Concordia Seminary 1930)
Ph.D. (Duke University 1947)
Secretary of Faculty
Honorary Honors Committee
Chief College Marshall

Hickory, NC
March 5, 1996 (Birthday of the Donor).

WITHDRAWN

Voltaire: Man of Justice

Courtesy of New York Public Library

F. D' Arouet Voltaire

Voltaire:
MAN OF JUSTICE

By ADOLPH MEYER

CARL A. RUDISILL LIBRARY
LENOIR-RHYNE COLLEGE

HOWELL, SOSKIN, PUBLISHERS

COPYRIGHT, 1945, BY ADOLPH MEYER

ALL RIGHTS RESERVED

Manufactured Entirely In The United States

PQ
2099
.M45
1945
C 2

Dec. 1997

CARL A. RUDISILL LIBRARY
LENOIR-RHYNE COLLEGE

To the memory of Irving Gottlieb
First Lieutenant USAAF
missing in action December 29, 1943,
this book is humbly dedicated

TABLE OF CONTENTS

Early Youth

O N A SUNDAY, the 21st of November, 1694, a son was born to the wife of a Parisian notary, François Arouet. The mother's name was Marguerite. On the next day the infant was taken to the church of St. André-des-Arcs where he was enrolled as a Christian and given the name of François-Marie. In time the world was to know him as Voltaire.

The birth had been premature. Frail and unbelievably tiny, the baby scarcely breathed. For almost a whole year life and death fought to possess him. Most of his early childhood he languished in bed, and all his life he was slight and thin, forever harassed by colds and fevers.

Of the antecedents of this child only the barest details are known. His father, shrewd and successful in his work, had behind him a long line of equally shrewd and success-ful forebears. We know of one Helenus Arouet, a master tanner, living in an obscure spot in old Poitou in the sixteenth century, as the family's most likely sire. Hard-working and ambitious, Helenus married the daughter of another master tanner. From their union came scores of other tanners, also some weavers and drapers, and, in time, some apothecaries. The Arouets grew and prospered, and as they accumulated worldly goods they also rose socially, emerging in time in the ranks of the higher bourgeoisie, or the upper middle classes. But no one in the entire clan seems to have been graced with any extraordinary talent other than the important one of making money, and not a single Arouet is today recalled for any distinguished accomplishment.

Voltaire's mother was born a Daumard, a family which, like the Arouets, was of the middle classes. The Daumards were not unlike the Arouets, too, in their ability to forge ahead and flourish. But on the social ladder of their class-conscious age the Daumards stood a couple of rungs or so higher than the Arouets, and hence deemed themselves their betters. In time they climbed even higher by buying a position in the lower nobility.

The portrait of Voltaire's mother has remained a little dim. Temperamentally, she appears to have been light-hearted and gay. Certainly her effervescent spirit contrasted strangely with that of her earnest, plodding husband. And if Voltaire inherited wit and mirth from anyone, it must have been from his mother rather than his father. Her charm readily won friends for her, even in the usually exclusive circle of the well-born. Men found her attractive, and she was fond of men; and in an age when flirtation was quite conventional, men clustered about her, even in her home—sparkling, sophisticated men, with poets and abbés in the vanguard. Marguerite Daumard's gayety was at bottom probably only a convenient disguise for her basic feelings. Actually her life was not very happy. Death had taken two of her four children. She herself had never been strong, and after the birth of her fifth child her fragile health broke completely. She died when her son was only seven.

Of Voltaire's father the picture, though meager, is somewhat more revealing. Industrious and diligent, the notary was a typical Arouet who labored vigorously to advance himself. In the furtherance of his business he found his wife's many cordial connections with the well-heeled *noblesse* quite helpful. Some of the notary's most illustrious clients, such as the high-born Richelieu, Saint-Simon, Béthune-Sully, Chateauneuf, and many others were also the good friends of Madame Arouet. The notary served his customers well, and though he never became wealthy, he at least made an excellent living and managed to keep his family well fed and comfortable. In time he acquired a town house in Paris and had, besides, a country place in nearby Chatenay.

Though he was sober and practical, the elder Arouet was not altogether insensible to more subtle values. He, too, had some aristocratic yearnings and these his understanding wife never failed to encourage. When, after seventeen successful years, he relinquished his work as notary and became Receiver of Fees and Fines in the Chamber of Accounts, a capacity in which he handled some of the king's money, François Arouet had his eye on social as well as business gains. His new position, besides increasing his income, gave him some social glamor, a distinction which pleased him no end. Soon after assuming his new office Monsieur Arouet honored his family with a coat of arms, an accomplishment which, he thought, now made the ambitious Arouets the social equals of the Daumards.

There were two other children in the family besides young François-Marie, a boy and a girl. The latter, called Marie—her full name was Marguerite-Catherine—was not quite eight, while her elder brother, Armand, was going on ten.

The Arouet home usually swarmed with people. The fact that the notary used his house for business as well as a residence caused a steady invasion by his squadrons of clients. Of these a number were also friends of the family, and their visits were thus often social as well as commercial. Among these visitors was Boileau, then a poet of considerable distinction. Apparently, however, he made less of an impression on Voltaire's mother than he had on the French Academy. "A good book, but a foolish man," was her terse characterization of the poet—an estimate which is generally confirmed today.

More to Marguerite's taste were such men as the amiable writer of frivolous songs, the Abbé Rochebrune, and the Abbés Chateauneuf and Gédoyn. They were always present at Madame Arouet's after-dinner assemblies, where the disputations were not only spirited, but at times, to the obvious delight of the hostess, quite heated.

François de Castagner, Abbé de Chateauneuf, was Voltaire's godfather. Cynical by nature, easy in morals, the Abbé lived as a hedonist, solely for the pleasure he derived from life. Most of his Christian precepts he had cast off long ago, and in their place he substituted an unholy skepticism. More than anyone else, it was Chateauneuf who left his mark on the youthful Voltaire; perhaps, indeed, he may even have set the future course of the boy's education. It was the Abbé who planted in the mind of his godson

the notion that the greatest offense against man is un-
reasoning belief—that nothing should be accepted on faith
alone. It was the Abbé who introduced Zozo, for so the
boy was called in the family circle, to the sacrilegious lines
of the *Moissade,* a poem which displayed Moses as a moun-
tebank and a fraud. This poem the boy knew by heart
when he was four years old.

It was the Abbé who saw the first signs of talent in the
youngest Arouet and who announced to the lad's astonished father that his heir was a genius destined for great
things. Deliberately the Abbé tapped his godson's nascent
wit by delicately fomenting verbal bouts between Zozo
and his brother, Armand. The Abbé and his cronies delighted in these clashes from which the younger Arouet
often walked off in triumph. Plainly the boy was the idol
in the Abbé's shrine, and the proud godfather loved to
exhibit his talented protégé before all his fashionable
friends. He took him to banquets of fine lords and ladies,
where the boy recited his verses and was praised and petted
in return. Once the Abbé brought the boy to the famous
Ninon de Lenclos, at one time a beautiful actress with
many lovers, but now creased with the years and over-
weight. Ninon must have been charmed by the boy, for
soon after she left him some 2,000 francs which, she stipu-
lated, he was to spend on books. When the boy's mother
died, the Abbé assumed full charge of his godson's further
education—the notary was both too sad and too busy to
interfere—and some three years later, when the time came
for young Arouet to go to school, it was the Abbé's persuasive suggestion which made the busy father choose the
famous Collège Louis-le-Grand for his son.

Through his godfather young Arouet became ac-

quainted with another cleric, the Abbé de Chaulieu, a
poet of some repute in his day. The two abbés were fowl
of the same feather. Like his irreverent ecclesiastic brother,
Chateauneuf, the poetic Chaulieu was one of the abbés
subsequently designated by Voltaire as "an indefinable
being, who is neither layman nor ecclesiastic." Chaulieu
quickly detected the boy's flair for verse and eagerly took
him in hand, teaching him how to scan and rhyme, and
how to use the more familiar classical metaphors. But
more important than that, the boy absorbed some of his
master's paganism. If the Abbé died, as Voltaire declared,
"unknown to the theologians," then many a thought of
his on pleasure, on stoic calm, and especially on the imbecilities of theology, lie buried in the rhymes of Voltaire.

Though the notary's son lost his mother when he was
barely seven, his boyhood was not without feminine influence. Even as a lad he was happy in the companionship
of women, a characteristic he sustained for the rest of his
life. Among the many callers at the Arouet home were
two women, Mademoiselle Bessières and her aunt. The
latter made an everlasting impression on Voltaire. "In one
week," he said, "she used to eat two or three biscuits, and
she lived almost like a parrot. She was dry, like the wood
of an old violin, and she lived in this state until she was
almost eighty with hardly any illness." Despite her gastronomic economy she was of a happy, radiant disposition,
bestowing a gracious gayety on the Arouet home, which
she apparently deemed quite her own. The young people
she took to her heart, calling them all "her children," and
bequeathing them, when she went to her last reward, as
her special legacy to her niece. The beneficiary took over
where her aunt left off, and soon Voltaire became her par-

ticular heritage. Throughout his childhood Mademoiselle Bessières came closer to being a mother to him than anyone else in the Arouet household.

François Arouet had some excellent reasons when he consented to send his youngest son to the Collège Louis-le-Grand. To begin with, the school was an old and trusted citadel of orthodoxy. Run by the learned Jesuits, it had a first-rate academic reputation. It was the largest and most fashionable school of its kind in all of France, a sort of Gallic Eton or Rugby. In its halls walked the heirs of the nation's aristocracy, dukes and counts, and even princes. They lived in special rooms, had special meals, and were tended by their own valets. All this impressed the bourgeois notary, and having learned long ago how powerful friends can lubricate a successful career, the sagacious man hoped that at Louis-le-Grand his son might at least make some useful contacts which might some day further his career.

François-Marie was not quite ten when he came to live at the Collège. He was small and frail, with mere filaments for legs. His face was hollow and white and it contrasted strangely with his blazing black eyes. Extremely nervous, young Arouet was a restless boy, though even at that age he detested systematic physical exercise, and did everything he could to avoid it. Full of boyish animal spirits, he constantly played pranks on students and teachers alike. He would sneak up behind an unsuspecting pedagogue and remove his wig, while the good man, unaware of his tonsorial nakedness, continued to be learned and dignified in the proper manner. When the season was right—and the coast was clear—Voltaire would drop chunks of ice into the school's holy water. Yet, he had a winning way and, just as his father had hoped, he easily made friends. Many of these schoolboy friendships blossomed into associations that endured for the greater part of Voltaire's life.

Endowed with a keen mind and a good memory, François-Marie was an excellent student. Curiously enough, he never radiated much enthusiasm for what he was compelled to learn. The fact that education should bear some relationship to the world in which the pupil lived was then unknown, and hence Voltaire concentrated mainly on Latin and rhetoric, with generous doses of religion and morals. "I did not know," he once declared, "that Francis I was taken prisoner at Pavia, nor where Pavia was; the very land of my birth was unknown to me. I knew neither the constitution nor the interests of my country; not a word of mathematics, not a word of sound philosophy. I learned Latin and nonsense." Outside the sacred and decorous classroom, however, where the school was less in the grip of its traditions, the situation was better. Here schoolmasters had a chance to be educators and a handful actually succeeded. Here the boy was no longer treated as an empty bowl to be filled with pre-digested knowledge, but as a human being with intellectual qualities that set him off from the rest of the herd. Three of Voltaire's teachers—Fathers Touremine, Thoulier and Porée—quickly discerned the boy's special qualities and they did everything to encourage them.

Father Tournemine edited a monthly magazine for the Jesuits and was not officially connected with the Collège. He was, however, an ardent bibliophile and spent most of his spare moments in the school library. There the young

Voltaire often sought him out to discuss literature and to show him samples of his latest verses. Some of the boy's big-muscled schoolmates, who preferred play and sports to literary discussion, used to jibe at his non-athletic interests; but one day Voltaire silenced them by telling them that "everyone jumps and amuses himself in his own way."

Father Thoulier had a reputation as a Latinist. He had dedicated his life to the study of Roman letters and particularly to Virgil and Cicero. Somewhat of a skeptic, he openly preferred Cicero and his Roman world to the Christian France of Louis XIV. He had become tired of teaching, and his pupils bored him. Voltaire, on the other hand, attracted him. "Read Cicero!" he urged his pupil. "Read Cicero!"

Of all Voltaire's teachers, however, it was Father Porée who stimulated him the most. Father Porée was an excellent teacher who, despite the rigorous formality prescribed for every Jesuit classroom, succeeded in making his classes interesting. Endeared to all his students, he was known everywhere as the Good Porée. His hobby was the writing of Latin playlets, and in an age when school dramatics were virtually unknown, he often presented them to the faculty and students. The parts were enacted by the students and occasionally young Voltaire had a chance to display his histrionic talents. For a time Porée was Voltaire's teacher of Latin rhetoric, and in this capacity he soon discovered his pupil's gifts for composing verse. He gave the boy every opportunity for developing these gifts. On one occasion Father Porée caught François playing with a snuff-box instead of paying attention to his Latin. To punish him the teacher not only confiscated the snuff-box, but for its redemption required a set of original verse. In a very short time the young penitent handed his master the following lines:

> Farewell, my poor snuff-box,
> I ne'er shall see thee more!
> To me, not any tears or prayers
> My treasure can restore.
> Farewell, unhappy snuff-box
> That on my heart I bore.
> Could gold and silver ransom thee
> I'd ransack Pluto's treasury.
> But O, my snuff-box, 'tis not he
> They'd have me now implore.
> Not Pluto, but another god
> Has locked and barred the door!
> They ask for verse, my snuff-box,
> They bid me write a song,
> Before thy smooth round face I see,
> For which I saved so long,
> So many a sou, my snuff-box,
> So many a silver crown . . .
> And still the Muse looks down her nose;
> Apollo wears a frown.
> Farewell, my poor old snuff-box
> (I've used that line before!)
> The rhymes run out. The spring runs dry.
> I ne'er shall see thee more.

On another occasion Father Porée set his class the task of composing some verses on the suicide of Nero. Young Voltaire condensed his efforts into these four lines:

A vile accomplice in my mother's death,
By mine own hand I am stricken into dust,
For, having plagued mankind till my last breath,
It struck me that self-slaughter might be just.

From classroom versifier Voltaire rose to the position of school poet. When a crippled soldier, who had served in the Dauphin's regiment, asked the Fathers to write some verses for him petitioning the king for a pension, the job was turned over to Arouet. Under the guidance of Father Porée the youthful poet fashioned a poem beginning:

> *Blood royal of our most royal king,*
> *His love and hope thou art,*
> *Who rules not the soil of France,*
> *But every Frenchman's heart.*

The same tone continued throughout the poem. Not only did it win a pension for the needy soldier, but it so flattered the vain Louis that he was moved to make personal inquiries about the boy who "could write such lovely poesy."

Not all Voltaire's teachers were as understanding as the Good Porée. One of them was Father Lejay, a dull pedant and a hard taskmaster. He seems to have been particularly exasperated by François-Marie. Once in the course of a debate some unexpected repartee from Arouet nettled Lejay. Leaping from his chair, he descended upon the offending boy. "Wretch!" he shouted as he shook him by the collar, "you will become the leader of the deists in France!"

Aside from this unfortunate incident most of Voltaire's

experiences at Louis-le-Grand were pleasant. He did very well in his studies and often stood first in his class. In the winter, however, he considered this a dubious honor, since the seat assigned to the best student was near the doorway and hence subject to incessant draughts. When the weather grew cold François-Marie relaxed his scholastic zeal, studying just hard enough to get a seat somewhere in the middle of the room as near to the stove as possible. By the end of the year, however, he usually stood near the top of his class. When commencement day arrived the notary's son carried off more prizes than any other student. Amid the applause of the delighted onlookers the poet Rousseau kissed him on both cheeks and predicted that he was destined to do great things.

When young Arouet made his triumphant exit from Louis-le-Grand he was not yet seventeen, but his mind was already swarming with grandiose dreams. He had resolved, for one thing, to make poetry his profession. With it he would travel the high road to fame and fortune. In addition, he had decided to give himself a leading role in the frolicsome social life of the lords and ladies adorning the Parisian salons. Guided by Godfather Chateauneuf and his clerical crony, Chaulieu, he had sampled a few of its flavors and had found them pleasing.

But when the elder Arouet got wind of his son's intentions he moved at once to correct them. His son, he insisted, was to be an Arouet like all the Arouets before him. Let him stop this silly blather about literature and settle down in something practical and profitable. His son, he announced, should study law. When the youth demurred and said he wanted nothing but a career of letters, old Arouet exploded. "Literature," he bellowed, "is a profession of a man who wants to be useless to society. Poets are a burden to their relatives. They die of hunger." When this failed to break his son's rebellion, the father continued to rave and roar, until the youth grudgingly capitulated.

It was a hollow victory for the notary. Voltaire's experience with the learned jurists only served to stimulate his dislike of them and their profession. The more he listened to their harangues the more certain he became that they were imbeciles. "What disgusted me most," he said, "was the profusion of useless things with which they wanted to load my brain." A lawyer, it seemed to him, was a man who for three years crammed into his head the ancient laws of Theodosius and Justinian "in order to know the practice of Paris."

For a time he gave himself to their lectures, reserving his spare moments, however, to compose verses. Now and then he made an occasional sortie into the treasured haunts of Chaulieu. The old abbé belonged to a club known as the Temple. Composed mainly of pleasure-loving reprobates like himself, the Temple included some of the biggest wigs in France, such as the Prince of Conti and the Grand Prior Philip of Vendôme. The Templars gathered often over lavish food and drink when, in addition to delighting their stomachs, they regaled one another with elegant conversation, eulogies to the ancient pagans and the latest bits of bawdiness from Versailles.

Voltaire was always well received at the Temple, for his repartee and charm made him a pleasant accomplice. Gradually his visits became more steady while his attendance at the law school slackened, until in the end it collapsed completely. He had never known such luxury.

The Temple was only a beginning. Soon invitations from all over Paris were addressed to the young man, invitations from the great seigneurs who were eager to embellish their parties with the clever *bons mots* which fell so readily from the lips of the notary's son. Voltaire's reputation for wit and for his verses increased steadily, and with it his self-assurance. The fact that the full enjoyment of his new delights demanded a considerable expenditure of money didn't seem to disturb the poet very much. Indeed, though the cautious notary kept his son's allowance at a perpetual low tide, the young man soon learned how to convert his financial precariousness into a social asset. Openly he advertised his empty pocketbook to all his moneyed friends, shaking them with laughter with his droll stories of Jewish pawnbrokers who made the sign of the cross and took their usury in advance before lending him any money. Then, as now, there were plenty of people who yearned to be literary geniuses, but who had only money and no talent. By polishing the poesy of the literary-stricken gentry, Voltaire was able to make an occasional addition to his slim capital. Most of his money, however, evaporated as rapidly as it came in.

As might be expected, a man of François Arouet's shrewdness was not entirely in the dark about his son's escapades. That the young fellow wasn't damaging his eyes over his law books the notary knew well enough. It was obvious, too, that his son was a roisterer, who kept obscene, unbourgeois hours. For the rising poet had no house-key, and every night the notary had to leave the front door unlocked. Once he tried the familiar trick of locking out his wayward heir, but that night Voltaire slumbered peacefully in a porter's chair in the Parisian court house.

With each outburst of his father's anger the son would promise to reform, and then would forget his promise. Eventually, when the senior Arouet realized what gay Paris was doing to his son, he decided to solve the problem once and for all. He would shift François-Marie to far-away Caen, in Normandy. Unfortunately, Monsieur Arouet fancied that distance alone would effect a cure, and that once out of touch with his high-living associates, the youth would forget his lust for gayety and become a sober-minded Arouet. Voltaire, of course, did nothing of the sort. Caen, then the Athens of Normandy, was as completely saturated with letters as it was with the salt air which came in from the beaches. Unmolested by an interfering father, Voltaire now turned to his literary work with full force. He wrote more than ever before, composing couplets and alexandrines, and even sweating out the first rough draft of a play. Before long, too, he had introduced himself in the homes of the town's leading families, and soon he was once more prowling from salon to salon, intoning his verses and tossing off quips for the benefit of the assembled ladies and gentlemen.

But Caen, for all its cultural efforts, was not Paris. The free and easy cynicism which made a hard life tolerable to an intellectual of the eighteenth century was absent at Caen. Almost inevitably the notary's son was destined to become suspect and gradually warning signals began to be hoisted over most of the salons which hitherto had harbored him. Even so, his sojourn might have continued blissfully and unscathed had he not made the fatal blunder of directing destructive criticism at the treasured rhymes of one Madame d'Osseville. The Madame happened to be the town's most self-important Muse, and when Voltaire failed to glow over her poetic efforts, she suddenly discovered that much of his own verse was aimed against God and common decency. As the literary leader of Caen Madame d'Osseville promptly set a righteous example. Henceforth her home was not open to him, and before long Caen's moral *haut monde* followed suit. From now on Voltaire was anathema. Only a Jesuit professor, a Father Couvrigny, continued to associate with the ostracized poet. Encouraged by Couvrigny, Voltaire stuck to his literary course and gave no heed to the scandal-mongering Madame d'Osseville. In due time his father began to urge him to return home, offering to buy for him a counselor's post to the parliament of Paris, if he would promise to settle down in a legal career. The notary's son, however, refused to be bribed. "Tell my father," he said to the bearer of the offer, "I do not desire any place which can be bought. I shall know how to make one for myself that will cost nothing." Not until the notary was willing to have his son return to Paris with no strings attached did Voltaire turn his back on Caen.

The brief interlude in Normandy left no visible mark on Voltaire. For him letters was still the only career, and the courtly life the only life. Yet in the obdurate father the determination still blazed to mold his son into a lawyer and an honest, solid tax-payer. François-Marie lost no time in reclaiming his old haunts. Soon the familiar gastronomic and literary routine was in full sway, and the storm clouds once again began to gather over the Arouet mansion. The belabored notary had in fact made up his mind to cast out his unchastened son forever, but before he could take that step the air began to clear. The unexpected came in the person of the Marquis de Chateau-neuf, a brother of the Abbé—now lamented and resting in his sacred grave. By the accidents of politics the Marquis had become ambassador to the Netherlands, and, as a good friend and client of the notary, he was willing to do him a favor by taking his son to the Hague. There the nineteen-year-old youth was to serve as the ambassador's handy man, besides learning something of the elusive mysteries of diplomacy. François-Marie gave the whole scheme his hearty approval and promised to do his best. Some day, he assured his father, he would be a master diplomat of whom they would all be proud. No doubt he meant what he said. He laid aside his careless ways, and plunged into his new work with eagerness. Officially he was listed as a "page," a sort of minor attaché without pay. His duties seem to have been mainly clerical, and since they were never very onerous, Voltaire had considerable time for leisure. This, as usual, he devoted mainly to writing and to the winning of new friends.

It was almost inevitable that in time he should meet Madame Dunoyer, a woman of some notoriety. She had written a seven-volume work entitled "Letters Historical and Gallant," and was also the editor of *La Quintessence,* a magazine specializing in scandal and gossip about prominent people. Her writings earned a good living for her, and since the poison in her pen had been known to destroy promising careers, she was not without influence among people in high places.

Madame Dunoyer had two daughters, the older of whom she had married off to a rich, elderly Parisian. Her younger daughter, Olympe, or as she was nicknamed, Pimpette, had been engaged for two years to one Jean Cavalier; but something had frightened Jean and he had fled to England. However, the ambitious mother had not given up hope of making an advantageous match for Pimpette, and when the new French ambassador arrived at the Hague, Madame Dunoyer was on the prowl for a suitable son-in-law. Introduced to the Dunoyer literary circle, Voltaire met Pimpette and promptly fell in love with her. Madame Dunoyer, however, emphatically disapproved of the penniless Arouet's suit. When the couple continued to meet despite her prohibitions, she complained to the Marquis de Chateauneuf. The ambassador, knowing full well the strength of la Dunoyer's political influence, forbade all further meetings between his page and Pimpette. When the two continued to meet anyway, the infuriated diplomat had his page confined to his quarters, while Pimpette's indignant mother did the same to her daughter.

But the lovers succeeded in writing to one another. "I am here as the King's prisoner," Voltaire wrote. "They may rob me of my life, but not of my love for you, my dearest." For a time the lovers were able to meet clandestinely. In fact, Pimpette even managed to elude the embassy guard and spend a whole night with her lover. Through his spies the ambassador became suspicious, and though he was without a shred of evidence, he decided to forestall any future complications by ordering his page back to Paris. "They have just told me that I leave tomorrow," he wrote to Pimpette, "though I expect there will be some delay. . . . Good-bye, my dear heart, this is perhaps the last letter I shall write from the Hague. . . . Good-bye, my adorable Olympe, good-bye my dear. If one could write kisses, I would send you an infinity by the courier. I kiss instead of you, your precious letters, in which I read my happiness."

When the young man returned to Paris he didn't dare go home. From friends he heard that his father had not only cut him out of his will, but was lying in wait with a warrant for his arrest, a *lettre de cachet,* to have him jailed in the Bastille. For a time the romantic lover went into discreet seclusion, meanwhile, however, setting his friends to work on his bellicose father. Under their steady pressure the notary softened somewhat. He was ready, he declared after a time, to forget about the Bastille, but his son would have to get out of France. Meanwhile Voltaire had not forgotten Pimpette. Indeed, he had written her several letters, trying to persuade her to join him. "I do not dare show myself," he wrote, "and they cannot make my father change his mind about his will in which he disinherits me. . . . I am in the depths of unhappiness. It is absolutely impossible to be more unhappy unless I am abandoned by you. . . ." Most of his letters remained unanswered, and when Pimpette finally did write it was a very tactful letter, advising him to seek a reconciliation with his father "even though this may mean returning to the study of law." Soon after, the notary received a very humble and submissive letter from his son. "I consent," it said among other things, "to go to America, and even live there on bread and water, if only before I go you will let me embrace your knees."

These honeyed words had their desired effect. The elder Arouet capitulated—but not completely. He was ready to forgive his son, provided the young man would cease his insanities, assume a life decent and becoming, and would dedicate the next few years to making himself an honest lawyer.

To prepare himself for this new life the notary's son was

sent as a law clerk to Monsieur Alain, a Parisian advocate, who besides agreeing to acquaint the young man with the finer juridic points, was also to furnish him with board and lodging. At the start François-Marie, now somewhat penitent and chastened, worked hard to restore himself to paternal grace. Indeed, for a time it began to look almost as if the notary had won his long-fought battle, and that Arouet the younger might yet amount to something. What buoyed up Voltaire, however, was not any pleasure he derived from his new occupation, but rather his lingering hope that Pimpette might yet come to Paris. He continued to send her ardent letters, but she didn't reply. Under the direction of her mother, Pimpette had already turned to another suitor, a Count de Winterfeld, whom she soon afterwards married.

When it became clear to Voltaire that his former sweetheart had forgotten him, his work in Monsieur Alain's office became more distasteful than ever. Voltaire was not designed to spend the rest of his life toiling over the complexities of contracts and mortgages or trying to decipher the unpoetic language of wills, torts and partnerships. The old yearning for self-expression asserted itself—that strange, inexplicable yearning which set him apart from his father and brother, from all the Arouets before him. As the months went by the young clerk gradually slipped into his old ways, concerning himself with legal practice as little as possible. The notary's son had made a close friend of a fellow-clerk, Thieriot, a gay fellow like himself, and a devotee of letters and pleasure in general. With Thieriot as an accomplice Voltaire abandoned himself to a wild and irresponsible life. Instead of working diligently for Monsieur Alain they composed epigrams burlesquing the legal profession; and instead of sweating over their law books they discussed poetry and plays. Their nights they devoted to roistering, and when they came home their shouting and ribald singing awakened the whole household. Finally, in sheer desperation Monsieur Alain dismissed the troublesome François-Marie, predicting at the same time a sad and dismal end for the youth.

Voltaire was so engrossed at the time in a new venture that he could not take his dismissal too seriously. The French Academy had offered a prize to the poets of France for the one writing the best ode to commemorate Louis XIV's generosity when he donated a new choir to venerable Notre Dame. For months Voltaire had toiled on such an ode, polishing and scrubbing it, until even the great minds of the Temple were convinced it was superb. But the judges, characteristically enough, thought otherwise. Instead of letting Voltaire carry home the bronze prize, they bestowed that honor on the doddering Abbé du Jarri, a man now forgotten by all save antiquarians. The Abbé's chief claim to fame rested in his two volumes of "Panegyrics of the Saints" and one on "The Eloquence of the Pulpit, or The Best Way of Preaching the Word of God." But more important than his cultural contribution was the fact that Abbé du Jarri happened to be a favorite at Louis' court, an attribute which had given his ode a quality altogether lacking in the poesy of his rivals.

As usual, the disappointed artists roared and bellowed for a time, only to quiet down in the end. But Voltaire refused to quiet down. The Abbé, he said very loudly, was an ignoramus. Hadn't he said in his victorious ode that the South Pole differed from its northern counterpart only in the blazing heat it generated? To show his utter disdain for the prize-winning Abbé, Voltaire bombarded him with broadsides of satire. He went even further, heaving his high curse on the academician La Motte who had awarded the prize to du Jarri in a mocking, obscene poem called *Le Bourbier*—"The Mud Puddle"—wherein he lampooned his victim so thoroughly that Paris resounded with laughter. But at bottom this was a rash act which might easily have proved fatal; for the Academy was then a privileged pet at the Court, and for anyone to poke fun at it was to invite catastrophe.

A timely invitation from a friend in the country helped to rescue the young poet from the rising storm. From one of Voltaire's old school chums, young Caumartin, who happened also to be a devotee of the Temple, the notary received a request to allow his son to spend the next few months with him and his uncle, Louis-Urbain de Caumartin, Marquis de Saint-Ange. The elder Arouet, susceptible to the honor of such an invitation, and glad to get his reckless François-Marie out of Paris, eagerly accepted the bid on behalf of his son. Delighted to escape from the conflict he had started in Paris, Voltaire sped to the ancestral chateau of the Caumartins, built by the sainted Henry of Navarre for his beloved mistress Gabrielle, but now presided over by the Marquis. Patriarchal in years and wisdom, the Marquis de Saint-Ange in his prime had been a jurist of national renown, and had, in fact, held some of the best posts in the land. The diarizing Saint-Simon reports that old Caumartin "knew everything in history, in genealogy, in court anecdotes, and remembered everything he ever heard or read, even to repeating in conversation whole pages." Most of this information the Marquis had gathered from his experience at Court and from what his ancestors, who had held high offices there, had disclosed. Like most veterans, once active but now on the sidelines, the old man never grew weary of reciting the special role he had played in a great and heroic past. Saturated with an intimate knowledge of the reigns of Louis XIII and Henry IV, the Marquis knew more about French history than the erudite doctors of the Sorbonne. From him Voltaire heard the whole colorful tale, from the weaknesses of inept monarchs to the plottings of their avid women and prehensile cardinals; from little known facts about the nation's dwindling finances to unfamiliar details about high politics among nations. It was from the Marquis de Saint-Ange that young Voltaire first heard the anecdote of Louis XIV and the disastrous Battle of Ramillies—how upon receiving the news of the French defeat the Grand Monarch sadly exclaimed, "Is it possible God has forgotten all I have done for him?"

The Marquis' idol among French monarchs was Henry of Navarre, and the castle of Saint-Ange was replete with mementoes of the great king. Erected by Henry himself, it had a library rich in rare documents about him and his time, while its walls were adorned with portraits of the king and his renowned compatriots, men like Coligny and Mornay and the king's minister Sully. Of these men Voltaire knew virtually nothing, and when his aged host narrated their exploits he was an eager listener. From Caumartin he heard the story of the bloody Massacre of Saint Bartholomew, of Henry's long struggle with the anti-Protestant League, of the religious wars which for so many years had bled France, of the dagger thrust by which a religious fanatic murdered Henry. The Marquis' enthusiasm for his subject was readily absorbed by his young

listener. While at Saint-Ange Voltaire conceived the idea
that the story of Henry was the natural subject of a national
epic which could be fashioned into a stirring poem; and
since French literature lacked such an epic, Voltaire made
up his mind that he would write one—that, in fact, he
would "give his country an epic poem such as Virgil had
given Rome when he wrote the *Aeneid*."

In the summer of 1715 news reached Saint-Ange of the
approaching end of Louis XIV. For most Frenchmen these
tidings were no cause for lament. On the contrary many,
unable to suppress their glee, got drunk publicly to celebrate the coming event. The fourteenth Louis had mis-
ruled France for the greater part of seventy-two years. His
was the longest of any reign in Europe. Launched in great
hopes, it had seen France soar to great heights, only to
behold that land totter and crash. Endless wars and extravagance abetted by their handmaidens, famine and
disease, had brought the once powerful nation to the brink
of ruin. The national treasury showed a deficit of a billion
francs, while in many cities the starving populace was
openly talking about rebellion. With Louis' end in plain
sight Frenchmen once more took heart and grew optimistic. Peace and a plentiful larder, many now believed,
would soon caress the land. As usual, the new prosperity
was expected to make its first appearance in the capital,
and to be on hand when it came hordes of expectant
Frenchmen began to make for Paris.

The nation's psychological trend affected Voltaire. He,
too, glowed with radiant hope and, like his compatriots,
he looked to Paris as the natural place for its fulfilment.
With opportunity knocking on everyone's door, he was
sure poets and playwrights would certainly not be over-

looked. The play which he had begun at Caen was still a mere fragment; but with the promise of great rewards to spur him on he knew he could finish it in a short time. Thus, buoyant, optimistic, and determined to be ready for the new era when it arrived, Voltaire returned to Paris to work feverishly on his play.

Louis died on September first, 1715, and a week later he was buried at St. Denis, for eleven hundred years the burial place of the kings of France. With Louis' passing France was faced with the problem of succession, for the heir to the throne, Louis' great-grandson, was still an infant in the crib. In his will the monarch had bequeathed the regency to Philippe-Auguste, one of the king's dozen illegitimate offspring and also his favorite. But the haughty peers, appalled at the thought of being ruled by a bastard, even though he was of royal origin, swept aside Louis' last wish and set up one of their own number as regent. He was Philip, Duke of Orleans. The nobles' arrogant act split France into two hostile factions, the one favoring Philip, the other declaring for the ousted Philippe-Auguste, Duke of Maine. There was little to choose between them. Certainly Philip, obese and dissipated, given to gross guzzling and gorging, was more interested in lush and riotous living than in the problems of state.

In this political dispute Voltaire's sympathies were prompted by sheer self-interest rather than by any principles of statecraft. The notary's son favored the Duke of Orleans largely because in the duke he saw a potential patron for his play, which he had decided to call *Oedipus*. But the play's theme happened to be incest and for Philip this was most distasteful. His distaste was natural enough, since everywhere in Paris, in salons and alleys alike, there was considerable gossip associating the Regent intimately with his own daughter, the dissolute Duchess de Berri.

When the Duke indicated his disapproval of what he deemed an immoral and pathological play, Voltaire promptly switched his political allegiance to the Duke of Maine. He concentrated his fire on the Duchess of Maine, who was then actively managing her husband's campaign for the Regency. A slight woman, but with the determination of a tigress, the Duchess was consumed by her ambition to seat her husband in the Regency. From her estate at Sceaux, on the fringe of Paris, she directed constant attacks on Philip. She was familiar with all the sharp practices of politics and she had assembled a corps of propagandists who unleashed a barrage of vitriol and innuendo against the hapless Regent.

With the help of two of his Temple confrères, the Abbé de Chaulieu and the Grand Prior, Philip of Vendôme, both of whom were close friends of the Duchess, the playwright obtained for himself an invitation to spend a few days at Sceaux. Life there Voltaire found altogether pleasant and to his taste. Gaudy parties, designed to promote the House of Maine, were given regularly. In this elegant world the notary's son glided about with the ease of a man born to the purple, charming the ladies, flattering the lords, and everywhere diverting attention to himself. Eager to enlist the nimble-witted poet in her bureau of literary snipers, the Duchess treated him with the charm and deference she usually reserved for field marshals and archbishops. When Voltaire brought up the subject of *Oedipus*, the Duchess appeared tremendously interested. The author, she insisted, must read it to her. When she finally heard it, she gave it ecstatic praise, calling it "a beautiful tragedy," and promising even to finance its production at an early date. In return Voltaire, of course, was glad to help the Duchess with an occasional pot-shot at the Regent. When, for example, Philip, in a burst of economy, announced to the astounded Parisians that he had sold half of the late king's five thousand horses, Voltaire promptly declared that the Regent would do far better if he got rid of half the asses adorning the royal court.

But most of the attacks coming out of Sceaux were neither funny nor gentle. They were, on the contrary, vicious and indignant, accusing the Regent of every imaginable crime, from assassination to blasphemy and incest. Ordinarily a mild and pleasant fellow, the Regent was aroused by this incessant raillery, and to stop the Duchess' literary onslaughts, he decided to make an example of her most significant writer. Thus, without bothering to separate the guilty from the innocent, Philip ordered the exile of Voltaire. Though the poet had actually never penned a poisonous line against the Regent, he was ordered to Tulle, an industrial town some three hundred miles from Paris, and noted even at that distance for the vile smell of its tallow works and tanneries. Even the poet's father, usually stern and implacable, was shocked at Philip's sudden harshness and personally implored the Duke to soften his sentence. The result was that Voltaire was exiled to Sully-on-the-Loire where at least there were fragrant gardens and lovely woodlands. There, the notary assured the Regent, his son would be under the surveillance of relatives who "would be able by their good advice to correct his imprudence and moderate his vivacity."

Instead of seeking out the benevolent kinsmen who would keep him morally and legally safe, the young man lived at the chateau of the Duke of Sully, one of the notary's clients. Here again the poet frolicked in the voluptuous delights of courtly living, feasting on exquisite foods and the best of Burgundies. Even more than at Sceaux, life at Sully was a festive affair. "You would be astonished, no doubt," the exile confided to the Marquise de Mimeure, "were I to tell you that in this beautiful woodland we have bright nights as at Sceaux . . . in the green salon of elms, lighted by innumerable lanterns where the other evening a magnificent supper was served, followed by a dance of more than three hundred masqueraders in superb costumes."

For the same lady he composed a verse:

> *I write from banks and woodlands green*
> *Where blither exiles once did dwell*
> *Than France for many a year had seen,—*
> *Les Manicamps and Les Chapelles;*
> *Who rhymed and talked the summer through*
> *And watched the Loire's bright ripples shine,*
> *And filled the sage's cup anew,*
> *Not with philosophy, but wine.*

Voltaire found the Duke of Sully to be "the most amiable of men. I am under the greatest obligation to him. His chateau is the most beautiful place in the world. There is a magnificent woodland in which rascals or lovers have amused themselves by carving their names on the bark of all the trees."

He recorded his impression in verse:

To see so many letters traced
So many love-knots interlaced
One would think d'Urfé's sentimental beau,
Caledon, had forsworn his reign
At Lignon for a new domain,
At Sully, where the moonlit waters flow.

Yet young Voltaire never abandoned himself completely to riotous living. His health, never sturdy at best, would scarcely have stood such treatment. Instead he balanced his periods of fun with hours of hard, steady work. The Sully chateau, like that of Saint-Ange, was rich in historical tradition. The chateau itself had been given by Henry of Navarre to his illustrious prime minister, a former Duke of Sully. Here, once again, there was a splendid library full of valuable data about Henry and his associates. With an eye on his projected epic poem about Henry, Voltaire cloistered himself in the Sully library, devouring its precious material and neatly storing in his notes what he wanted to remember. Thus he worked with the diligence of a determined scholar while the lords went ahunting, "passing the lovely days," as he put it, "in assassinating partridges."

Several months were thus spent in exile. In the summer, things had been pleasant enough, but with the approach of fall the Duke and his guests returned to Paris, and the once lively chateau became very quiet. To his old friend, the Abbé de Chaulieu, Voltaire said: "I write you from a place that would be the most agreeable had I not been exiled to it . . . and where there's nothing wanting for my perfect happiness save the liberty of leaving." That "liberty of leaving" he now set out to obtain. He had been exiled on suspicion, and to remove that suspicion he composed flattering verses about the Regent. "Beneficent toward all," he wrote to Philip, "to me alone severe, you doom me to rigorous exile." Then, remembering no doubt how in ancient Macedonia an unjustly treated citizen had dared to appeal "from Philip the drunk to Philip the sober," the poet subtly added: "But I dare appeal from yourself to yourself. I implore your justice, not your clemency. . . ." He sent copies of his verses to the Regent's friends. "Cast an eye over it," he asked them, "and tell me frankly if it is worthy of such a Prince." To one he declared: "It shall *not* see the light until *you* deem it worthy of publication." To another he said: "If I had the honor to be better known to you, you would see that in this piece I speak as I think." His campaign bore excellent fruit. Before the end of autumn the Regent lifted the ban and Voltaire returned to his beloved Paris.

Back in his home town, Voltaire received a rousing reception. His friends had missed his merry talk and were glad to have him back. Only the notary had some somber doubts. "Perhaps," he wrote to his business chief, the President of the Chamber of Accounts, "you may have heard that it has pleased the Regent to recall my son from his exile. The exile distressed me much less than does this precipitate recall, which will complete the ruin of the young man, intoxicated as he is by the success of his poetry, and by the praises and welcome bestowed on him by the great, who, with all the respect I owe them, I must regard as the ones really poisoning him."

Voltaire was still anxious to slip out of the paternal yoke which would hold him to a dull, bourgeois profession. To be less hampered in his movements he took a oom at the Green Basket, a modest inn in the shadow of

Notre Dame. He continued to frequent the salons in Paris and he also made longer jaunts to Sceaux where the Duchess' propaganda bureau was still hammering away at the Regent. In her plottings to regain the regency for her husband the crafty little woman had ensnared a new and potent accomplice, the sinister Cardinal Alberoni, virtual dictator of Spain. With him the Duchess was laying plans for a *coup d'état* which would make her the virtual ruler of France during the minority of Louis XV. And since she was now playing for higher stakes than ever, the Duchess had no time for the production of *Oedipus*.

The Regent, Philip, was not altogether ignorant of what was going on. In fact his suspicions concerning the House of Maine and its literary shock troops had never abated. His secret constabulary, one of the best of its kind in Europe, kept him closely informed about what went on at Sceaux. Whenever Voltaire showed himself at the Maine estate, his activities were recorded in the chronicles of the police, and thus the Regent was aware that the Duchess' leading poet had again become a conspicuous figure at her court.

In the spring of 1717 two compositions were flung at the Regent which attracted more attention than any that had appeared previously. One was known as the *Puero Regnante*—"The Reigning Boy":

> *A boy reigning;*
> *A man notorious for poisonings*
> *And incests;*
> *Councils ignorant and unstable;*
> *Religion more unstable;*
> *The treasury empty;*

Public faith violated;
Infuriate wrong triumphant;
Danger of general sedition imminent;
The country sacrificed
To the hope of a crown;
All inheritance basely anticipated;
France about to perish!

The other was called the *J'ai vu,* or the "I-have-seen":

I have seen the Bastille and a thousand other prisons filled with brave citizens, faithful subjects! ... *I have seen* the people wretched under a rigorous servitude! ... *I have seen* the soldiers perishing of hunger, thirst, indignation and rage! ... *I have seen* the devil in the guise of a woman (Madame de Maintenon) during the kingdom, sacrificing her God, her faith, her soul, to seduce the spirit of a too credulous king! ... *I have seen* the altar polluted! ... *I have seen* the blackest of all possible acts, which the waters of the entire ocean could not purge, and which posterity will scarcely be able to believe—bodies stamped with the seal of immortality removed by profane and sacrilegious hands from that sojourn of gracious men, Port Royal[1] ... *I have seen* the prelacy sold or made the reward of imposture! ... *I have seen* nonentities raised to the highest rank! ... *I have*

---

[1] *The Society of Port Royal, a group of Jansenist scholars, had been brutally broken up by Louis XIV, the bones of their dead disinterred and cast to the dogs.*

seen—and this includes all—the Jesuit adored! . . .
I have seen these evils during the fatal reign of a
prince whom formerly the wrath of Heaven accorded to our ardent desires! . . . *I have seen* all
these evils, and I am not twenty years old.

The two pieces swept through Paris like a tornado.
Whether the *Puero Regnante* was merely the fragmentary draft of some unfinished verse is not known. At any
rate it was the boldest attack yet made on the Regent. Not
only did it repeat the old and familiar charges of murder
and incest, but the line "all inheritance basely anticipated"
clearly hinted of designs on the life of the boy-king. As for
the *I-have-seen,* while it was not aimed at Philip himself,
it was a direct assault on the late Louis and at everything
for which he stood, and hence *lèse majesté.* The police
scoured every nook of Paris in search of the guilty author,
but they found no clue. Philip, however, was determined
to put his hands on the wretch who had so grossly abused
him. Calling in his leading spy, Captain Beauregard, the
Regent ordered him to track down the culprit at all costs.
The Captain had met Voltaire several times at one of the
popular coffee houses. Knowing that the young writer was
commonly suspected as the author of the slanderous lines,
the Captain called on him to see what proof he could
smoke out. To build up his case against the unsuspecting
Voltaire, the spy encouraged him to talk freely against
the Regent. And talk he certainly did. The mere mention
of Philip's name seemed to ignite the poet's anger.

"Since I cannot get my revenge on the Duke of Orleans
in a certain way," he is reported to have said to Beauregard, "I will not spare him in my satires." When the Captain, feigning ignorance, asked what the Regent had done

to the poet, Voltaire flew into a rage. "What!" he exclaimed, "you don't know what that *bougre* did to me? He exiled me because I let the world know that that Messalina of a daughter of his was a prostitute."

Except for such indignant outbursts, however, the poet said nothing which might have proved him guilty of the attack on the Regent. Indeed, Voltaire always insisted stoutly that he was not the author and that the pieces were miserable. When Captain Beauregard failed to get the information he wanted he decided to save his face with the Duke by fabricating his own evidence. A few days after his conversation with Voltaire, the Captain submitted a detailed report wherein, under solemn oath, he accused Voltaire of having confessed the authorship of the libelous pieces and of having uttered "a quantity of other things unfit to be recorded."

A little later, one fine day in May, while strolling through the Palace Gardens, the poet met the Regent.

"Monsieur Arouet," said Philip, smiling blandly and playing on the *I-have-seen,* "you have seen many things, no doubt, but there is one thing, I'll wager, I can show you which you have *never* seen."

"Indeed? And may I ask, Monseigneur, what it is?"

"The inside of the Bastille."

"Ah, Monseigneur," said the young man, "allow me to consider that as already seen."

Early the next morning while most of Paris was still asleep Voltaire was arrested on a *lettre de cachet* and taken to the Bastille.

This prison was not as terrible as is commonly thought. What made it so feared and hated was not any brutality it may have manifested toward its inmates, but rather the arbitrary, unjust methods which had lodged them there. They were in the Bastille on the king's order and they could be released only at his pleasure. It happened on occasion that records went astray, or that accusers died, with the result that some unfortunate prisoner remained in the old fortress indefinitely, or even forever. The prisoners themselves were treated fairly decently. Indeed, as prisons went in those days, the Bastille was in some ways extraordinarily humane. Only confirmed and vicious lawbreakers were roughly handled. For them there were dark dungeons in the prison's damp cellar with heavy chains and other ingenious devices to make them suffer. As for the rest, their treatment varied with their social standing. Technically, they were not "prisoners" but the "king's guests" in the "king's hotel," and as such they were supposed to be treated with courtesy. With certain limitations, some were allowed to roam about the prison at will. They could play games and even gamble for sizable stakes. They could buy almost anything they wanted, from special attendants to wait on them to a sumptuous and well-prepared dinner.

Voltaire's lot was far from melancholy. Lodged in one of the prison's high towers, he had a large, comfortable room, equipped with cot, table and a couple of chairs. There was even a fireplace. His first request was for a copy of Homer, some handkerchiefs, a couple of cravats and a flask of his favorite toilet water. He was allowed to associate with other guests of the king and, characteristically, he soon made friends with several. Nor did he overlook the prison's head warden, or governor. They were on excellent terms, and at times Voltaire was even his dinner guest.

All these benefits did not mitigate the hard fact that he was a prisoner and that day in day out he beheld neither earth nor sky. Nor could they diminish the psychological hurt he suffered as an innocent man in prison. He read a great deal, particularly Homer and Virgil. But he wrote even more. "His prison," said Frederick the Great, "became his Parnassus, to which the Muses resorted." The epic poem he had envisioned under the roof of the inspiring old Marquis de Saint-Ange, and for which he had assiduously collected material ever since his sojourn at the Caumartin chateau, now took actual shape. Tentatively he called it "The League," meaning thereby the anti-Protestant League against which Henry of Navarre had fought so valiantly. Henry, the leading character in the poem, was depicted as a brave and tolerant king who devoted his life to stamping out religious bigotry. The baleful effects of intolerance Voltaire made the keynote of the epic:

> Religion, raging with inhuman zeal,
> Arms every hand, and points the fatal steel.
> To me, however, it will least belong
> To prove the Roman or Genevan wrong.
> Whatever names divine the parties claim,
> In craft and fury they are both the same.

Into his poem Voltaire poured his full energy, even rising at night to work on it. "I have the devil in me," he announced later, "but of course one should have, to write verse." It is said—though there is little evidence to support it—that his jailers at first denied him paper and ink and that consequently Voltaire memorized whole cantos of "The League" before writing them down.

When he wasn't concentrating on the composition of his epic, the young poet often turned to lighter verse. He even burlesqued his arrest in a comic poem. The day he was imprisoned happened to fall on Pentecost, a day set aside by the Roman Church to commemorate "the descent of the Holy Ghost upon the Apostles." Voltaire began his poem by having his valet, drunk the evening before, cry out when he heard the approaching police: "Master! The Holy Ghost has come! It is he, and no mistake, for I have read he comes into people's homes with a thundering racket!" Roused from his sleep, the drowsy poet saw at the foot of his bed "not a pigeon nor a dove, the Holy Spirit's tender and faithful bird, but twenty crows, ravenous for their prey." Continuing in this vein, the poet discovered that these "crooked monsters shaped in hell" were in reality the police come to take him to prison.

Voltaire stayed in the Bastille for eleven months. When he learned the cause of his incarceration he wrote letter after letter to the Regent imploring justice. His friends, too, sent appeals on his behalf. But all their fervid efforts failed to penetrate Philip's iron front. Indeed, even with the discovery of the real author of the *I-have-seen,* an overwrought, neurotic Jansenist named Le Brun, Voltaire continued to be detained. Hearing of Le Brun's confession, Voltaire's father, who for a long time had been fairly certain of his son's guilt, went in person to the Duke of Orleans to plead for his son. The notary's act bore good fruit, for on April 10, 1718, the governor of the Bastille was informed that "the intention of his Royal Highness is that the Sieur Arouet, *fils,* a prisoner in the Bastille, be set at liberty and relegated to Chatenay, near Sceaux, where his father, who has a country house there, offers to take charge of him." Thus the notary's influence grew.

Prison life had not changed Voltaire very much. He came out of the Bastille neither bitter nor rebellious. Whatever resentment he may have felt at his unjust imprisonment was slight. Never for a moment was he indignant over the system which made such injustice possible. Nor had Voltaire's talent for flattery been dimmed. No sooner was he at Chatenay than he started a campaign to get back to Paris; for at the capital his play, *Oedipus,* had been accepted and was ready to go into rehearsal. His first gentle strike for full freedom he made in a letter to the Lieutenant of Police, to whom he wrote: "The first use I must make of my liberty is to write to thank you for having given it to me. I think I have profited by my misfortunes, and I venture to assure you I am indebted to His Royal Highness for my imprisonment as for my freedom. . . . I have never spoken of that prince but to express my admiration for his genius." He signed the letter "with the profoundest respect—your most humble servant—your most humble and very obedient servant."

This letter was followed by another, similarly unctuous, to the Regent's minister, the Count de Maurepas. "I do not ask you to shorten the period of my exile," he wrote, "nor for permission to pass one hour in Paris. The only favor I solicit is that you will be so good as to assure his Royal Highness that I am as much obliged to him for my imprisonment as for my liberty, and that, as I have profited by the one, I shall never abuse the other."

All this correspondence he signed "Arouet de Voltaire," a name which for some reason he adopted soon after his dismissal from the Bastille.

His pleas, however, failed utterly to lubricate the wheels

of justice. Meanwhile, having got wind of the news that it was Captain Beauregard's perjury which had helped to send him to the Bastille, he wrote another letter to the Minister, pleading for permission to come to Paris for just two hours, "to throw myself," he said, "at the feet of His Royal Highness." This time permission was granted.

A strange contrast they must have made—the Regent, fat and sluggish, bored by life's abundance; the poet, thin and vivacious, eager to make a good impression.

"Be prudent," the Regent said, "and I will take care of you."

"I should be delighted," was the quick retort, "to have His Majesty charge himself henceforth with my *board,* but I beg your Royal Highness not to trouble yourself any further with my lodging."

Voltaire's reply amused Philip, but it failed to change the Regent's mind. Voltaire's banishment from Paris remained in effect for six months after his release from the Bastille. Finally, on October 12, 1718, permission was granted by His Royal Highness "for the Sieur Arouet de Voltaire to come to Paris whenever he pleases."

On his return to the capital Voltaire plunged immediately into rehearsing *Oedipus.* The first performance had been announced for the following month of November, but already interest in the play was high. With his natural talent for attracting attention, the notary's son was easily his own best press agent. Long before he had composed the last couplets of *Oedipus* he had drawn his friends into feverish discussions of the faults and merits of his play, getting them to compare it with the finest works of Sophocles. They made loud and frequent predictions of its inevitable success—but also made occasional suggestions for its improvement. To this drumfire of discussion, Voltaire added a few notes of his own, with particular stress on the high qualities of the author. His unjust imprisonment in the Bastille he exploited for its full publicity value. The fact, moreover, that the subject of *Oedipus* was racy inevitably caused controversy and made many people eager to see the play.

The French theatre of Voltaire's time was quite different from anything we know today. Only the aristocracy patronized the dramatic arts, the masses going to plays only on rare and special occasions when the king footed the bill for the entire audience. What drew the nobles to the theatre in the main was not any great interest they had in the drama, or even an urge to be agreeably diverted, but rather the opportunity it afforded them for self-display. Bigwigs courting popular favor used the theatre as their showcase, coming day after day even to the same performance, simply to be in the public eye. Nor was the theatre the decorous place it is now. Often it was a thunderous arena where opposing factions tried to outshout one another in their reactions to the lines of a play. In the case of a new play large sums were frequently wagered on its chances of success or failure. Hence a first night was commonly more like a political convention than a dramatic performance. An opening night without organized claques for and against the play was unthinkable. Indeed, spectators were generally asked did they come to hiss or applaud, and were seated accordingly in the proper section.

The dramatic fare offered in the theatre of Voltaire was strictly tragedy or melodrama, comedy being considered beneath the dignity of the effete nobility. Most plays were written in sonorous alexandrine rhyme, rigorously trussed to the dramatic requirements of ancient Aristotle. Of plot there was little, and of characterization even less. Actors and spectators alike doted on long, windy speeches, each one rendered for its own effect like a piece of elocution. What the audience seemed to relish, in short, was grand opera without music. The fact that some French dramatists, like Racine and Corneille, overcome such obstacles and wrote moving drama, is a high tribute to their creative genius.

On the night of November 18th, 1718, *Oedipus* was performed for the first time at the Comédie. The house was packed. The audience, fashionable and glittering, represented the best blood of France. Even the Regent, having apparently overcome his scruples about the play's moral tone, made his appearance. At his side sat his mistress of the moment, while in the royal box, not far away, was his wife. The opposition, too, was well represented by the Duke and Duchess of Maine and a good many of their political adherents.

The story of *Oedipus* was not new to the French. Its theme had been employed successfully by Corneille and by the great Sophocles in ancient Greece. Like the *Oedipus* of these two writers, that of Voltaire was substantially the story of the familiar ancient fable. In this it was prophesied that Laius, king of Thebes, and his queen, Jocasta, would have a son who would murder his father and marry his mother. When a prince was actually born to the royal couple, they sought to avert the predicted tragedy by doing away with the infant. But their plans miscarried and the babe was brought to the king and queen of Corinth, who adopted it and gave it the name of Oedipus. Grown to manhood, Oedipus learned of his fatal destiny from an oracle. Believing the king and queen of Corinth to be his parents, he fled from their domain and set out for Thebes. On his way he met an old man, quarreled with him and killed him, not knowing, however, that the slain man was his father. Approaching Thebes, Oedipus was stopped by a Sphynx. Crouched on the mountainside overlooking the road, this creature stopped all passers-by and asked them a riddle. Those failing to solve it, it killed, and the terrified Thebans had vowed to have as their next king whoever would destroy the monster. To Oedipus the Sphynx propounded its well known riddle, "What is it that is four-footed, then two-footed, and finally three-footed?" Oedipus replied: "Man, for as a child he crawls on all fours, as a mature man he walks on two legs, and as an old man, he uses a staff." Oedipus' correct answer broke the spell of the Sphynx which plunged to its death in a chasm. Arriving in Thebes, Oedipus was hailed as the city's savior, and true to their oath, the Thebans made him their king. Following the custom of the land, Oedipus married the widowed Jocasta, and in time she bore him four children. After a number of years plague and famine struck the city, and the frightened Thebans implored their king to appease the gods. But an oracle revealed that the plague would disappear only after the assassin of the former king was identified. Commanded by Oedipus to name the murderer, an aged high priest accused Oedipus himself. Jocasta, refusing to believe the charges against her husband, tried to explain away the accusation as a dream. But when the identification was complete, the horror-stricken Jocasta hanged herself. Crazed by the realization of his double crime, Oedipus gouged out his own eyes. "I was the slave and tool of an unknown power. O pitiless gods! Yours are my crimes!" Voltaire made him say as he wandered in darkness to expiate his crimes.

Voltaire's *Oedipus* captivated the spectators from the first scene to the last. Fully familiar with the psychology of his partisan audience, the poet began his play with a few loyal salutes to the little boy king, thereby compelling the entire house, regardless of private political opinion, to applaud. In his other political allusions, generously sprinkled throughout the work, Voltaire was not so clear. In fact he deliberately dressed most of them in double meaning, thus evoking hearty hand-clappings from the Regent's friends and foes alike. What he said about the reverend clergy made the sacred men writhe at times, but since his lines were always about pagan Greeks and never about holy Christians, no cleric could properly complain. Skeptics, of course, could think as they pleased about such matters, and hence when they heard such lines as

> *Our priests are not what the foolish people think*
> *Our credulity makes all their science,*

they applauded with delight.

Throughout the performance the rafters of the Comédie re-echoed with applause and when the last speech had ended there came a tremendous ovation. *Oedipus,* plainly, was a hit of the first magnitude. Dukes and princes gathered about the twenty-four-year-old playwright, eager to shake his hand and make flattering speeches. Baron de Goertz, an emissary from Sweden, and a friend of the Duchess of Maine, threatened to kidnap the young poet to exhibit him to the Swedish Charles XII who, the Baron said, "doesn't know what a poet is."

There is a legend that Voltaire's father witnessed his
son's triumph, that there were tears in the old man's eyes,
and that throughout the play he kept on muttering to
himself, "The rascal! The rascal!" Another legend holds
that in the last act Voltaire himself donned a costume and
appeared on the stage carrying the train of Jupiter's High
Priest, enlivening the solemn dialogue by strutting behind
the High Priest with mock solemnity, peeping under his
train, and perpetrating similar horseplay not calculated
to add to the dignity of the serious pontiff.

Oedipus ran for forty-five consecutive nights, thereby
breaking all existing records. Voltaire himself attended
every performance, diligently studying the various reactions of his audiences. "Each production of my *Oedipus*,"
he said, "was for me a severe study in which I gathered the
approval and the criticism of the public, and studied the
public taste to form my own."

The Parisians of 1718 flocked to see Voltaire's *Oedipus*
not for what it said about the king of Thebes, but for
what they thought it said about the rulers of France.
When he mocked the sacred clergy of ancient Thebes, his
audiences were certain that what he really had in mind
was the clergy of his own day. The very fact that Voltaire's
first purpose was to please his audience is what has made
him negligible as a dramatist. He did please his audiences;
but in doing so he has failed to please posterity. In satis-
fying the spectators Voltaire showed great cleverness. The
operatic poesy, so esteemed by the theatre-goer of 1718,
Voltaire produced with singular skill. The fact, too, that
Oedipus appealed to so many divergent tastes had something to do with its popularity. Those hostile to the Regent
came to gloat over its ugly theme which, they insisted,

could only refer to Philip and his daughter, the Duchess de Berri. But Philip's supporters loudly howled this down as nonsense, and to prove their point they kept going to the play and recommending it to others. The Duchess de Berri attended five successive performances, while her father went more than once.

Realistic Parisians, knowing Philip and his daughter to be no saints, were quick to seize their opportunity: Regent-Oedipus they publicly dubbed their ruler, while his daughter became Berri-Jocasta. But the Regent gave no heed to such flippancies. Instead he pretended not to know what it was all about. On Voltaire, Regent-Oedipus pinned a huge gold medal, besides giving him a pension of some 600 livres. In January he even summoned the author to the Royal Palace to give a special performance of his play for the benefit of the little boy-king. The Duchess de Berri came to this performance, too, as well as the entire court, several high ministers and cardinals and some ambassadors in full regalia. The future monarch of France, a child of eight, however, was not particularly impressed with France's latest dramatic hit.

Voltaire's triumph was financial as well. The play's various performances netted him some 4,000 francs, to which he added further revenue from the printed edition of *Oedipus*. Tactfully he dedicated this to the Regent's mother. With his usual appreciation of the value of self-advertising he sent complimentary copies to the Regent, the Regent's daughter, the Regent's sister the Duchess of Lorraine, the Duke and Duchess of Maine, George I, king of England, and to several others. Most of his newly gained money he invested in a promotion scheme of one John Law, a speculative venture against which the conservative notary stoutly advised him, but by which everyone in France, from the Regent down to the lowest tailor and cobbler, was seeking a quick and easy fortune.

Voltaire's success naturally made him a sensational social figure. Pampered by lords and ladies, he had to rush from one banquet to another. Presents came from everywhere, even from George I of England, who sent the dramatist a handsome watch. With so much adulation heaped upon him, his cockiness rose to new heights. Slipping unceremoniously out of his bourgeois past, Voltaire felt himself on a par with the dazzling magnificoes who apparently were so eager to have him in their midst. When the Prince de Conti wrote a poem in his honor he graciously accepted it. "Monseigneur," he vouchsafed, "you will be a great poet. I must request the king to give you a pension."

With his first literary creation ecstatically received, Voltaire set out to duplicate his triumph with another play, *Artémire*. His labors on the new piece and on the still unfinished epic, "The League," together with his many social activities made him an extremely busy man.

In the spring of 1719 his social and literary routine, now running quite smoothly, was suddenly disturbed by a summons from the Regent. Philip was in a stormy frame of mind. The machinations and conspiracies against him by the Duchess of Maine and her theological confederate, the Spanish Alberoni, had been uncovered, and the Duchess as a consequence was now compelled to spin her political reflections in the Bastille. What further aggravated Philip was the unsolved authorship of three new, outlandish tirades against his private life. Known as the *Philippics*, they repeated more frankly than ever the hackneyed charges of murder and incest. In a vivid scene they pictured Philip trying to poison his nephew, the boy-king. Though the Regent was unquestionably dissolute, he was nonetheless a devoted uncle and utterly innocent of any foul designs on the life of the future king of France. When Philip saw the odious verses for the first time, he burst into tears. "This is too much," he sobbed, "this horror is stronger than I."

Unlike most of the libels cast at the Duke of Orleans, the *Philippics* were clearly the work of a master craftsman; and the name of the possible author which immediately occurred to every suspicious mind was Voltaire. While Philip hesitated to accept this damning hypothesis, he was also unwilling to reject it. Voltaire, he knew, had been a frequent associate of the discredited Duke and Duchess of Maine; and he had never ceased being a comrade of their outstanding political allies. For the harassed Regent and his circle these facts seemed enough to incriminate the poet. Hence the Duke ordered Voltaire to leave Paris; he was free to go anywhere he pleased, but let him stay away from the capital until further notice. It is said that as Voltaire was leaving the city a violent thunderstorm burst overhead and that he remarked to a fellow-traveler that "the kingdom of heaven sounds as if it, too, has become a regency."

Once more a refugee from his native town, Voltaire for a while visited the country homes of his well-born friends. "I pass my life," he announced, "from chateau to chateau." He stopped first at Sully. Here he hoped to experience once more the delights of that lovely rustic paradise. But he came also to work and spent many studious hours in the Duke of Sully's library, unearthing fresh material for his national epic. Most of his sojourns with his friends were decently short until he came to the castle of the Duke and Duchess of Villars. The poet had been introduced to the Duchess during that unforgettable first night of *Oedipus* and since then he had seen her on several occasions. A young and dashing woman, the Duchess was the wife of a man almost as old as he was famous, the veteran marshal who had led the late Louis' soldiers in many of their numerous assaults and even more numerous retreats. The Duke bristled with anecdotes of that bygone era, and probably had a larger stock of exclusive stories concerning the fourteenth Louis than any man in France. Like most veteran campaigners, the old soldier was always ready to reminisce and, as usual, Voltaire was an avid listener.

Marshal Villars' hospitality was more than matched by that of his wife. A flirtatious woman, and romantically minded, she used every trick in her repertory to attract Voltaire. Yet the Duchess had no intention of letting the poet become her lover—not because she had any moral qualms, but simply because it pleased her more to flirt with him. For a time Voltaire felt himself in love. He lost his usual inclination for work. Instead of composing new lines for his epic he wrote love poems for the Duchess. He called her his goddess, whose husband, alas, was Mars. But Voltaire was not designed for deep passion. Before long he began to be amused at himself. His amorous display toward the Duchess he characterized as "unfortunate." He had felt "the desire of the moth for the star." To his friend, Madame de Mimeure, he wrote: "You make me feel that friendship is a thousand times more precious than love. It seems to me that I am not made for the passions.

I find something ridiculous in my being in love, and I think it more ridiculous in those who should be in love with me. It is all over. I renounce it for life."

With Paris still a forbidden city he continued to wander from chateau to chateau. From the Villars estate he returned to his beloved woodlands at Sully. For a time we see him with the Caumartins at Saint-Ange; then we meet him on the sumptuous domain of the Duke of Richelieu. He returned frequently to the Villars where, now that he had renounced love, he found the Duchess an amiable and sympathetic companion. But not all of his time was devoted to leisure. On *Artémire,* with which he hoped to make a triumphant return to the capital, he labored with persistency, driving himself from morning till night to finish the play. In addition he kept his literary hand busy with occasional verses, besides pouring forth a stream of letters to his correspondents, now scattered in many lands.

Meanwhile doubts over his investments had begun to assail him. "Is Law," he asked one of his friends, "a god, a scoundrel, or a quack who poisons with the drug he distributes to all the world? It is a chaos which I cannot see through. . . ." On what was largely a hunch he disposed of his holdings at a substantial profit. "For my part," he said, "I give myself up to no other chimera than those of poetry."

In February, 1720, good news came from Paris. The author of the *Philippics,* a poet named La Grange-Chancel, had been discovered, and Voltaire was free to return to his native city. As soon as he was back he plunged into the task of getting *Artémire,* his new tragedy, ready for production. Despite the enormous success of *Oedipus,* its author's dramatic ambitions had been far from satisfied. He had used for his maiden effort a story centuries old and familiar to every educated Frenchman. Even the play's dramatic high point was borrowed almost bodily from the ancient work of Sophocles. In his new drama Voltaire sought to overcome his lack of originality by writing a piece which was completely his own.

The plot was extremely simple—to modern eyes, in fact, it must seem threadbare. Artémire, queen to Cassandra, who ruled in the days of Alexander the Great, has been accused falsely of infidelity during her husband's absence. Consumed by jealousy, the king made up his mind to die. Just after the mortal wound was inflicted, Cassandra discovered his wife to be innocent.

Voltaire had placed high hopes on this play. Before putting it into rehearsal he had read it at Sully and at Villars, and everywhere it received lavish applause. When the Abbé de Bussi attended a reading he is reported to have wept so copiously that he caught a cold from his own tears. But when the play opened at the Comédie on the 15th of February it was accorded a very poor reception. Before the end of the first act the audience openly hissed; and before the drama's mid-point the tumult became so violent that the author had to plead with the spectators for silence. *Artémire* ran for eight nights, after which it was embalmed in permanent obscurity. Measured by the most tolerant yardstick, *Artémire* was a bad play and deserved to fail. A contemporary critic found that "this tragedy in which Voltaire had nothing to depend on save his own genius, would not have the destiny of his *Oedipus*. It is too much work, especially for a young man, to have to invent the plot, the characters, the sentiments, and the arrangement, to say nothing of the versification." Yet even had *Artémire* been a perfect masterpiece, its road would still have been hard. For Mr. Law's fantastic bubble had burst at last, scattering financial wreckage all over France. No one had any ready money and even the lords, usually so light-hearted, were cast into deep gloom.

Although luck had been kind to Voltaire and had spared him from financial annihilation, the failure of *Artémire* had been a heavy blow. Plagued also by indifferent health, he grew increasingly nervous and irritable. Even the discovery of the true author of the *Philippics* and Regent Orleans' apology for having once again exiled the wrong poet, failed to pull the dejected man out of his neurotic swamp. His easy *bonhommie* had vanished, and also a good part of his self-confidence.

For a time he tried to occupy himself with his epic poem, but with only half a heart. He had begun to realize, too, that getting permission to publish "The League" would be most difficult. Certainly it would be too much to expect the Church to approve a poem which openly denounced it as bigoted and intolerant—which, in fact, depicted Henry of Navarre's fight against the Catholic League as a noble crusade. To outwit the Church authorities Voltaire resorted to a subtle stratagem. Recalling that Regent Orleans was a descendant of the valiant Henry of Navarre, the poet set out to obtain the ruler's personal endorsement of his epic about Henry and thus block in advance any opposition from the clerical brethren. He wrote to the Regent, begging for an audience so that his Royal Highness might listen "to some fragments of an epic on the illustrious ancestor whom you most resemble." He was, he told the Regent at the end of his letter, "your very poor Voltaire." Philip liked the compliment and when he heard the fragments of the epic on his illustrious ancestor, his pride expanded even more. But the Duke was much too sagacious to mix sentiment with politics; hence, though he confessed to admiring Voltaire's poem, he found he could not possibly approve it for publication.

With Philip's literary judgment, tempered as it was by the exigencies of politics, Voltaire had no quarrel; but when his friends, moved in the main by good intentions, began to hack critically at his work, Voltaire's nerves snapped completely. "It is only fit to be burned," he exclaimed in a sudden fit of despair and tossed the script into the flames. His amazed and horrified friends stood petrified as they saw it smoke. One of them, Hénault, rushed to draw the smouldering manuscript from the fire before the flames did too much harm. "Your poem," he later reminded its author, "cost me a pair of lace ruffles."

Unable to ease his harassed state of mind with the usual antitoxin of work, Voltaire turned his heels on Paris to abandon himself altogether to the frivolity of chateau life. He spent most of his summer at the country home of the Duke and Duchess of Villars. Here his dejected spirit found the solace and refreshment it craved. Late in December his wandering came to an abrupt stop when he was suddenly summoned to Paris where his old father was dying.

François Arouet died on New Year's day in 1720. Around his bedside, awaiting the end, were his children—Marguerite-Catherine, now married and the mother of two girls; her husband, Monsieur Mignot, employed like his father-in-law in the Chamber of Accounts; Armand, the elder brother, a fanatical Jansenist, who wore hair shirts and believed in miracles; and the thin-faced Voltaire, pleasure-loving skeptic whose only faith was reason.

Two days before his death the notary had resigned his position in the Chamber of Accounts to Armand, an office yielding some 13,000 francs a year. His property he divided equally among his three children, deducting, however, some 4,000 francs from Voltaire's share, for money he had paid out at various times to hold off the poet's creditors.

To his very end the notary had little faith in the ability of his sons to carry on the practical affairs of life. "I have a pair of fools for sons," he once lamented, "one in verse, the other in prose!" To guard them against a premature residence in the poorhouse he appointed his chief, President de Nicolai of the Chamber of Accounts, as trustee for the estate. Voltaire's patrimony, moreover, the shrewd notary bound up securely with chain and padlock so that it could not opened until the youth was thirty-five, and then only after he had satisfied the watchful trustee that "he had accepted a regular course of life."

In the belief that a dead man's wish might carry weight where a living man's efforts had failed, the aged notary closed his will with a solemn warning: "To the utmost of my power I exhort my two sons to remember the advice I have given them more than once, and by which it seems to me that they have profited but little, namely, that good sense desires and commands us to accommodate ourselves to the capacity of those to whom we think ourselves superior in intelligence and knowledge, and that *we ought never to make them feel our superiority.*"

Voltaire's first act, once his father was buried, was to

provoke a bitter dispute with President de Nicolai.

The father's anxiety, at his death, over young Voltaire's future was certainly not without just cause. At the age of twenty-eight the young man had accomplished little. He had made some money, but his income was at best precarious. In his chosen profession of letters he was still an unknown quantity. To his credit stood *Oedipus,* a successful play; counterbalancing it was *Artémire,* a bad failure. His ideas were also disturbing to the father, for in a world intellectually dominated by theologians he leaned toward a skepticism and rationalism which the notary regarded as a dangerous and unholy way of living. Moreover, Voltaire had become a playboy in whose tinsel world only poets and princes counted, and in which it was altogether fitting for the latter to contribute to the support of the former.

With the passing of his father Voltaire felt a touch of insecurity. "I shall be obliged to work to live," he wrote to Thieriot, "after having lived to work." Yet living had never exacted a large price from him. In his easy chateau existence he had lived in the manner of a grand seigneur. Now his financial prospects caused him to appeal to Philip the Regent, who gave him a new pension of 2,000 francs, besides a smaller one, drawn from the Regent's privy purse.

Meanwhile Voltaire began a campaign to obtain a soft governmental berth, concentrating for that purpose on Philip's prime minister, Cardinal Dubois, a man of doubtful character, but with ecclesiastic benefices yielding him a revenue of more than 1,500,000 francs a year. "If I could induce Your Eminence," Voltaire wrote to the Cardinal, "to employ me in something, I entreat you to believe, you would not be dissatisfied with me, and I should be eternally grateful to serve Your Eminence."

Not unmoved by Voltaire's appeal, His Eminence offered him a small assignment in espionage which the young man eagerly accepted. Specifically, Voltaire's task was to spy on a spy, a certain Levi Salomon, supposedly in the employ of the Emperor. The poet's venture into professional sleuthing was apparently a success, for the Cardinal promptly gave him an opportunity to enlarge and extend his operations. In the next summer he was to go as the prelate's special confidential agent to Cambrai where he was to pry into the affairs of some of the diplomats attending an international conference. Voltaire was delighted, and, anxious to continue in high grace with his employer, he journeyed to the royal palace at Versailles to make preparations for his mission. There, while rummaging through some confidential documents one day in the office of the Minister of War Le Blanc, he encountered his early nemesis, Captain Beauregard. The Captain appeared to be on excellent terms with Minister Le Blanc, and had in fact come to be his dinner guest. When he saw the poet, now a fellow spy, Beauregard was quite willing to let byones be bygones and greeted him as an old friend. But the poet would have none of him. "I was well aware that spies were paid for their services," he said as stiffly as possible, "but I did *not* know their compensation was to eat at the minister's table!"

Voltaire's caustic pronouncement reaped a prompt response. A few days later while returning to his quarters, he was suddenly pounced upon by the Captain, a dynamo of a man, who beat the poet with his walking stick, leaving a permanent dent in Voltaire's nose. In time Voltaire was able to drag his assailant to court, but he was never able to live down the humiliation of having been publicly caned.

In July of 1722 Voltaire undertook his trip to Cambrai, but he did not travel alone. Instead he went in the company of a young Marquise de Rupelmonde, the wealthy widow of a Flemish nobleman and the daughter of the governor of Metz. In the marquise there was an odd mixture of effervescence and sobriety. She liked fun and social gayety, but she also dabbled in philosophy and literature. She was traveling to the Hague on business, and hearing of Voltaire's journey to the Low Countries, she invited him to "share a place in her carriage." Her generosity extended even further, for she insisted also on paying all her escort's bills besides having her attendants wait on him, while he, as usual, endeavored to repay his benefactress with his charm.

The journey to Holland, however, was destined to be more memorable for its philosophic results than for its philanthropy. When the Marquise asked him what he believed in religion Voltaire put his answer into a poem, calling it "The Epistle to Uranie," but subsequently changing it to "For and Against." In it he told the Marquise that she was not to take the holy books seriously as history, but rather as a series of legends. As such they were, he said, artistic and at times even beautiful—but as history they were imbecilic. It was ridiculous, he declared, to believe that the Creator of man "drowned the fathers and died for his children." It was ridiculous, too, to attach divine significance to the lowly life and death of Jesus.

Such nonsense Voltaire advised his questioner to leave to the sacred theologians. Instead let her

Believe that the eternal wisdom of the Most High
Has engraved with his hand, in the depths of your
heart
The Religion of Nature.
Believe that your soul, in its native simplicity,
Will not be the object of God's eternal hate.
Believe that before his throne, at all times, in all places
The heart of the just person is precious.
Believe that a modest Buddhist monk, a charitable
dervish
Will find more favor in his eyes
Than a pitiless Jansenist
Or an ambitious Pope.
Ah! what indeed does it matter the name under
which we pray to him?
He receives every homage but by none is honored.
Be sure he does not need our assiduous services.
If he can be offended, it is only by unjust deeds.
God judges us by our virtues, not by our sacrifices.

When the Marquise and her companion arrived at Cambrai, they found the city in a festive mood, with dances and dinners as prominent on the diplomats' agenda as their talks in conference halls. With a little deft wire-pulling on Voltaire's part, a gala production of *Oedipus* was performed, which was attended by high-ranking dignitaries of state and church. Voltaire reported all these happenings in great detail to his chief, Prime Minister Dubois, who happened also to be the Archbishop of Cambrai, even though in his entire episcopal life the prelate had never set foot in that city.

"We arrive," Voltaire wrote, "in your metropolis, where,

I believe all the ambassadors and all the cooks of Europe have given one another rendezvous. It seems that all the ministers of Germany are at Cambrai for no other purpose than to drink to the health of the Emperor. As for the ambassadors of Spain, one of them hears two masses a day, and the other directs a troop of actors. The English ministers send many couriers to Champagne, but few to London. . . . May the gentlemen of the Congress, in drinking at this retreat, assure the peace of Europe!"

For six weeks Voltaire helped the diplomats in their bibulous efforts. Then, his own mission on behalf of the Cardinal completed, he traveled northward to Brussels. There Voltaire called on Jean-Baptiste Rousseau, once esteemed as the Horace of France, but now languishing in exile. In his younger days Rousseau had been an acidulous skeptic, a terrifying smasher of idols, and a hero to the youthful Voltaire. But now, approaching old age, he had put aside his hammers and axes and had embraced a moral, Christian life. Where once he had created cynical strophes debunking Moses, he now composed humble apothegms to the Holy Ghost.

At the outset the two poets expressed great admiration for one another. Voltaire, still harboring some traces of his early hero-worship, treated his fellow poet with great deference, calling him Master, and going arm in arm with him to the theatre. On Sunday he outdid himself and went to mass with his host, though on this occasion Voltaire's impious gestures and grimaces almost caused his forcible ejection from the church.

The fraternal feeling of the two poets, already strained by this episode, was ruptured completely when they began to discuss their rhymes. Not suspecting that the once iconoclastic Rousseau had become devout, Voltaire proceeded —so he thought—to regale his host with his deistic "For and Against," but before he got very far Rousseau stopped him. "Spare yourself the trouble of reading any more," he ejaculated. "It is a horrible profanity!" Somewhat later Rousseau read his "Ode to Posterity." "That is an ode, Master," Voltaire commented, "which in my opinion will never reach its address."

In October Voltaire arrived at the Hague. He had come to the Dutch capital to make arrangements for the printing of his national epic, "The League." He still hoped to obtain the "privilege" to publish the poem in France, but, should this be refused, he intended to make the Dutch edition serve the readers of both countries. He had no difficulty finding a willing printer. For a number of weeks Voltaire gave himself almost wholly to the task of putting the final touches on his manuscript, getting it ready for the printer and softening such passages which might be objectionable to the Paris censor. The success of his venture excited him. His spirits had never been higher. "There is no better place than the Hague," he wrote to Madame de Bernières. "One sees nothing but fields, canals and green trees; it's an earthly paradise from the Hague to Amsterdam. I have gazed with respect on this town, which is the storehouse of the Universe. There were more than a thousand vessels in the port." He saw "the prime minister on foot . . . without lackeys, in the midst of the people." There was "not one idler, not one pauper, not one dandy, not one ruffian." Between his work on "The League" and his tours of sight-seeing, Voltaire passed his life, he said, "between labor and pleasure," thus living, as he put it, "Holland fashion and French fashion." "We

have a detestable opera here," he confided to Madame de
Bernières, "but by way of compensation, I see Calvinist
ministers, Arminians, Socinians, Rabbis, Anabaptists, who
discourse to admiration, and who, indeed, are all in the
right."

As the time drew near for his homeward journey Voltaire concentrated more and more on getting subscriptions for his forthcoming epic. He made his Parisian
friend, Thieriot, his assistant, and kept him busy circulat-
ing sample parts and soliciting sales. Before setting out for
Paris, moreover, he instructed his friend to send him "the
exact prices paid in France for an escalin, a florin, a pan-
tagon, a ducat, and a Spanish pistole," coins then current
in Holland and selling at a premium in France.

The poet's trip back home was made on horseback, with
two saddlebags full of foreign coins and a head full of
ideas. Voltaire was in no great haste to get to Paris, for
this, too, was in essence a business trip. While Thieriot
in the capital was taking subscriptions for "The League,"
and endeavoring at the same time to influence the censor
to permit its publication, Voltaire was covering the chateau
trade from Holland to Brabant, skirting the German frontier down to Paris. Wherever he appeared he distributed
circulars extolling his national epic and inviting literary
connoisseurs not to miss the opportunity to subscribe to
the great work.

Back in Paris, he disposed of his foreign coins at a good
profit, thereby more than paying for his long trip from
the north. But his stay in the capital was brief. Before long
he was once more touring in search of subscriptions, working his way a hundred miles south of Paris toward Orleans.

Not far from that celebrated city, at La Source, he was the guest of Lord Bolingbroke and his French wife. Because of his Jacobite sympathies Bolingbroke had been ostracized from English politics and had retired to France. Here, on a large and magnificent estate, he lived the comfortable life of an affluent English gentleman. Voltaire was careful to read his national epic to the Bolingbrokes. The Lord and the Lady liked the poem; and the author, for his part, liked its admirers. "This illustrious Englishman," he reported to Thieriot, "has all the erudition of his own country and all the polish of ours. I have never heard our language spoken with greater accuracy or vigor. . . ." He added that the Lord knew the History of the Ancient Egyptians as he knew that of England, and that he was familiar with Virgil as well as Milton. "It is hardly becoming of me," Voltaire declared to Thieriot, "to say that Madame and himself have been infinitely satisfied with my poem. . . . They place it above all the poetical works which have appeared in France." "But," Voltaire added, "I know how to discount such extragant praises."

Meanwhile the author of "The League" had made no headway with the censor. Flattery and subtle persuasion had left that moral custodian completely cold. Yet Voltaire continued to be optimistic. He softened and sweetened his work as best he could, deleting the sharper passages, and trying in every way to make his diatribe against religious bigotry palatable to the clergy. He worked assiduously on the Regent and on his Cardinal Archbishop Dubois. Finally he dedicated the work to the boy-king, reminding His Majesty that "every work in which the great deeds of Henry IV are spoken of ought to be offered to Your Majesty," for "it is the blood of that hero which flows in your veins." Yet in the end permission to print was refused.

If "The League" could not be published in France, Voltaire's contract with his Dutch printer had to be canceled and all money returned to the subscribers. Rather than do that, the poet decided to take his chances with the law, and set out to have his work printed in secret. To get it ready for a printer he rented quarters in the house of Madame de Bernières in the *Rue de Beaune*. There he planned to work in quiet solitude. But before long he found himself "in a cruel position." "I have no wish to quit Madame de Bernières," he wrote to Thieriot, "and yet it's impossible for me to live in her damned house, which is as cold as the pole in winter, stinks of dung like a stable, and where there is more noise than in Hell itself." Yet live in this "damned house" he did; and a month later he even rented another room in it for Thieriot.

Meanwhile, some seventy miles from Paris, at Rouen, one of Voltaire's former school mates, Cideville, now a magistrate, had found a man who could be persuaded to print the forbidden work. To assist in the job of putting his poem into print Voltaire made frequent quick trips to Rouen, leaving Thieriot to act for him in Paris during his absence. The process of printing "The League" was lamentably slow. Not only was all the work done by hand, but with the necessary stealth and secrecy involved in the proceedings, almost a half year was needed to put its two hundred or so pages into type.

In Paris, under the supervision of Thieriot, work on bindings for two thousand volumes had been started. To divert all suspicion, should any of his instructions to his Parisian friend accidentally fall into hostile hands, Voltaire was careful to allude to his poem as his "son," or even his "little bastard," while the bindings for the book became its "coat." "The child," Voltaire said, "was to be decently clothed."

Getting the printed pages to Paris, once they were ready, was again no simple matter; for the roads between the capital and Rouen were lined with police, in plain clothes and in uniform, as well as squadrons of local customs officials who would have been delighted to pounce on such a choice morsel as the prohibited "League." However, with the help of his good friend Madame de Bernières and her husband, Voltaire hoped to accomplish his end. The Bernières were in the express business, moving goods in large vans between Rouen and Paris, and also in barges up and down the Seine. Concealed in the Bernières vans and barges, Voltaire's forbidden poem was smuggled into the capital. The dangerous work was at best exasperatingly slow, a few bundles being brought at a time. Once in Paris, they were sneaked into Madame de Bernières' house on the *Rue de Beaune* where Voltaire and Thieriot carefully hid them.

During these months Voltaire had plunged into the composition of another play. He called it *Mariamne,* setting the scene in Palestine, with Herod as the leading character. The chief feminine role of Marianne he wrote for France's leading actress, the young and gifted Adrienne Lecouvreur. Voltaire laid down his customary publicity barrage, touting his play and its author very highly even before the piece had been finished. Following the practice he had employed so successfully in the case of *Oedipus,* he made arrangements to give an advance reading of *Mariamne* before a distinguished audience. For this purpose he got himself an invitation to the Chateau de Maisons, on the outskirts of Paris. The reading was scheduled for early November, and the occasion was to be somewhat of a celebration, with three days of dining, drinking, music and dancing.

Two days after his arrival at Maisons the playwright was suddenly taken with a fever, which by evening was recognized as smallpox. At once there was consternation, and a wild exodus from the chateau. Only Adrienne, the actress, remained at the poet's bedside, meanwhile having summoned Thieriot. Doctors, deeming the frail poet's chances for life beyond hope, were reluctant to treat him, leaving him, as he said, awaiting death "with sufficient tranquility, regretting, however, to go without having put the last hand to my poem and to Mariamne, and sorry to leave my friends so soon." But the thin man surprised the doctors and the embalmers, and after a month's illness he was strong enough to leave for Paris. He had not gone a hundred steps from the chateau when fire broke out in his room and a large part of the building was burned to the ground.

His illness and his narrow escape from the flames shattered Voltaire's nerves, and for a while he believed he had only a short time to live. He had always been something of a hypochondriac. From early youth he had derived a melancholy satisfaction from his aches and pains, and had swallowed pills and tonics and elixirs in fantastic amount. No new nostrum escaped him. Indeed, on one occasion when the poet found a bottle of untried medicine in the room of one of his friends, he couldn't resist the temptation to walk off with it and try it. Like many such invalids he devoted a good deal of his time to observing and discussing his health. In a letter to the Baron de Breteuil, one of the longest letters Voltaire ever wrote, he minutely described his smallpox and his cure. "Eight times," he wrote, "the doctors gave me emetics; and instead of the strong cordials usually recommended in this malady, made me drink a hundred pints of lemonade. This treatment, which you will think extraordinary, was the only one which possibly could have saved my life—and I am convinced that the majority of those whom this fearful disease has killed, would be alive had they been treated as I was."

Soon after Voltaire's return to Paris, "The League" made its surreptitious appearance. Early in 1724 copies of it began to circulate and before long the illicit book became a common topic of conversation. As usual, the fact that the book was forbidden made it desirable. For educated persons it became required reading, and soon no secret drawer was complete without it. Even old Mathieu Marais, a very effete and proper person, who despised Voltaire for his bourgeois background, read the book. "I have read it," he confided to his diary. "It is a wonderful work, a magic piece of the mind, as beautiful as Virgil. Behold our language in possession of an epic poem. . . . I do not know how to speak of it. I cannot think where Arouet, so young, could have learned so much. . . ."

As in all of Voltaire's writings the plot of his national epic, which in the mind of his admiring countrymen elevated him far above Milton and Dante, is childishly simple. Henry, king of Navarre, and Henry III, king of France, are laying siege to Paris. Henry of Navarre seeks help from Queen Elizabeth to whom he relates the misfortunes of France, laying particular emphasis on religious bigotry and the massacre of Saint Bartholomew, which he describes in great and vivid detail. Discord, an allegorical figure, arms Jacques Clément who murders Henry III, thus making Henry of Navarre the legitimate heir to the throne. But Henry, a Protestant, is not acceptable to the Church and is opposed by the Catholic League. The spirit of the great French king, Saint Louis, appears to Henry and conducts him to the Palace of Destiny, where Henry sees his posterity as well as the great men of France. At Ivry des Ligueurs Henry defeats his foes; but instead of assuming the responsibilities of his sceptre, Henry abandons himself to pleasure in the Temple of Love with his mistress, Gabrielle d'Estrées. However, in time he is moved by the misery and starvation of the people of Paris. Enlightened by Truth, he becomes a Catholic and enters Paris to rule as Henry IV of France.

It is not surprising that old Mathieu Marais should have compared Voltaire's work with that of Virgil, for both in structure and in incident, "The League" was modeled after the "Aeneid." Nor should it be difficult to understand why Voltaire's contemporaries should have esteemed his epic poem so highly. In an age impregnated with theological controversy Voltaire's strophes had universal appeal. To a France, harassed so long by misgovernment, Voltaire's portrayal of the heroic Henry IV came like a vision of hope. The poet's assault on religious bigotry and intolerance gave no quarter, and its readers almost inevitably admired its daring, if not its logic. "The League" listed every crime perpetrated by intolerant religion since the dawn of history. It showed mothers offering to Moloch the burning entrails of their own children; Iphigenia led by her father to be sacrificed at the altar; the early Christians hurled from the top of the Roman Capitol and driven into the arena; Jews burned every year for "not abandoning the faith of their fathers." The poem depicted in detail the horrible massacre of Saint Bartholomew, showing civilized men turned to beasts by intolerant religion, "invoking the Lord while slaughtering their brothers, and, their arms wet with the blood of innocent children, daring to offer to God that execrable incense." It pictured religion used by an unscrupulous clergy to further its ambitions, even at the cost of civil war. "To him who avenges the church all becomes legitimate; murder is just; it is authorized; nay, it is commanded by Heaven!" The Roman Church was described as a power "inflexible to the conquered, complaisant to conquerors, ready, as interest dictates, either to absolve or condemn." Yet only weaklings fear the power of the church. "A great man," Queen Elizabeth was made to say to Henry, "ought not to dread the futile thunders of Rome."

The police hunted diligently for the book, but obviously they could never be expected to trace some two thousand volumes scattered throughout France. Though they came upon a single copy here and there, the book continued to excite readers for a long time. The Pope pronounced his solemn curse and anathema on it, but with little practical effect. The poem was imitated, pirated, and in the end even parodied. "Everybody," said Voltaire, "is making epic poems; I have brought poems into fashion." Meanwhile he continued to reap renown and an excellent revenue.

Flushed by his triumph with "The League," Voltaire offered his new tragedy, *Mariamne,* to the public in March, 1724. The story was set in Palestine and had for its leading personages King Herod and his young wife, Marianne. Essentially a melodrama, the play related in detail the suffering and injustice wrought by the brutal Herod. No sooner was Mariamne his queen than Herod tried ruthlessly to dominate her. Before her eyes he killed her father. He murdered her brother. His constant brutality failed to break the spirit of the queen; instead it made him an abhorrent sight to Mariamne. Herod's mad passions and excesses reached beyond his household, so that he became universally hated. Fearing for her life and that of her children, Mariamne prepared to flee from the court. When the king heard of her plan he vowed to destroy her and her children, but upon seeing her he was stricken with remorse, and on his knees begged her forgiveness. At this moment the people of Jerusalem, having heard of the plight of the queen, stormed the palace to rescue her. But the rebellion was quickly put down. Convinced that Mariamne had conspired against him, Herod ordered her execution. Immediately after her death the king received proof of her innocence and fell into a fit of belated remorse.

The theatre was crowded for the opening performance, but the expectant multitude was disappointed. Mindful of French delicacy, which abhorred physical violence on the stage, Voltaire presented none of Herod's butcheries to his sensitive audience. Instead, he told the spectators about them in the dialogue. Unfortunately, the repetition of Herod's atrocities became wearisome and the audience grew impatient. But what really wrecked the play was Voltaire's utter lack of dramatic sense. Though the drama dealt ostensibly with Herod and talked considerably about him for the first two acts, the leading character failed to appear until the play was more than half over. By this time the restless audience had become thoroughly hostile. Toward the close of the tragedy, when the hapless Mariamne raised the cup of poison to her lips, a wag in the pit cried out, "The queen drinks!" and the rest of the play could not be heard for the noise and tittering. Aware of his dramatic blunder, Voltaire withdrew his piece. Mathieu Marais, who only a short time ago had raved so ecstatically over "The League," now wrote in his diary: "Dramatic poetry differs from epic, and one man has not all the talents."

After *Mariamne's* failure Voltaire sought solace at Forges, a place famed for its curative waters and the fashionable world which drank them. Imagining once again that he was close to death's door, the poet took the cure which apparently was not to his taste. "There is more vitriol," he announced, "in a single bottle of Forges water than in a whole bottle of ink. . . ." His discomfort was somewhat mollified by the presence of his friend, the Duke of Richelieu, who was also taking the cure. Through the Duke, the poet made the acquaintance of Madame de Prie, the mistress of the Duke of Burgundy and a woman of no little influence at the Royal Palace. Voltaire paid gallant court to Madame de Prie for most of the summer, even writing a little skit for her, *Indiscretion,* a light satire on court life. In return the Madame held Voltaire in high esteem and made sure that he was invited to her more important functions.

Shortly before the appearance of "The League" the Regent's Prime Minister, Cardinal Dubois, died; and a few months later Philip went to his grave. The King of France, Louis XV, a boy of fourteen, had been betrothed to Maria Leczinska, six years the King's senior and the daughter of the dethroned King Stanislas of Poland. The wedding had been scheduled for early September of 1725.

With this turn of events Voltaire was highly satisfied, for in Maria he foresaw a possible sponsor for "The League," and the consequent removal of the censor's ban. In addition he had visions of being able to squeeze his way into some kind of courtly sinecure. Thus reasoning, he hurried to Versailles to lay the groundwork for his scheme. "I shall write verses for her (the Queen)," he wrote to Madame de Bernières, "if she is worth the trouble," though, he added, "I should rather write verses for you if you loved me."

Putting his most elegant flattery into rhyme, he paid glowing homage to Madame de Prie, now generally said to be the power behind the throne. The Madame was human enough to be vulnerable to Voltaire's blandishments, and saw to it that he received an invitation to the royal nuptials at Fontainbleau. There from his strategic observation post Voltaire gave detailed reports to his friends of what went on behind the scenes. "Everyone," he wrote, "is enchanted by the Queen's goodness and politeness. . . . She fainted a moment in the chapel, but only for form's sake. . . ." Yet all the while his eyes were fixed on his goal. "During the first days of this hubbub I shall avoid having myself presented to the Queen," he wrote. "I shall wait until the crowd has subsided and Her Majesty has recovered a little from her bewilderment. . . . Then I shall try to have *Oedipus* and *Marianne* played to her. I shall dedicate them both to her. She has already sent me word that I should take that liberty."

Voltaire's campaign was not without competition. "All the poets in the world," he informed Thieriot, "have come together at Fontainebleau. Every day the Queen is assas-

sinated with odes, sonnets, as well as marriage songs. . . .
I imagine she takes the poets for court fools. . . ." In the
midst of this swarm of courtiers, job-seekers, and compet-
ing poets, Voltaire made little progress. Indeed, as time
went on, he found himself "in low humor and not daring
to show it, seeing many ridiculous things, but not daring
to tell of them." When his *Marianne* was produced, the
Queen was moved to tears. His skit, *Indiscretion,* made her
laugh. But that apparently was the limit of Her Majesty's
reaction to the hopes of Voltaire. "Every day," he lamented,
"they give me hopes which yield me little nourishment."
The Queen, he informed Thieriot, "speaks to me frequently; she calls me 'my poor Voltaire.' A fool would be
content with all that, but unfortunately I have sense
enough to feel that praise is of small account, that the
role of a court poet has always something in it a little
ridiculous, and that it is not permitted to be in this country of ours without having some kind of status."

In November of 1725, however, Voltaire's luck changed.
"The Queen," he now could announce to some of his
friends, "has just given me from her privy purse a pension
of 1500 livres. . . . This is the first step to obtaining the
things I ask. . . . I count on the friendship of Madame de
Prie. I begin to have a reasonable hope of being able
sometimes to be useful to my friends."

As the year 1725 approached its end Voltaire was filled
with even more than his usual self-confidence. At the age
of thirty-one he was generally regarded as France's most
promising poet. He had given France its first national epic,
and while that poem was still under the censor's ban, it
was nonetheless highly praised. He was a fairly successful

dramatist; he was a friend of the powerful Madame de Prie; and his work had been recognized by a royal pension. His capacity for being affable and charming had made him the pet of the *noblesse,* and had even gained entree for him at the Royal Palace, through whose glistening halls he glided in the same way he had passed through the chateaux of dukes and princes. He had shed his bourgeois background as easily as he had shed his bourgeois name. Voltaire the poet deemed himself the equal of those whom the accident of birth had made noble.

One night in December of 1725 while Voltaire was chatting with some people at the opera, the Chevalier de Rohan-Chabot, of the eminent and powerful House of Rohan, a man of forty-three, quarrelsome, bullying, and also somewhat of a coward, began to jeer at Voltaire's name.

"Monsieur Arouet, Monsieur Voltaire—what *is* your name?" he sneered.

The reply came quickly: "Whatever my name is, I know how to preserve and honor it."

Rohan mumbled incoherently and went off; but the incident was not closed.

Two days later the men met again at the Comédie in the dressing room of Adrienne Lecouvreur. Once again Rohan asked his impertinent question. "The Chevalier has had his answer," was Voltaire's retort. Furious, Rohan raised his walking stick, while Voltaire's hand darted to the little sword he carried at his side. But at that moment Adrienne very conveniently fainted and the group dispersed.

Eighteenth-century France was still in the grip of a medieval caste system, and for a bourgeois to talk back to a noble was unthinkable. Voltaire's tongue had carried him too far. To humiliate a privileged aristocrat in public was fraught with danger.

A few days later, while Voltaire was dining at the home of the Duke of Sully, a servant brought him a message telling him he was wanted in the street. He went out, was seized by a gang of men and mercilessly beaten in the sight of Rohan, who directed operations from his carriage. "Spare the head," he jeered. "It is still good enough to make the people laugh."

When Voltaire was finally released he dashed back, disheveled and bleeding, into the Sully dining room where only a few moments before he had been diverting the guests. In an excited torrent of words he poured out his agonizing story. But the high-born company was indifferent; the barrier of caste had suddenly begun to manifest itself. The Duke of Sully, in whose home Voltaire had the standing of one of the family, had witnessed the whole episode. Voltaire implored his help, which, he believed, could send Rohan to jail. Yet neither Voltaire's pleas nor a sense of justice moved the Duke. Sully and Rohan were cousins. Yet even if they had not been related, they were socially of the same stratum, and bound against a bourgeois by a common code.

What made Voltaire's plight even more painful was the barbarous custom of the age which treated a person's misfortune as a fitting object of ridicule. For the next few days wherever the poet appeared he was greeted by laughter and derision. The very people who had chuckled at his quips and admired his brilliance, now laughed at his misfortune. The Prince de Conti, who not so long ago had composed an ode eulogizing the author of *Oedipus,* now remarked with a shrug of the shoulders "the blows were well received and badly given." "We would be unfortunate, indeed," said the Bishop of Blois, as he took a pinch of snuff, "if poets had no shoulders"; while old Marais wrote in his diary: "No one pities him, and those he thought his friends have turned their backs on him. . . . And so, at last, behold our poets, through the fear of the stick, reduced to their legitimate work of learning and pleasing."

The few friends who remained loyal were powerless. Even the formidable Madame de Prie was helpless. "I am really very sorry for poor Voltaire," she said. "At bottom he is right." But the Rohan clan was too influential even for her, and the best she could do was to advise the poet to get out of Paris lest matters grow worse. Get out of town he did, hiding for the next two months on the fringe of the capital, and secretly practicing swordsmanship.

Under the law Rohan had made himself liable to long imprisonment. The law was not invoked and Rohan continued to circulate as before. But the law which had remained dormant in the case of Rohan began to be very active in the case of Voltaire. The authorities, suspecting Voltaire might seek revenge, ordered the police to arrest him the moment he showed any inclination to make trouble. From the police record we know that he appeared suddenly one day at Versailles, apparently looking for Rohan, but he vanished just as suddenly as he had come. Later he was reported living in Paris, taking fencing lessons. "Several times," says the police report, "during six weeks he has changed his residence and his quarters. We have information he lives in bad company. It is said he has dealings with some soldiers of the guards and that several ruffians frequent his lodgings. . . . It is certain he has very bad designs."

His designs, indeed, were not seraphic. Denied help from the courts, Voltaire had made up his mind to take the only road open in those days to a man of honor—to avenge the insult by a duel.

Not long after, he appeared unexpectedly at the theatre, where in the box of Adrienne Lecouvreur he saw Rohan. For once he wasted no time on sugary blandishments. "Monsieur," he said, "if some affair of interest has not made you forget the outrage of which I have to complain, I hope you will give me satisfaction for it." Rohan accepted the challenge, but the duel never took place. For at once the pressure of the Rohan family exerted itself, and on the next day, the 17th of April, according to the police records, "the Sieur Arouet de Voltaire" was arrested and "by order of the king" taken to the Bastille.

The Voltaire who was lodged in the Bastille was no longer the carefree poet with whom we are familiar. Gone was his easy confidence; gone his airy flippancy. For the first time in his life Voltaire had become deeply serious. While he was still in hiding he wrote to Madame de Bernières, "I have reached the limit; I am waiting only to get well to abandon this country forever. . . . I wish to return to Paris only to see you, to embrace you one more time, and let you see that I am loyal both in friendship and in misfortune." His determination to leave France was not merely a whim. A few days after his arrest he wrote to the Minister of the Department of Paris: "The Sieur de Voltaire very humbly represents that he was assaulted by the brave Chevalier de Rohan, that ever since he has constantly sought to repair not his own honor, but that of the Chevalier, which has proved very difficult. . . . With earnestness . . . he requests permission to go at once to England."

A fortnight after his arrest Voltaire was released on condition that he leave France at once. Two days later, accompanied by one of his jailers, he was driven to Calais, whence he was to embark for England. Before he crossed the Channel he chatted with the lieutenant of police.

"What do you do with people who forge *lettres de cachet?*" he asked.

"We hang them."

"That is fine," flashed Voltaire, "in anticipation of the time when those who sign genuine ones shall be treated the same way!"

England

VOLTAIRE caught his first glimpse of the English shore on a beautiful day in May. He himself recorded that the sky was without a cloud, "a soft breeze tempering the sun's heat and disposing all hearts to joy." Sailing up the Thames as far as Greenwich, he set foot on English soil some five miles below London. The day of his arrival happened to fall on the king's birthday, with all England apparently celebrating it. The Thames, Voltaire reported, was covered for six miles with rows of merchant vessels, their sails fully spread, in honor of their majesties who were gliding down the river in a golden barge, surrounded by boats on which bands were playing lively tunes, and followed by countless small craft rowed by men in elaborate costumes. "There was not one of these oarsmen," Voltaire commented, "who did not assure me by his face, his dress, and his excellent physical condition that he was a free man and lived in plenty."

Such were the first impressions made by a strange land

on the avid eyes of the exiled Voltaire. His movements in the days that followed are uncertain and at times even confused. Apparently he cloistered himself for a while in a village somewhere near Dover where he concentrated on the study of English. From one of his notebooks, recently discovered, we know that after only a couple of months in England, the poet was using English well enough to record his private notes.

By mid-October we find him installed at Wandsworth, not far from London, but in the interval he seems to have made a secret and somewhat mysterious trip to France, where, it is believed, he hoped again to challenge the Chevalier de Rohan to a duel. "I sought but one man," he wrote to Thieriot, "whose cowardly instinct concealed him from me, as though he had discovered I was on his tracks." His hopes failed to materialize, however, and the dread of being discovered caused him, as he put it, "to leave in more haste than I had come."

When he returned to England he found a letter from Mademoiselle de Bessières, telling him of the death of his sister, Marguerite-Catherine. Voltaire had been very fond of his sister. After his mother's death, she had been closer and kinder to him than any of the Arouets. Later on, she had a family of her own and her main interests were necessarily under another roof. She was not yet forty when she died, and the news of her passing shook Voltaire badly. To his friend Madame de Bernières he wrote: "My sister should have lived and I should have died. It was destiny's mistake. I am saddened by her loss. You know my heart, you know how fond I was of her. I was sure she would be the one to wear mourning for me." To another friend he confided that his sister's passing had suddenly made him realize how little he himself was worth.

To add to his afflictions, soon after his arrival in England he lost most of his money. He had depended for funds on some bills of exchange on a Jewish broker, whom circumstances had forced into bankruptcy. "At my coming to London," he wrote to Thieriot in his quaint English, "I found my damned Jew was broken. I was without a penny, sick to dye of a violent ague, stranger, alone, helpless, in the midst of a city wherein I was known to nobody; my Lord and Lady Bolingbroke were into the country. I could not make bold to see our ambassador in so wretched a condition. I had never undergone such distress; but I am born to run through all the misfortunes of life. In these circumstances my star, that among all its direful influences pours on me some kind refreshment, sent to me an English gentleman unknown to me, who forced me to receive some money that I wanted. Another London citizen that I had seen but once at Paris, carried me to his country house, wherein I lead an obscure and charming life since that time, without going to London, and quite given over to the pleasures of indolence and friendship. The true and generous affection of this man who soothes the bitterness of my life brings me to love you more and more. All the instances of friendship indear my friend Tiriot to me. I have seen often my lord and lady Bolingbroke; I have found their affection still the same, increased in proportion to my unhappiness; they offered me all, their money, their house; but I refused all, because they are lords, and I have accepted all from Mr. Falkener, because he is a single English gentleman."

Everard Falkener was a well-to-do silk merchant living quietly in his country home at Wandsworth. He and Voltaire became close friends, and the Frenchman stayed with him apparently for some time, perfecting his English, "enjoying honest talk and wholesome wine," besides predicting that some day his host would be ambassador to Turkey. Falkener knew the methods of business and commerce and took delight in revealing this significant phase of English life to his guest. Yet Falkener was more than a successful business man who prattled about sales, commissions and net profits. He was evidently a man of refined tastes, who adorned his house with paintings and rare objects of art and whose library was filled with fine books on every conceivable subject. A well-educated man, Falkener talked with ease and intelligence about letters and politics, and Voltaire drew heavily on his friend's knowledge. The conversations with Falkener and his friend comprised innumerable subjects and Voltaire, with his usual meticulous care, jotted them down into his notebook. He made no effort to arrange his entries logically, but left them helter-skelter just as they came to his mind. Thus in one breath they reveal conditions in Lapland, a choice bit of gossip about the Pope, from which they saunter to some extemporaneous rhymes of the Earl of Rochester. Written in English, the notes ranged from short sentences and terse apothegms to anecdotes and observations. As might be expected, a good many of Voltaire's remarks dealt with his impressions of the English.

"The English," he wrote, "is full of thoughts, French all in miens, compliments, sweet words, obsequious with pride, and very much self concern'd under the appearance of a pleasant modesty. The English is sparing of words, openly proud and unconcerned; he gives the most quick birth as he can to his thoughts, for fear of losing his time.

English tongue, barren and barbarous in its origin, is now plentiful and sweet, like a garden full of exotik plants." Voltaire's keen interest in religions of all kinds brought forth several comments. "England," he found "in the meeting of all religions, as the royal exchange is the 'rendezvous' of all foreigners." As for the Quakers, "it seems that one does deal in England with the quakers as with the peers of the realm, which give their verdict upon their honour, not upon their oath."

Contrasting England with his own country, Voltaire wrote: "We arrive at the same work by different ways; a chartusian friar kneels and prostrates himself all along before me, a quaker speaks to me always covered, both do so to follow the Gospel in the most rigorous sense." Regarding the Jewish faith, it "is the mother of Christianity, the grandmother of mohametism. When I see Christians cursing Jews, methinks I see children beating their fathers." Now and then we find a burst of skepticism, as when he described the founders of religion to be "ignorant supported by more ignorant men." "Dunces," he said, "are the founders of all religions; men of wit founders of all heresies; men of understanding laugh at both." And, "to get some authority over others one must make oneself as unlike them as one can. 'Tis a sure way of dazzling the eyes of the crowd. So the priest appears in long gown, etc."

While at Wandsworth, Voltaire made good use of his host's library. He read and investigated every conceivable subject, but his favorite field was history. The high points of his readings, like those of his conversations, he carefully recorded in his notes. The range covered the whole sweep of history from the ancient Greeks and Romans to the world in which he lived. There were, he wrote, "three

plauges in London under Elizabeth, Charles the First and
Charles the Second." As for Cromwell, Voltaire found that
he "built nothing. There is no monument remaining of
him. His body together with those of Ireton and Bradshaw
were taken out of their coffins at Westminster, and drawn
upon hurdles to Tyburn where they were hanged by the
neck for some hours, their heads chopt off afterwards and
perched on Westminsterhall, 30 January 1661, a year after
the restoration." To which he added that "the same army
that cut off Charles the first and Lawd (*sic*) was ready to
make an arbitrary king of Charles 2 and a pope of the arch
of Cant. . . ."

It was at Wandsworth that Voltaire discovered the
Quakers, a sect hardly known to Catholic France. They
interested him immensely, though at times their earnestness amused him no little. He often went to their meetings
and as time went on made friends with many of them. One
of them, Edward Higginson, a teacher in a local Quaker
school, has told how the fiery Frenchman used to argue
with him on the subject of water baptism until, to clinch
the argument once and for all, the schoolmaster produced
a text from St. Paul. "Some time after," Higginson said,
"Voltaire being at the Earl Temple's seat in Fulham, with
Pope and others such, in the conversation fell on the subject of water baptism. Voltaire assumed the part of a
Quaker, and at length came to mention that assertion of
Paul. They questioned there being any such assertion in
all his writings; on which a large wager was laid, as near
as I remember £500; and Voltaire, not retaining where it
was, had one of the Earl's horses, and came over the ferry
from Fulham to Putney. . . . When I came he desired me
to give him in writing the place where Paul said, *he was*

not to baptize; which I presently did. Then courteously taking his leave, he mounted and rode back"—and, we may assume, won his bet.

From his retreat at Wandsworth Voltaire made occasional jaunts to London, which was only a short carriage-ride away, and there he probably saw Bolingbroke and his circle. But the noise of the capital upset his sensitive nerves and consequently Voltaire was always glad to return to his "obscure and charming life quite given over to the pleasures of friendship and indolence." By the end of October he had not only mastered the English language, but had even absorbed some of the English spirit. "All that is king," he wrote to Thieriot, "or belongs to a king, frights my republican philosophy. I won't drink the least drop of slavery in the land of liberty," and "I fear, I hope nothing from your country. All that I wish for is to see you one day in London."

By November, however, Voltaire forsook his rural cloister and established himself in London at the Bolingbroke home in Pall Mall. From the start the Frenchman was athirst for a full knowledge of the English, and in quest of it he prowled about ubiquitously. We see him in Maiden Lane and Covent Garden, in coffee houses and at Quaker meetings. In London Voltaire saw the last rites of Isaac Newton, and the spectacle of the renowned scientist being laid to rest in Westminster amid the shrines of England's departed royalty made an indelible impression on the Frenchman. He explored every corner of the city. Once, getting out of bounds, he lost his way and found himself surrounded by a hostile crowd. "French dog" and "frog eater" were some of the milder insults hurled at him. But Voltaire was equal to the occasion. Leaping on a nearby doorstep, he plunged into a harangue beginning: "Brave Englishmen! Am I not sufficiently unhappy in not having been born among you?" The crowd's jeers turned to applause and wild enthusiasm; and in the end they insisted on carrying the little Frenchman to his quarters.

When the poet left France he had several letters of introduction, including one from Horace Walpole, the British ambassador to France, and one from Lord Bolingbroke, then still a resident at his chateau near Orleans. These letters helped to open the doors of some of England's most exclusive homes. On Bolingbroke's return to his homeland, Voltaire became a frequent guest at his friend's London mansion, and there he was further introduced to some of England's most eminent men and women. During this time Bolingbroke was often with Swift and Pope, and occasionally Voltaire joined them. Unfortunately for us there was no Boswell on hand to record their conversations. Of Voltaire's relation to these men only the most fragmentary details have come to us. The French writer was an admirer of the work of Pope even before his exile. In September, 1726, while returning from a visit to Bolingbroke, Pope was injured when his carriage overturned. When Voltaire heard of the mishap he wrote a gracious letter to the victim. "I am concerned beyond expression," he said, "for the danger you have been in, and more for your wounds. Is it possible that those fingers which have written the 'Rape of the Lock,' and the 'Criticism,' which have dressed Homer so becomingly in an English coat, should have been so barbarously treated? Let the hand of 'Dennis,' or of your poetasters be cut off. Yours is sacred, I hope." The two writers exchanged mutual compliments by mail, and soon afterwards they met for the first time, probably at the Twickenham villa. Rather interesting is Voltaire's comparison of Bolingbroke and Pope. "I think oft of Mr. B. and Mr. P.," he wrote in his notebook. "They are both virtuous and learned, of equal wit and understanding, but quite contrary in their ways. P. loves retirement and silence, virtuous and learned for himself. B. more communicative, diffuses everywhere his virtue and his knowledge. P. is a dark lanthorn: tho it is illuminated within, it affords no manner of light, or advantage to such as stood by it: the other is an ordinary lamp which consumes and wastes itself for the benefit of every passenger."

Voltaire thought very highly of Pope as a poet; indeed, he esteemed the author of the "Dunciad" above all others. "Pope," the Frenchman once declared, "drives a handsome chariot with a couple of neat nags, and Dryden a coach and six stately horses."

Of Voltaire's relations with Swift, we know virtually nothing. The redoubtable Dean of St. Patrick's was in London during the summer of 1726 to put the finishing touches on "Gulliver's Travels"; but the two men didn't meet until the next year. Voltaire considered Swift "one of the most extraordinary men that England has produced." He was particularly fond of comparing the creator of Gulliver with his French counterpart, Rabelais. "Rabelais, without his nonsense," was the way Voltaire described the English writer. Yet his admiration for Swift didn't prevent him from hurling his critical darts at "Gulliver's Travels." When the second part of this work appeared he sent it to Thieriot, but advised him to "stick to the first, the other is overstrain'd." "The reader's imagination," he wrote, "is pleased and charmingly entertained by the new prospects of the lands which Gulliver describes to him, but that continued series of new fangled follies, of fairy tales, palls at last upon our taste; nothing unnatural may please long." He went on to explain that " 'tis for this reason that commonly the second parts of romances are so insipid." When, in 1727, Swift planned a trip to France, Voltaire hastened to assure the Englishman that "I shall certainly do my best endeavors to serve you and to let my country know that I have the inestimable honor to be one of your friends." The death of George I, however, caused the contemplated trip to be canceled.

Voltaire's circle of literary acquaintances in England seems to have been fairly large. He knew Gay, who showed him his immortal "Beggar's Opera" before it was produced. Pemberton showed him his "A View of Isaac Newton's Life" before its publication. He was acquainted with Mrs. Conduit, Newton's niece, who, it is believed, told him the story of the falling apple which he preserved for posterity in his writing. He was also a friend of Berkeley, as well as Hans Sloane, president of the celebrated Royal Society. He knew the poets Thomson and Young. In Dorsetshire, at the country home of Bubb Dodington, Voltaire and Young became embroiled in a dispute over the merits of Milton's "Paradise Lost." Voltaire, who deemed most of Milton's poem to be nonsense, attacked it fervidly. Young undertook to defend it. Voltaire objected with special vehemence to the episode of Sin and Death sitting in conversation in Hell. Young had the last word, however, closing the argument with an epigram directed at Voltaire:

> *You are so witty, profligate and thin,*
> *At once we think you Milton, Death and Sin!*

While in London Voltaire called on the dramatist Congreve, now an old man, gouty and blind, and no longer interested in the vanity of fame. "I am just an English gentleman," he said, untouched by Voltaire's bland compliments. "If you had the misfortune of being a simple English gentleman," Voltaire retorted, "I should not have taken the trouble to see you." "He had one fault," Voltaire subsequently declared, "that of not esteeming sufficiently his first profession of author, which had made his fame and fortune."

Omnivorous as always in his social diet, Voltaire met the great English in other than literary fields. He visited Walpole, who cared nothing at all about literature, but who was Prime Minister; he met the famous Chesterfield, the first Viscount Palmerston, and Lord Hervey. To Lady Hervey, who was renowned for her beauty, Voltaire addressed his only poem composed in English:

> *Hervey, would you know the passion*
> *You have kindled in my breast?*
> *Trifling is the admiration*
> *That by words can be express'd.*
>
> *In my silence see the lover—*
> *True love is by silence known;*
> *In my eyes you'll best discover*
> *All the power of your own.*

Despite its ardent declarations Voltaire's little madrigal was not intended as anything more than a flowery compliment.

The French poet was also acquainted with the Duchess

of Marlborough, whose husband not so many years earlier had slaughtered the armies of the ambitious Louis XIV. Voltaire had met the Duchess while she was in Flanders collecting material for her memoirs. When he visited her at Blenheim, she received him cordially and even tried to charm him into helping her with her memoirs. She was busy, she told him, "mending the character of Queen Anne." She explained that she had come to love her again "since these good folk have become our rulers." When Voltaire objected to the partisan nature of her memoirs, she flew into a rage and snatched the manuscript out of his hands. "I thought," she later explained, "he had sense; but I find him at bottom either a fool or a philosopher."

The high point of Voltaire's social contacts was reached in January, 1727, when "the famous French poet, who was banished from France," was introduced to King George II. On the word of the London *Daily Journal* we may assume that His Majesty "received him very graciously."

That Voltaire should in time gravitate to the English theatre was of course inevitable. From Colley Cibber, who later became Poet Laureate, he obtained seats in the Drury Lane Theatre where he became a fairly regular patron. At the start his English was still too uncertain for him to follow the dramatic developments on the stage; hence he generally armed himself with a printed copy of the play, reading it as it evolved. He probably saw most of the more important plays, including Addison's "Cato," Congreve's "Double Dealer," Wycherley's "Country Wife," besides several of Shakespeare's tragedies. Voltaire's reactions to the English playwright were somewhat mixed. The fast pace of the Shakespearean drama hypnotized him; its color fascinated him; and its characters stirred him; but its form, so unorthodox to his classic eyes, left him cold. At bottom his conservative French taste was an insurmountable barrier to his complete capitulation to the great English bard. "Julius Caesar" was his particular delight. "What was my rapture," he wrote, "when I saw Brutus, still holding in his hand a dagger stained with the blood of Caesar, call together the Roman people, and from the Roman rostrum address them. . . ."

Shakespeare's dramatic freedom pleased Voltaire and appalled him. He admired that "happy lack of restriction which allows you to write tragedy in unrhymed verse . . . and when necessity demands it, to create new words. . . ." A Frenchman, in contrast, was "a slave to rhyme, sometimes obliged to write four verses to express a thought which an Englishman could give in a single line. The Englishman says what he wants to, the Frenchman only what he is able to; the one runs in a vast race-course, the other walks in fetters on a narrow slippery road!"

On the other hand he was constrained to tell Lord Bolingbroke that "almost all of the tragic authors in your country have lacked the purity, the order, the decorous plot and style, the elegance, and all of those fine points in dramatic art which have established the preeminent reputation of the French theatre since the great Corneille." When he applied this conservative yardstick to the plays of Shakespeare they became incomprehensible. "These pieces," he declared, "are monsters in tragedy. There are some plays, the action of which lasts several years; the hero, baptized in the first act, dies of old age in the fifth. You see upon the stage wizards, peasants, drunkards, buffoons, grave-diggers digging a grave, who sing drinking songs while playing with skulls. In a word, imagine what you can of the most monstrous and the most absurd, you will find it in Shakespeare."

While Voltaire was in England his literary enterprises were by no means cast aside. Soon after he landed he wrote to Thieriot, "I had in mind at first to print our poor Henry ('The League'), but the loss of my money is a sad stop to my design. . . ." Though he averred himself to be "weary of courts," in time he overcame his prejudices at least enough to seek their help in putting out an English edition of his epic poem, which he had decided to rename the *Henriade,* after its leading character. As in France, Voltaire campaigned relentlessly for his favorite poem. To Thieriot he wrote that he intended "to give the publick the best edition I can of the *Henriade.*" Whenever he could get his name into the public prints, he always made sure that it was coupled with the beloved *Henriade.* Not a single item about him in the English press from the day of his arrival to the day of his departure failed to mention the *Henriade;* and most of them also spoke of him as "the famous poet who was exiled from France." When he was presented to the King the London *Daily Journal* not only chronicled that plain fact, but added also that "they say he (Voltaire) received notice from France not to print his poem of the League; a prosecution still pending against him, by the Cardinal de Bissy, on account of the praises bestowed in that book on Queen Elizabeth's behavior in matters of Religion, and a great many strokes against the abuse of popery and against persecution in matters of faith."

Early in 1727 Voltaire started a drive for subscriptions for a lavish *de luxe* quarto edition of his national epic, enthusiastically harnessing most of his distinguished friends to the venture. Prime Minister Walpole took time off from the affairs of state to solicit subscriptions; while Bolingbroke, Chesterfield and hosts of others did the same. Probably never in the history of English books has an epic poem, written by a Frenchman, been promoted by such aristocratic salesmen. To kindle an interest in his *Henriade* Voltaire bolstered his usual publicity effusions with a brace of essays, composed in English, one entitled "On the Epic Poetry of the European Nations from Homer to Milton," and one called "An Essay upon the Civil Wars of France," which was in part the subject matter of the *Henriade*. "As to the present Essay," Voltaire explained, "it is intended as a kind of Preface or Introduction to the *Henriade*." He added that this was almost entirely printed. Everything, it seems, was ready but the illustrations; and these Voltaire felt he "must recommend here as particular Master-Pieces of Art in their kind"—which they were, indeed. Both essays were written in a lively, readable prose, but at bottom they were the obvious work of a literary promoter rather than a literary historian. Actually Voltaire was very much interested in the subject of his essays; and he devoted the entire summer to their study and composition. Yet this, of course, was far from enough, and the work that resulted revealed the unmistakable signs of haste and superficiality. Since the essays were intended to attract English readers for the *Henriade*, Voltaire was careful to feed their vanity. Addison he called the "best Critic and the best Writer of his age"; Pope's translation of Homer he bathed in luxurious praise; even to Milton, most of whose work he disliked, he accorded high tribute. But behind all his blandishments was the thought that the forthcoming *Henriade* was superior in every respect.

CARL A. RUDISILL LIBRARY
LENOIR-RHYNE COLLEGE

Before the book was finally published Voltaire canceled its former dedication to Louis XV and now offered the book to Queen Caroline of England. "It is," he wrote, "the fate of Henry IV to be protected by an English queen. He was assisted by that great Elizabeth who was in her day the glory of her sex." Where once he had reminded the fifteenth Louis of France that the blood of the heroic Henry flowed in Louis' veins, he now asked Queen Caroline "by whom can his (Henry's) memory be so well protected as by her who resembles so much Elizabeth . . . ?" One other change was made in the English *Henriade*: the name of Sully, which had appeared prominently in the French edition, was everywhere deleted. The English *Henriade* was published in March, 1728, with a list of subscribers that dazzled the eye. Headed by King George and Queen Caroline, it included the name of virtually every dignitary in the realm. Lord Bolingbroke took twenty copies, as did Lord Peterborough; while Chesterfield was down for ten. The venture was a huge success. Every copy of the magnificent quarto edition was sold before publication; and three octavo editions were printed in as many weeks.

The *Henriade* was acclaimed "the best Epic poem of the year"; and before the year was over Voltaire made a profit of at least ten thousand francs, besides getting a pension from the King and a letter from the grateful Queen together with her portrait.

Though he concentrated on the *Henriade*, Voltaire as usual had several other irons in the fire. He had been so moved by Shakespeare's "Julius Caesar" that he felt impelled to dramatize the theme for the French theatre. Not that he intended to employ the dramatic liberties of the

CARL A. RUDISILL LIBRARY
LENOIR-RHYNE COLLEGE

great English dramatist—that would have required a dramatic revolution which the conservative French would never have countenanced. Voltaire's version of the Roman tragedy was called "Brutus," and its first act was probably written in 1727 while he was with Falkener at Wandsworth. Besides working on his new tragedy, he had also begun to write a history of the Swedish Charles XII. In gathering material for this work he not only read omnivorously; but just as he had collected unpublished material on Henry of Navarre from his friend, the old Marquis Caumartin de Saint Ange, he now garnered information about Charles XII from Baron Frederic Ernest Fabrice, a man who had been closely associated with the late Swedish monarch. The Baron had been in Charles' diplomatic service, and had so pleased his master that the two became intimate friends. After Charles' death the Swedish nobleman went to England where, for a time, he stayed at Chesterfield's house in Saint James' Square. The Swedish nobleman and Voltaire moved in the same social spheres, and it was undoubtedly in this way that they met. What attracted the French writer to the Baron, however, was not so much his social quality as his vast knowledge of Charles and his reign. Like the Marquis de Saint Ange, Fabrice never tired of relating anecdotes and reminiscences about his royal friend, and Voltaire listened attentively. There were others in England who were also in a position to give Voltaire first-hand information about the Swedish king, and these people the Frenchman turned to literary account. There was, for one, the former English minister to Sweden, Jeffreys. Then there was Lord Bolingbroke, whose familiarity with the court of Charles was a rich source of information. Even the Duchess of Marlborough was drafted into Voltaire's service. From the Duchess Voltaire obtained the description of the interview which had taken place a score of years earlier, between her husband and Charles at a time when England and her allies were trying to discover what part Sweden would play in an anticipated war. By tapping these springs of information, and by diligently checking and rechecking them against other sources, Voltaire was in effect using the modern method of historical research.

In addition to his projected history of Charles and his tragedy "Brutus," Voltaire had begun to record his impressions of England. He was composing them, however, not for immediate publication, but was putting them, instead, into a series of letters addressed to his friend Thieriot. In time he hoped to be able to assemble these letters in book form and to offer them to his fellow-countrymen.

It so happened that Voltaire's sojourn in England came at a climactic point in that nation's history. Caressed by peace and plenty after the upheavals of the Revolution and the long and bloody wars on the continent, the nation had emerged victorious, conscious of its freedom and confident of its power. Ruled by an enlightened aristocracy, it was in competent hands. With the advent of George I, moreover, England had acquired a king more concerned with his German domain than his British realm, with the result that the power of Parliament made gigantic strides until, in the end, it emerged supreme. Unprecedented freedom and tolerance were the products of this parliamentary surge to power, religious and political persecution becoming almost obsolete. It was possible under such beneficent conditions for Swift to be in the employ of the

State Church and yet be allowed unmolested to heave his critical thunderbolts at the government itself.

With political liberty and religious tolerance came a great intellectual and aesthetic renaissance. The remarkable discoveries of Newton seemed to enlarge the horizon of speculation; men of letters occupied offices of state; and the great nobles busied themselves fostering trade and commerce, and building palaces of great splendor. This was the England of Swift and Pope; of Walpole and Carteret; of Butler and Berkley. It was the England that created "Gulliver's Travels" and the "Dunciad," both of which appeared during Voltaire's stay.

This national culture Voltaire encountered on all sides. He found it not only in the high places among the Bolingbrokes and the Walpoles, but in the streets of London. National consciousness pervaded the coffee houses; the market-places; the Royal Exchange, where the world's gold poured so lavishly into the English till. It was in the Quaker meeting houses, where the brethren sat in awed silence awaiting the inspiration of the Holy Spirit. It was visible in every tavern in the land where free Englishmen gathered over their English ale and beef. It was discernible in the press, in every gazette and periodical which openly expressed itself on all sorts of controversial matters.

It was only natural that Voltaire, smarting from the cruel injustice inflicted upon him by the cynical, feudal regime of his own country, should have been stimulated by the luxury of unaccustomed freedom. "Reason," he wrote soon after his arrival, "is free here and walks her own way. No manner of living appears strange. . . ." "You will see," he said in a letter to Thieriot, "a nation fond of their liberty, witty, learned, despising life and death, a nation of philosophers; not but there are some fools in England . . . but by God, English wisdom and English honesty is above yours." He added that it was a country where people "think freely and nobly, unrestricted by servile fear." "If I followed my inclination it would be there that I would live with the sole inclination of learning to think."

Voltaire's enthusiasm for the English was reflected in his letters about them to Thieriot. They were not, however, simply an account of his observations in the island kingdom. At bottom they were a criticism of France itself. They were the propaganda of an earnest reformer; for Voltaire was convinced that France could learn a great deal from England. Given like causes, he reasoned, the results should be the same; hence France, like its Anglo-Saxon neighbor, could achieve freedom, tolerance, prosperity.

To prepare the way Voltaire endeavored to show his countrymen the reasons for English superiority. His letters are a detailed exposition of English life in its full and vivid actuality, as he saw it. We behold Quakers and business men, members of Parliament, philosophers and scientists. We attend a performance of "Julius Caesar." The theory of gravitation is explained, as are the effects of vaccination. We read of the witticisms of Bolingbroke, of the poetry of Pope, and the philosophical theories of Locke, besides detailed discussions of English literature and science.

Altogether Voltaire wrote twenty-five letters. Knowing French fastidiousness in matters concerning their King and Church, Voltaire was careful not to attack these directly, but only by subtle inference. To make his treatise attractive he flavored it generously with a pungent humor which few Frenchmen could resist. The following account of his visit to a Quaker is a typical example of his method:

"The Quaker was an old man of fresh complexion, who had never been sick, because he had always been continent and temperate. In my life I have never seen a presence more noble or more engaging. He was dressed, like all those of his persuasion, in a coat without plaits at the sides, or buttons on the pockets and sleeves, and wore a broad-brimmed hat like those of our ecclesiastics. He received me with his hat on, and advanced towards me without making the least inclination of his body; but there was more politeness in the open and humane expression of his countenance than there is in our custom of drawing one leg behind the other and carrying in the hand what was made to cover the head.

" 'Friend,' said he to me, 'I see that thou art a stranger; if I can be of any use to thee, thou hast only to speak.'

" 'Sir,' I said to him, with a bow and a step forward, according to our custom, 'I flatter myself that my reasonable curiosity will not displease you, and that you will be willing to do me the honor to instruct me in your religion.'

" 'The people of thy country,' he replied, 'make too many compliments and bows, but I have never before seen one of them who had the same curiosity as thou. Come in and take dinner with me.'

"I still kept paying him bad compliments, because a man cannot all at once lay aside his habits; and after a wholesome and frugal repast, which began and ended with a prayer to God, I began to question my host.

"I began with the question which good Catholics have

put more than once to Huguenots: 'My dear sir,' said I, 'have you been baptized?'

" 'No,' replied the Quaker, 'nor my brethren either.'

" 'What! *Morbleu!* You are not a Christian, then?'

" 'My friend,' he mildly rejoined, 'curse not. We do not think that Christianity consists in sprinkling water upon the head with a little salt.'

" 'Good Lord!' said I, shocked at this impiety; 'have you forgotten, then, that Jesus Christ was baptized by John?'

" 'Friend, once more, no cursing,' replied the benign Quaker. 'Christ received baptism from John, but he baptized no one. We are not John's disciples, but Christ's.'

" 'Ah!' I cried, 'how you would be burned by the Holy Inquisition! In the name of God, my dear sir, let me have you baptized!'

" 'Art thou circumcised?' he asked. I replied that I had not that honor.

" 'Very well, friend,' said he, 'thou art a Christian without being circumcised, and I without being baptized.' "

When Voltaire struck out at the social and economic abuses existing in France he discarded his satirical mask. "You do not hear in England," he wrote, "of one kind of justice for the higher class, a second for the middle, and a third for the lowest; nor of the privilege of hunting on the land of a citizen who is not allowed to fire a shot in his own fields. Because he is a nobleman or an ecclesiastic, an Englishman is not exempt from paying certain taxes; all imposts are regulated by the House of Commons, which, although second in rank, is first in power. . . . The peasant's feet are not blistered by wooden shoes; he eats

wheat bread; he is well clad; he is not afraid to increase
the number of his cattle, or to cover his roof with tiles,
lest his taxes should be raised the following year."

A few pointed words sufficed to sketch the differences
between the English and French attitudes towards business.
"In France," Voltaire declared, "anyone who wants to can
become a marquis, and whoever arrives in Paris from the
depths of the provinces with money to spend and a name
ending in 'ac' or 'ille' may talk of 'a man like me,' 'a man
in my position,' and look down with disdain on a merchant. The trader himself hears his vocation spoken of so
contemptuously that he is foolish enough to blush for it.
Yet I know not which is the most useful to a state, a carefully powdered nobleman who can tell the exact hour
when the king gets up and goes to bed, and who gives
himself the airs of a great man while performing the part
of a slave in the ante-chamber of a minister; or a trader,
who enriches his country, gives orders from his desk for
Surat and Cairo, and contributes to the welfare of the
world."

Nor did Voltaire overlook the chance to remind his
countrymen that in England the intellectual was esteemed
higher than the warrior. "Who was the greatest man, asked
a distinguished company, Caesar, Alexander, Tamerlane
or Cromwell? Somebody answered that it was undoubtedly
Isaac Newton. This person was right, for if true greatness
consists in having received from heaven a powerful understanding and using it to enlighten oneself and all others,
then such a one as Newton, who is hardly to be met with
once in ten centuries, is in truth a great man. It is to him
who masters our minds by the force of truth, not to those
who enslave men by violence; it is to him who understands

the universe, not to those who disfigure it, that we owe our allegiance." Voltaire's more daring words on the army and the employment of force he prudently put into the mouth of a Quaker. "Our God," he said, "who has bidden us to love our enemies and suffer evil without complaint, assuredly has no mind that we should cross the sea to cut the throats of our brothers, because murderers in red clothes and hats two feet high enlist citizens by making a noise with two little sticks on an ass's skin tightly stretched."

What with his literary labors and his social and business excursions, Voltaire led a busy life. He abandoned himself with his customary zeal to his multifarious activities, with the usual bad effect on his health. As soon as he was through with the work involved in getting the *Henriade* published, he fled from the turmoil of London for the peaceful shelter of Wandsworth, where he hoped to regain his strength and energy. But the harsh English climate affected him more and more. Before long Voltaire was informing his doctor that he "grows worse and worse in England"; while to his friends he was writing that he wwas sick to death." Aggravating his poor physical condition was undoubtedly a psychological factor. The long years away from his native land had begun to tell on him: he was thoroughly homesick. The lustre of England had begun to tarnish. It was not quite the Utopia he had once imagined. Here, too, he had seen poverty and squalor —not as much as in France perhaps—but they existed just the same. He had seen Englishmen impressed into the navy. He knew all about England's exploitation of Ireland —it was during his stay in England that he read Swift's satire, "A Modest Proposal for Preventing the Children

of Poor People in Ireland from Being a Burden to Their
Parents or Country," wherein the embittered Swift proposed that the starving Irish children should be bought
and eaten by the rich English landlords. Despite the cordial reception accorded him in high places, Voltaire was
aware of a racial antipathy towards him on the part of
most Englishmen. He missed his favorite haunts of old—
the theatre, the Temple, the company of his friends. He
missed the Gallic exuberance which made the French
spirit what it was and without which no real Frenchman
could be happy. Thus, where two years before he had
written to Thieriot, "I hope nothing from your country,"
he now implored his friend to "write me oftener than I
write you. I live in a retreat about which there is nothing
to tell, while you are in Paris where every day you see new
extravagance which might still please your friend who is
unhappy enough not to be able to enjoy them."

By the middle of 1728 Voltaire had decided to return
to France. "Write no more to your wandering friend," he
instructed Thieriot, "for at an early moment you will see
him appear. Prepare to come at the first summons." Since
he was still under the ban in France, he had to move secretly; hence we do not know exactly when he crossed the
Channel, though it was probably early in 1729.

In the middle of March, 1729, Voltaire appeared some
fifteen miles from Paris, at St. Germain-en-Laye. He had
given himself an alias, Monsieur Sansons; and he lodged
with a wig-maker. "You must ask for Sansons," he wrote
to Thieriot. "He inhabits a hole in this barrack. There is
another for you, as well as a bed and short rations."

After a brief stay with the wig-maker, Monsieur Sansons
moved to Paris, where he continued to live in hiding. A

few of his friends—"the indispensable ones"—Voltaire let in on his secret, in part because of his natural longing for them, but in part also because he hoped their influence with the Court might bring about an annulment of his warrant of exile. His hope was justified, for in April of 1729 he was informed that his warrant had been canceled and that he was free to circulate in Paris.

England had left its mark on Voltaire. The mood which had engulfed him when he walked out of the Sully house that night of the Rohan episode had never left him. It had helped, no doubt, to make him receptive to the freedom and tolerance of England; but having tasted these delights, he was determined to have them forever.

Before his exile Voltaire had been an ambitious courtier, interested chiefly in himself, and concerned largely with the superficialities of life. Now this was changed. The injustice which Rohan and his caste had heaped upon him; the disaffection and disloyalty of his aristocratic friends; the callousness of the state—all these had planted in him a deep and passionate earnestness. England had given Voltaire a new point of view by which he could judge his own country. The yardstick which he applied to the civilization of his own land had been vitally tempered by his experiences in England, the most civilized land he knew. Voltaire had left France a promising poet; he returned a philosopher. Moreover, he returned not as a Frenchman; nor even as an Englishman; he came back a cosmopolitan. "What belongs to good sense," he declared, "belongs to all the nations of the world."

Back in Paris, he lost no time in giving expression to his "English ideas." Like most travelers he derived great

pleasure in discussing the unusual things he had encoun-
trede—but some of these happened to be freedom, justice
and tolerance. His friends, alarmed at his conversion to
what seemed dangerous and radical doctrines, strove to
lead him back to the old and trusted paths. But their efforts failed. In time Voltaire's outlandish beliefs began to
be the topic of Parisian gossip. Eventually they reached
the ears of Lieutenant of Police Hérault. Summoning
Voltaire before him, the Lieutenant solemnly warned the
returned exile against his unheard of freedom of speech.
"But," said Voltaire, as if he didn't understand what
Lieutenant Hérault had in mind, "I write nothing, I print
nothing which can render me liable to censure or pursuit
on the part of the government."

"Whatever you write," the Lieutenant replied, "you will
never succeed in destroying the Christian religion."

"We shall see," said Voltaire.

Under the ever-present shadow of the suspicious authorities, Voltaire thought it wise to wait with the publication
of his English observations. He devoted himself, instead,
to the work of completing "Brutus" and the history of
Charles XII. For diversion he went to the opera and the
theatre; or he would join the intellectuals who gathered in
Parisian drawing-rooms; now and then he would sally
forth for a session with his Epicurean cronies at the Temple. He still enjoyed gay dinner-parties, but his failing
digestion had begun to impose a necessary moderation
upon him.

Soon after his return to Paris Voltaire began to discover
anew that the loyalty which he accorded so unstintingly to
his friends was not always reciprocated. The treatment he
had received from some of them during the Rohan affair

should have taught him that. Yet in the matter of friendship Voltaire was a perennial optimist. Steadfastness in friendship was a basic principle in his code; anything else seemed out of the question. His new disappointment came when he visited a young actress whom he had once befriended. Though her acting had been mediocre, Voltaire never ceased to encourage her, and had helped her obtain parts in several plays. She was Mademoiselle de Livri, but during the poet's stay in England she had become the Marquise de Gouvernet. Her matrimonial triumph had given her sudden delusions of grandeur; and when her former benefactor called to extend his good wishes, she had her Swiss butler tell him she was not at home. Voltaire took the rebuff lightly, but soon afterwards he addressed a long, light-hearted poem to the foolish woman. "Where is the old time flown," he asks,

> When, in a hackney-coach, we two
> Without a lackey, rode alone?
> And you, my dear, were simply you?
> A cafe in Bohemia then
> Was all we needed, you and I,
> To make the great gods envy men,
> And lift a mortal to the sky,
> Youth had a magic in that day,
> Could change the simplest food and wine
> To nectar and ambrosia,
> And make a roasted bird divine. . . .
> Ah, madame, how your life today
> Has quite forgot those midnight chimes!
> Honor and wealth have barred the way
> To wastrel poets and their rhymes. . . .

Your footman, with the powdered hair,
Who tells me lies now, at your door,
Phyllis, I see him standing there
Like Time's own image evermore,
To keep, with the great frozen stare,
The little gods of love aloof,
Whose roselike wings would never dare
To flutter 'neath your palace roof. . . .

No, madame, all these rooms bedight
With Persian rugs and Chinese art,
And fragile vases from Japan,
The jeweled star upon your heart,
The delicate painting on your fan;
Your mirror, throwing back the light
Of great prismatic chandeliers;
And those two sparkles, hard and bright,
The diamond pendants in your ears;
The glittering chains that make your bliss,
And all your pearls in clusters strung,
Are not worth one forgotten kiss
You gave when you were poor and young.

Voltaire's experience with the marquise was compensated for by a stroke of good fortune. In the course of a dinner with some friends the conversation turned to the subject of a national lottery. Planned by France's Controller General Desfort, it sought to liquidate certain city annuities. A mathematician, Condamine, who happened to be one of the guests, pointed out that Desfort's scheme had been unscientifically organized; and that anyone buying up all the tickets would make a million francs. None of the diners took the mathematician seriously—that is, none except Voltaire. As soon as the dinner was ended, the poet hurried to some of his moneyed friends and told them what Condamine had said. In a flash papers were being covered with figures by men who seemed to have gone mad. Convinced finally that Condamine was right, they formed a stock company with Voltaire as one of the shareholders. The tickets in the lottery were then bought up and the prizes demanded. When the unfortunate Controller General realized his mistake, he refused to pay; but the claimants sued him, and after a short battle in the courts, they emerged victorious. Voltaire's share in the victory was some 250,000 francs, which he promptly set out to augment.

Voltaire's sudden ascent to wealth opened the way to a new career. What he had learned in England about trade and commerce served him well; and before long he was playing the part of a successful capitalist. He invested in ships that sailed all over the globe; he imported goods from Barbary, Cadiz and America; he equipped and provisioned large armies. All kinds of speculative enterprises attracted him. Once he rode two nights and a day to buy fifty shares of the Duke of Lorraine's public funds, which were supposed to be sold only to the Lorrainers, but which he managed to obtain nonetheless. "I have trebled my gold," he wrote not long after to his friend Hénault, "and trust soon to enjoy my doubloons with people like you."

Yet Voltaire's quest for wealth had a purpose beyond that of the mere accumulation of money. To write as he pleased, to express himself freely, he needed independence —and the cornerstone of this independence was financial security. "I have seen so many men of letters poor and de-

spised," he declared, "that I made up my mind long ago
that I would not increase their number." "In France," he
added, "a man must be anvil or hammer,"—and he had no
intention of being an anvil. Although Voltaire was relentless in his pursuit of profit, he was also very generous. He
lent substantial sums without demanding a cent of interest.
To impoverished actors and authors he often gave money
outright. Many of them he placed on a sort of private pension list, giving them fixed stipends at regular intervals.

Voltaire's wealth made little difference in his literary
activity. He toiled as hard as ever, and aside from enjoying the hitherto unknown thrill of financial security, there
was little change in his living. His play "Brutus" had been
scheduled for production early in 1730, but just before the
opening night, reports reached the playwright that his old
enemy, de Rohan, had organized a cabal to hiss the play
off the stage. "Unwilling," as Voltaire put it, "to give the
brave Chevalier this pleasure," he withdrew his drama.

Soon after, grim events were to remind Voltaire once
more of the vast differences between England and France.
The beloved actress Adrienne Lecouvreur, twenty-eight
years old, collapsed while playing to a crowded house—
and four days later she was dead. Voltaire rushed to her
bedside and comforted her during her suffering. The priest
of Saint Sulpice came to administer the final sacrament;
but when the dying actress would not make the formal
renunciation of her profession required by French ecclesiastic law, he denied her absolution. By her refusal Adrienne had forfeited her right to be buried in consecrated
soil. Instead, her body was seized by the authorities, and
during the night it was dumped into an unmarked grave in
some waste land along the Seine beyond the city limits of

Paris. A few policemen and a couple of street cleaners were the witnesses. To hasten the process of annihilation they poured a sackful of quicklime over the body. The soil over the grave was trampled down to remove all traces of it.

This barbarous act stunned Paris; for Adrienne had been as generous as she had been charming, and her friends were countless. The sensitive Voltaire was overwhelmed. When words came to him at last, he wove them into an elegy. "They deny a grave," he said, "to one who in ancient Greece would have had an altar." "When she was alive, France hung in ecstasy on her lips—dead she is a criminal." The freedom and tolerance of England crept into his thoughts. "Is it only in England," he asked, "that mortals dare to think? O rival of Athens, London, happy land! No art is despised there! Lecouvreur would have been buried among kings and heroes and men of genius. There the spirit of Greece and Rome lives on. But the laurels of Apollo wither in the sterile fields of France."

Not content with mere words, the poet summoned his actors and urged them to go on strike. "Announce to the world," he exhorted them, "that you will not exercise your profession . . . until you, the paid servants of the king, are treated like other citizens in the king's service." The actors promised to take action; yet their fear of reprisals from the authorities cowed them, and in the end they did nothing. Voltaire himself was made to feel the clerical fury. Stung by his tribute to Adrienne, the Church took steps to punish him. But before it could exert the full pressure of its might against him, the poet had left town.

He returned when the storm was over; but in his heart

there raged another storm. All his emotions were now centered in an overmastering determination to fight the bigotry and obscurantism which enveloped his country. He had resolved with all his might to awaken "that feeble nation . . . sleeping under the dominance of superstition." His first move was to send Thieriot to England to arrange for the translation and publication of his "English Letters." The task was quickly accomplished; and by the end of 1730 the successful Thieriot returned from his mission, bringing with him some 10,000 francs in royalties for the book.

In the meantime the poet addressed himself to the task of making the French version of the "English Letters" acceptable to the censor. He chopped and pruned them; and wherever possible, he eliminated the more disquieting pronouncements. He rewrote portions of the book entirely, toning them down, and sprinkling them with sweetness. "I have been obliged," he remarked to a friend, "to change all that I had written on Mr. Locke, because, after all, I wish to live in France, and I am not permitted to be as philosophic as an Englishman. In Paris I have to disguise what I could not say too strongly in London. This circumspection, unfortunate but necessary, obliges me to erase more than one passage, sufficiently amusing, upon the Quakers and Presbyterians."

In the hope of gaining the support of the powerful Cardinal de Fleury, Voltaire read to him some letters on the Quakers—first, however, taking the precaution "to cut out all that could alarm his devout and sage Eminence." The Cardinal, Voltaire announced, "found the residue pleasant enough—but the poor man doesn't know what he missed." Yet despite everything the poet could do, the censor maintained his iron front: the letters could not be printed in France.

The projected history of Charles XII fared better, the royal privilege being granted in the spring of 1730. In the fall the laborious job of printing an edition of 2,600 copies was completed; but just as the book was about to greet its public the censor suddenly rescinded his privilege to print. The reason for this unexpected action remained an official secret. All that Voltaire could learn was that he had said things which might prove offensive to King Augustus II of Poland. When he argued that he had done nothing of the sort, he was told that he had compared Augustus unfavorably with the former King Stanislas, father of the Queen of France. He had written, for example, that "Stanislas, instead of punishing prisoners of war, contented himself with kindly reproaches. He even gave them some money to carry them on their way and showed by this generosity that Augustus had good reason to be afraid of him as a rival." When Voltaire insisted that this was the truth, the censor shrugged his shoulders and reminded him that truth and politics were not always compatible, and that at that moment the foreign policy of France happened to favor Augustus. "It seems to me," declared Voltaire, somewhat piqued, "that in *this* country Stanislas ought to be considered rather than Augustus."

With two of his works doomed by the censor, the frustrated author decided to take matters into his own hands. He turned once again to Rouen, the birthplace of the forbidden *Henriade*. There he found a willing printer and bookseller by the name of Jore, a venturesome man who on several occasions had run afoul of the law for publishing prohibited books. Monsieur Jore agreed to bring

out the "History of Charles XII"; in fact he was even
willing to print the "English Letters." Voltaire quickly
came to terms with the printer, and some time in March
the poet vanished from Paris, leaving behind him an explanation that he was on his way to "the cathedral city of
Cantorbéry," in England, to arrange for "a magnificent
edition of Charles XII." He got no further, however, than
the city of Rouen. To sidetrack any suspicion on the part
of the curious, he announced himself to be an English
lord, forced into exile for his political views, and anxious
to live in seclusion. He rented a dingy room in the shadow
of Rouen's beautiful cathedral. For twenty cents a day he
acquired the services of a "valet" whose duties were concerned more with carrying proof between the author and
his printer than with enhancing his master's comfort.
That comfort, to judge from Voltaire's own words, must
have been slight:

> *The spider weaves my tapestries.*
> *My bed is hard and full of fleas.*
> *The sheets are short; the chair's a wreck.*
> *The bottle with the broken neck,*
> *Wherein a dripping candle stands*
> *Was put there by your pilfering hands*
> *To keep things darker, I suppose,*
> *My hostess with the turned-up nose.*

With the coming of spring Voltaire exchanged his desul-
tory quarters for a room in a thatched farmhouse amid
the fragrance of blossoming trees. Here he lived, as he
said, "as in the age of gold, on herbs, fresh eggs, milk and
cheese." The functions of his valet were now performed

by one of the farm hands, who thrice a week carried the author's proofs to Rouen.

In this rural solitude Voltaire's work gained momentum. His *Charles XII* made splendid progress. To fill out the moments when he wasn't correcting proof, Voltaire began work on two new tragedies, *Eriphile* and *Julius Caesar*. Though he missed Paris, he informed Thieriot that he was "the happiest man in the world,"—adding, however, that the circumstances of his life had also made him "the most unfortunate." At the same time he sent his friend the manuscript of his verses dedicated to Adrienne Lecouvreur.

"I cannot resist," he wrote, "sending you this piece, for which you have so often asked me." He continued in typically ironic verse:

> *The pious folk, as in duty bound,*
> *With fagot and fire will ring me round,*
> *And zealously roast my body whole,*
> *All for the good of my wretched soul.*

In all of his letters he was careful to preserve the fiction that he was in England. "I join my feeble voice," he said, "to all the voices in England to make the difference felt between their liberty and our enslavement; between their wise hardihood and our weak superstition; between the encouragement given the arts in London, and the shameful oppression under which they languish in Paris." A few weeks later Thieriot received another letter, in which Voltaire reported himself—once again—to be "at death's door." He explained, however, that he was "quite unperturbed."

I write, my friend, with a fever-shaken hand;
But, with a constant mind that smiles at death,
Free of false bonds, far from my native land,
Careless of courts, I draw a lighter breath,
Patient in ills, gay in life's motley chances,
To foolish pride a light farewell I wave;
And though I've always one foot in the grave,
The other kicks and dances.

Voltaire's closeness to his grave was nothing more than a slight fever—an illness so slight that his work was not even interrupted. Only a few weeks later, in fact, he was able to announce the completion of his two plays. "In Paris I couldn't have done that in three years," he wrote with delight to Thieriot. "But you know well enough what a prodigious difference there is between a mind in the calm of solitude and one dissipated in the world."

The poet returned to Paris in October. Soon after his arrival huge parcels, containing the forbidden *Charles XII*, were delivered at the Versailles residence of the Duke of Richelieu. Too powerful to fear the wrath of a censor, the Duke had permitted Voltaire to address the parcels to the Richelieu home. From there the Duke's valet brought the book safely past the customs officials guarding the entrances to Paris. The work was quickly distributed, and before long its readers were proclaiming it a masterpiece.

That judgment was not unmerited. For in his history of Charles XII, as in his "English Letters," Voltaire revealed the true nature of his genius. The fundamental quality of that genius was not, as he so fondly imagined, that of a dramatist; nor was it that of an epic poet or a writer of light verse. It was as an observer of society and

of the whole civilization of his era that Voltaire displayed
his greatest talent. His study of Charles XII is much more
than a simple portrait of an interesting Swedish king; it
is a cultural cyclorama, a detailed and vivid account of
European civilization as it revolved about the Scandi-
navian monarch. Voltaire's narrative marches from one
end of Europe to the other; it crosses over to Asia and to
the New World. We behold not only Charles of Sweden;
we see the peasant girl who becomes Catherine I of Russia;
we attend a secret interview between Charles and Marlborough on which hangs the destiny of Europe. There is
an account of Peter the Great, fighting against the obstacles
of nature to build a city on the marshlands of Neva. There
are discussions of the Astrakan peasants and Chinese
coolies, of Turkish viziers and Russian patriarchs. There
are treatises on the futility of war, the abuses inherent in
personal government, and the evils of superstition.

Voltaire had a genuine understanding of the historical
method, an understanding which he had revealed once
before when he gathered material for the *Henriade,* but
which he now put to better use. Voltaire transcended the
school of historical writing which was content merely to
compile events; he widened the scope of history from its
narrow political and military confines to a survey of the
entire landscape of civilization.

Basically, *Charles XII* was history—but it was history
tinged with social criticism. Once again Voltaire trained
his guns on the antiquated social, political and religious
conditions in France. He may have recorded in his book
that it was Charles XII who "seldom took a more active
part in the council than to cross his legs upon the table";
yet every Frenchman who read between these lines knew

that at bottom Voltaire was criticizing the indolent and privileged *noblesse* of his own country. "The Grand Vizier," Voltaire wrote—again with the French nobility in mind—"was the son of a peasant. . . . Such parentage is never one to be ashamed of among the Turks. They have no nobility. They have neither hereditary posts requiring definite duties nor family titles. Service alone is supposed to account for all advance." "The Sultan," he told his countrymen—with an eye on the intrigues of the French Court—"need never fear that he will be bothered by useless appeals and unimportant petitions, for there is less writing in an entire year in Constantinople than in a single day in Paris." With France still under the yoke of the Ancient Regime, and serfs callously exploited by their overlords, everyone in France knew what Voltaire was attacking when he wrote that in Poland "the common people are slaves." "Such," he added, "is the destiny of man that by one means or another, the majority is always subjugated by the minority. The peasant does not sow for himself, but for the lords, to whom he belongs, as do his fields and his labor; and these lords can sell him, or butcher him, as they do the beasts in the fields."

Nor did Voltaire diminish his attack on religious hypocrisy and superstition. As in his previous onslaughts he was careful to immunize himself by aiming his criticism not at the Church of Rome, but at that of the Russian orthodoxy. "Few Muscovites," he wrote, "dare to eat a pigeon, because the Holy Ghost is painted in the form of a dove." In Russia, "as elsewhere, there are disputes upon religion; the greatest being on the question whether the laity should make the sign of the cross with two fingers or with three." "Confession," Voltaire said, "was practised, but only in the case of the greater crimes, when absolution seemed necessary. . . . They believed themselves pure before God when they received the benediction of their priests." After which, Voltaire added, "they went directly from confession to commit theft and murder." These same people "had scruples about drinking milk on a day of fasting."

The fire with which England had ignited Voltaire's thinking glowed afresh in *Charles XII* when he came to the subject of royal power. Let kings remember, he announced, "that being public men, they owe an account of their actions to the public. . . . This is the price at which they purchase their greatness." "The princes who have the most right to immortality are those who have done some good to men." "Let a prince wage war; let his court be troubled with intrigues; let him buy the friendship of one of his neighbors and sell his own to another; let him at last make peace with his enemies, after certain victories and certain defeats; his subjects, elated by the excitement of events, think they are living in the most remarkable epoch since creation. What then? The prince dies. A different policy is pursued; and the intrigues of his court, his mistresses, his ministers, his generals, his wars, and himself are buried in oblivion." As for Charles, "his life ought to teach kings that a peaceful and happy government is better than all his glory." "There is certainly no sovereign," was Voltaire's comment, "who reading the life of Charles XII, ought not to be cured of the mad lust for conquest. For where is the sovereign who can say 'I have more courage and virtue, a firmer spirit, a hardier frame; I am better versed in warfare; I have better troops?' And if, with all these advantages, and after so many victories, this king was so ill-starred, what can be hoped by other princes with the same ambition, but with inferior gifts and resources?"

The censor's ban on *Charles XII* was never rigidly enforced. Not only was the book allowed to circulate freely, but revised editions and translations soon began to appear. Beyond any doubt Voltaire's first work in French prose helped to enhance his prestige considerably, particularly among the intelligent members of the bourgeoisie. Burdened by the injustices of the Ancient Regime, tired of its waste and extravagance, smarting under its despotism and intolerance, the upper middle classes were eager to read Voltaire's criticism of the things that irked them. They readily understood his comparisons of good and evil; for these were not the fragile strands of some delicate, philosophic gossamer, but the lucid account of an actuality which they knew and felt.

Ever since his return from England Voltaire had stayed away from the chateaux he had once enjoyed so much. But after the strain of getting out his book was over, the author felt the need of resting his capricious nerves; consequently when an invitation came to stay for a time in the home of the Countess de Fontaine-Martel, he gladly accepted. The Countess was a witty old woman, of easy morals, and with an income of more than 40,000 francs. All her life had been dedicated to pleasure, and to obtain it she entertained on a grand scale. Her nightly suppers, to which she invited only the most diverting people of her time, were renowned throughout France. Although Fontaine-Martel's hospitality was profuse, she would tolerate no young men in her home. "I believe," Voltaire said, "she has me in her house only because I am thirty-six, and too much of an invalid to have love affairs." He established himself in the

Countess' luxurious mansion toward the end of 1731, and before long he was running it as if it were his own. He became his hostess' *major domo*, presiding over her dinners, enjoying her box at the opera, and riding about town in her carriage. He managed her private theatricals, directing the plays, but also producing pieces of his own. He delighted his aged hostess with Rabelaisian stories; and occasionally he extolled her in his verses:

> *A woman from all foibles free,*
> *You, by the charms of wit engage,*
> *And reason like an ancient sage.*
> *Your wisdom's not that monster dire*
> *Whom rancor and fell rage inspire,*
> *Envy's sad sister who, with eyes*
> *Malignant, into all things pries;*
> *Who, like a hag, with ceaseless rage*
> *Rails at the pleasures of the age,*
> *But that blessed wisdom, which with ease*
> *The humors of men can please;*
> *Which makes Life's every moment charm,*
> *And of its darts can Death disarm.*
> *On all sides, madam, you behold*
> *Beauties, when ugly grown and old,*
> *Because by lovers they're neglected*
> *Turn saints at last, to be respected.*
> *But you, more knowing, justly shun*
> *The error into which they run.*
> *You don't in vigils spend the night.*
> *In cheerful suppers you delight.*
> *The pleasing folly of the muse*
> *Instead of casuists you peruse.*
> *And in the place of monk, elect*

Voltaire your conscience to direct.
Preferring still as foe to care
The opera house to house of prayer.
But that which makes my bliss complete,
With you blessed Freedom seeks retreat.

Voltaire's new life pleased him. The diversion for which he had yearned he found abundantly in the Countess' soothing generosity. In her home, he declared, he found "Liberty, decent, tolerant and serene, conjointly with her sister, Gayety, never bitter in her satire, neither prudish nor dissolute."

In spite of his many activities Voltaire found time to produce *Eriphile*. Since he had captivated his first audience with *Oedipus*, fourteen years ago, he had composed nothing but dramatic failures. But the memory of that first and only triumph was still a powerful spur; he had worked hard on his new play—perhaps he had worked too hard. For *Eriphile* displayed all the signs of studied craftsmanship; its form was correct; its rhymes polished. Like nearly all Voltaire's plays, *Eriphile* was a technical tour de force. But beyond that it was nothing. It was artifice rather than art; it neither soared nor glowed, but pressed, like a preposterous weight on one's tired senses. It is hard to believe that this play, so clever yet so dull, should have been inspired by Shakespeare's immortal "Hamlet." Only its scene and persons were different; in plot it was essentially the same. With his sharp eye for stage effect, Voltaire even introduced a ghost. But this innovation shocked the conservative French; and though the apparition was on the stage for only a few brief moments, its mere presence was denounced as unpardonable. Following his usual practice, Voltaire tried to resuscitate his ailing drama. He drastically rewrote most of three acts and added a long prologue; but despite all his doctoring, *Eriphile* continued to languish. Finally, in May, 1732, Voltaire mercifully withdrew the piece.

The play's poor showing caused Voltaire's friends almost as much anxiety as it did him. Some of them even tried to dissuade him from writing any more plays. The mantle of Sophocles, they insisted, was not for his shoulders; instead of wasting his efforts on the composition of dramas, let him create more epic poems like the *Henriade* and more histories like *Charles XII*. Voltaire's answer to all these criticisms was another play—*Zaire*.

Meanwhile the hope that he might yet be allowed to publish the "English Letters" was not fully extinguished. All that was required to make it a bright and consuming fire was some fresh fuel—and early in the year, this had been unexpectedly provided when a vacancy occurred in the French Academy. Once more Voltaire's optimism leaped high; for he was convinced that if he could get himself elected to the Academy his prestige would be too great for the censor to press his opposition to the "Letters" any further. Voltaire's ambition to become one of the Forty Immortals was not pretentious. His achievements may not have been of the highest quality; but they certainly were not surpassed by any of his leading rivals. To make sure that his claims to membership would not go unnoticed, Voltaire sought the help of some of his powerful friends. The Duke of Richelieu, whose influence at the Court was considerable, exerted himself in the poet's behalf; and shortly before the appointment was to be made, the Duke was able to assure Voltaire that he was virtually elected. Unfortunately for Voltaire, an unexpected catastrophe put a sudden end to his roseate dream. The poem, "For and Against," which he had written almost a decade ago for the Marquise de Rupelmonde, and which, because of its declarations against revealed religion, he had carefully kept from the public, now mysteriously burst into print. Who was responsible for its publication is not known; yet whoever it was, he could not have chosen a more appropriate moment to harm Voltaire. Not only did the poem's appearance wreck whatever chance its author might have had of becoming an Academician, but it aroused his old enemy, the Church, to new and overwhelming fury.

"What do you think of it?" d'Aguesseau, the Chancellor of France, asked his secretary.

"Monseigneur," answered the holy clerk, who had also seen the unpublished "English Letters," "Voltaire ought to be shut up in a place where he could have neither ink nor paper. That man has a mind which could destroy a state."

In complete agreement with this sentiment was the Archbishop of Paris, who lodged a formal complaint with the police against the poem and its author. Yet Voltaire had no intention of going to jail; hence when he was summoned by the authorities to explain his connection with the offending verses, he brazenly denied having had anything to do with them. He even went so far as to insist that the poem had been written by the *Abbé de Chaulieu*—now, unfortunately, in his grave. Police Lieutenant Hérault, who harbored a secret admiration for Voltaire, pretended to accept his explanation and, despite the protests of the Archbishop, allowed the matter to drop.

Meanwhile Voltaire had begun to write his new play, *Zaire*. Reproached by his friends for not putting more love into his pieces, he had decided to compose a romantic love tragedy. "There shall be enough love this time," he announced, "and not mere gallantry." It was his desire, he said, "that there may be nothing so Turkish, so Christian, so amorous, so tender, so infuriate as that which I am now putting into verse for the pleasure of the public. . . . We shall love, we shall baptize, we shall kill. . . ." The subject so fascinated him that he could think of nothing else, and in three weeks the play was ready for rehearsal.

The play has been compared with "Othello," but aside from its central theme of consuming jealousy, and a few speeches here and there, it bears little resemblance to Shakespeare's tragedy. It is the story of Zaire, a Christian captive in Jerusalem. Raised by the Mohammedans, she is unaware of her Christian origin. The Sultan, Orosmane, falls in love with her and asks her to become his wife. She is on the point of entering his seraglio when her brother, Nerestan, arrives. He tells her of her Christian background, and explains to her that ever since her birth her father, now aged and dying, had been a prisoner of the Moslems. Zaire promises her brother that she will not marry a Mohammedan, but will, instead, be baptized a Christian. Torn between her faith, her loyalty to her kin, and her love for Orosmane, the vacillating Zaire arouses her lover's suspicions. She tries to meet her brother in a secret rendezvous; but Orosmane learns of her plan. Not knowing the identity of Nerestan, whom he suspects to be a rival lover, the jealous Orosmane murders his sweetheart. When, shortly afterwards, Zaire's brother is made a prisoner by the Sultan's men, the tragic truth at once becomes clear.

The end of the drama is reminiscent of "Othello." Over-whelmed by the horror of his crime, the Sultan stabs him-self.

For the first three performances the fate of *Zaire* was in doubt. There had been applause; but it had been half-hearted, and it had been adulterated with hoots and cat-calls. Sensing some of the play's defects, Voltaire under-took some quick revisions. The more unfavorable lines he deleted altogether. At the play's fourth showing his repair work was at last rewarded—and *Zaire* became a hit. Over-joyed at his triumph, Voltaire wrote to his friend Cideville that "never was a piece so well acted as Zaire. . . . I wished you were there; you would have seen that the public did not hate your friend. I appeared in a box and the whole pit applauded me. I blushed; I hid myself; but I should be a rogue, did I not confess to you that I was touched." Somewhat amazed by the magnitude of his triumph, Vol-taire protested—quite rightfully—that the less fortunate *Eriphile* "had been far better written." Correctly, too, he put his finger on the main reason for *Zaire's* popularity. "All the ornaments, all the spirit, all the forces of poetry," he asserted, "are not worth, so it is said, one touch of sen-timent."

Soaring once more into the interstellar space of fame, Voltaire was summoned by the King and Queen to direct performances of "the tender *Zaire*" at their palace in Fon-tainebleau. The poet was touched by this unexpected trib-ute; and in full appreciation of it he remained at the royal chateau for nearly two months. For the assembled dignitaries he produced not only his latest hit, but also his less successful *Mariamne*. All the while he was, he said, "floating in the vapors of vainglory." Not content with being the author and producer of *Zaire,* Voltaire—ever on the alert for additional glory—assigned himself one of the parts, that of Lusignan, the heroine's old and dying father. The role so affected his overstrung nerves that at the moment where the aged man recognizes his children, Voltaire melted so completely into tears that he forgot his lines. The prompter, who was weeping too, was unable to give him his cue; and for a few tense moments it looked as if *Zaire* might suddenly turn into an unintended tragedy.

Voltaire had barely left the Royal Palace when he was called to the bedside of his benefactress, the Countess Fontaine-Martel. She had been fatally stricken; yet to the end she maintained her cynicism. Only with great reluctance did she allow Voltaire to summon a priest—"so that she might die according to the rules." Even death was not without its lighter side to this pleasure-loving woman. "What time is it?" she asked as the end approached. Before Voltaire could answer—"Praised be God!" she said, "whatever the time, there is somewhere a rendezvous."

After the death of "the good Martel," her chief mourner continued to occupy her house. To relinquish its comfort was of course not easy; but for the moment Voltaire was too engrossed in his literary projects to give any time to the search for new quarters. He was still tinkering on his "English Letters"; he was working on a burlesque of Joan of Arc, *La Pucelle;* and he had started a new play. In addition he had put *Zaire* into book form, with a dedication to his English friend, Falkener. "I offer," he said, "this tragedy to you as my countryman in literature and my intimate friend. At the same time I take pleasure in being able to say to my own nation in what esteem merchants are held among you; how much respect is felt for a profession which makes the greatness of the state. . . . I know this profession is despised by our *petits-maitres;* but you know also that our little lords are the most ridiculous species that creep upon the surface of the earth."

This dedication brought forth a torrent of roaring criticism. Voltaire's foes, who had never ceased their attacks on *Zaire,* now turned their fire on the author for having inscribed his work "to a merchant and a foreigner." The poet was not unmindful of these fulminations, although outwardly he appeared undismayed. It was an imperturbability which he could well afford; for within the quiet confines of his study he was preparing a tremendous counter assault. He called it the "Temple of Taste," and to his friend Cideville he confided that he was building it of "mud and spittle."

In February Voltaire informed Cideville that "this little chapel of Taste . . . had become bit by bit an immense cathedral." By April his "rock-pile of scandal" had become a new edifice. The Keeper of the Seals, who had read the "Temple of Taste," had found nothing in it which was "contrary to the state, to religion, or to morals." Hence Voltaire confidently expected his work to be approved for publication, and allowed it to be printed while it was still in the censor's hands awaiting his decision.

The "Temple of Taste" is a long burlesque in prose and verse wherein Voltaire dissected some of his leading contemporaries. The piece has been likened to Pope's "Dunciad" and to the prose of Swift, to both of which its satirical qualities give it some resemblance. It is the story of Voltaire's pilgrimage to the Temple of Taste which lies somewhere in the Land of the Fine Arts. For his traveling companion he has chosen the king's minister, Cardinal

Fleury, who had frowned on the "English Letters." On their journey to the Temple the two travelers encounter artists, poets, philosophers; they see musicians, scientists, architects and theologians—all eager to be admitted to the Temple of Taste. They behold "connoisseurs of pictures who go into raptures at God the Father in his eternal glory, painted very courtly in the manner of Watteau." They meet a "swam of commentators, who restore passages and compile huge volumes about a word they do not understand." These men are not interested in getting into the Temple, for to them "taste is nothing." "Our task," they boast, "is to elaborate . . . what others think. As for us, we do not think at all." As the journey proceeds, there are discussions of the latest French craze for Italian music; the excessive ornamentation bestowed on new buildings; priests whose claim to fame is based on their ability to incite people to burn books; and editors and critics who, "like insects, are only noticed when they sting."

When the two pilgrims arrive at the Temple they observe a great crowd before its gates clamoring for admission. It is a motley assortment of frauds and incompetents, devoid of all critical sense and good taste. Among these "barbarians," these "modern Visigoths," Voltaire included many of his own contemporaries. Not content to employ mere innuendo, he singled out his victims by name and gleefully poured boiling oil upon them, while he stood by to watch them kick and squirm.

Chief among these unfortunates was Voltaire's old foe, the poet Jean-Baptiste Rousseau. The two men had been sniping at one another ever since their quarrel at Brussels a decade ago. Rousseau had been an acidulous critic of *Zaire*, which he had denounced as "an odious mixture of

piety and libertinage." Voltaire now took his revenge by
putting Rousseau into the mad throng trying to get into
the Temple. There Rousseau is depicted, "supported by
two little satyrs, and crowned with laurels and with
thistles." "I have come," he says, in a horrible, croaking
voice, "to laugh, to sport and to play, and to make merry
till the dawn of day." When Criticism, the Temple's guard,
fails to recognize Rousseau, he tells her he has just arrived
from Germany; and to identify himself he recites some of
his verses. Yet try as he will, he can do nothing more than
burlesque his own poetry. He finishes by breaking into the
well-known croaking notes of Aristophanes' *Frogs*: "Brek-
ke, kake, ko-ax, ko-ax, ko-ax!" "Bon Dieu! What a horrible
jargon!" cries Criticism. She is about to bar the preposterous Rousseau from the Temple, when she is told that
the Muses have changed his voice into that of a frog as a
punishment for his malice. Finally, out of consideration for
his early verses, she permits Rousseau to enter, reminding
him, however, that "poets do not go to Germany." Barely
within the Temple, Rousseau turns pale for before him
stands a man against whom he had directed so many spite-
ful epigrams.

> *This was the learned Fontenelle*
> *Who could in all the arts excel;*
> *And on each branch of science threw*
> *A light that pleased, because 'twas new.*

Full of rage, Rousseau goes off to write another epigram,
while Fontenelle "looks upon him with that philosophic
compassion which a broad and enlightened spirit cannot
help feeling for a man who knows only how to rhyme."

Shortly after the publication of the "Temple of Taste," Voltaire moved to new quarters, directly opposite the city gate of St. Gervais. His new abode was dreary and shabby, in sad contrast to the luxury which had surrounded him in the home of the lamented Countess. He now lived, he said, "in the worst house in the worst quarter of Paris." To Thieriot, who was touring England, he wrote that he would much prefer to be with him "in the land of liberty"; but that inasmuch as his health prevented him from traveling, he would content himself "with thinking freely in Paris, since writing is forbidden." "I shall let Jansenists and Jesuits mutually damn one another; parliament and councils exhaust themselves with decrees; men of letters tear each other apart, more cruelly than priests fighting for a benefice."

Voltaire's plan to lead a life of quiet contemplation was not easy to carry out; for soon we find him complaining to Cideville that he was "more deafened by the noise of church bells than a sexton." "But," he added resolutely, "I shall make so much noise with my lyre that the sound of the bells will be nothing to me."

The noise of his lyre was to surpass his highest expectation. For soon it became evident that the satire he had unleashed in his "Temple" was not to pass unchallenged. "Here is a little villain of a writer," Marais wrote into his ever-ready diary, "who ought to be sent over the sea again." Voltaire's more powerful victims sought the help of the Court against the libelous rhymester. Its pressure was soon discernible, for before long it was announced that the censor had refused to give Voltaire permission to print his "Temple of Taste," and had outlawed all existing copies of that work. Spurred on by their success, the poet's enemies now conspired to have him sent to prison. "This 'Temple of Taste,'" its unhappy author wrote to Thieriot, "has roused those whom I have not praised enough and still more those whom I have not praised at all. . . . Add to that the crime of having printed this bagatelle without a permit, and the anger of the minister against such an outrage; add to that the howlings of the Court and the menace of a *lettre de cachet,* and you will have only a faint idea of the pleasant position I am in and the protection given here to literature."

With such a storm beating upon him from all sides, Voltaire sought refuge in seclusion. His solace, as usual, was work—hard and indefatigable toil that filled his hours from morning till night. He wrote the greater part of his new play, which he called *Adelaide du Guesclin;* he composed the verses for Rameau's opera, *Samson;* and he completed a treatise on the philosopher Pascal. Early in July he sent the manuscript to Rouen, to his printer Jore, who was to include it as the twenty-fifth of the "English Letters," but to which it bore no relationship at all. To his friend Cideville, Voltaire wrote that he considered his scheme a bold one, for "this misanthropic Christian, sublime though he is, is for me only a man like any other when he is wrong, and I think he is wrong very often."

The "Remarks on the Thoughts of Pascal" were the first important expression of Voltaire's philosophy. The work, its author took pains to explain, was not directed against Pascal the scientist, for whom he had great esteem, but against Pascal the Jansenist. It was, Voltaire said, "against the author of the *Pensées* in which, it seems to me, he has attacked humanity much more cruelly than he has attacked the Jesuits."

A brilliant mathematician and physicist, Pascal lived in the seventeenth century, at the dawn of one of the greatest scientific eras. A narrow escape from death in a carriage accident so unnerved him that for months he was emotionally unstrung. When he recovered, he interpreted his experience as a divine warning—a warning he proceeded to heed by renouncing all interest in natural science. He now sought refuge in the consolation of religion and philosophy. Growing more and more somber in his views, he became in time the leader of the Jansenists, championing their teachings with a fervor and austerity akin to that of Jonathan Edwards. Terrified by the world's colossal wickedness, he sought partially to atone for it with incredible acts of self-torture. He prayed incessantly; he undertook long periods of fasting; he wore coarse hair shirts over which he bore a ponderous iron breast-plate with points that pierced his flesh. He died before he was forty, a sacrifice to his own harshness and self-denial.

As Jansenism's most eloquent spokesman, the devout Pascal attracted Voltaire's acute interest. He regarded him, indeed, as the formidable protagonist of a view of life almost completely opposed to his own. Hostile to the general idea of revealed religion, Voltaire rejected the Jansenist doctrines of the fall of man, redemption, predestination and grace. These he considered absurd theological inventions. As an advocate of reason, Voltaire was out of sympathy with Pascal's teachings that man could understand himself, and be understood, not by reason but by intuition.

Pascal regarded man not as an animal, but as a unique creature—a "finite creature with the ignominious mark of the infinite upon him." Because man was endowed with reason, he became more wicked than other creatures; because he was forever striving for an unattainable, mythical perfection, man was destined to be unhappy. His only hope lay in salvation; and to obtain this, it was his obvious duty to renounce all earthly pleasures, for only thus could he hope for divine grace and eternal bliss.

Voltaire regarded man not as a unique creature, but as an animal, different from his fellow animals only in degree. Like other animals, man had his limitations; but unlike them, he was highly organized. He had more feelings, more desires, more emotions. Intellectually, he was plainly superior. Man became a mysterious creature only when he persisted in knowing his beginning and his end; he became mysterious when he tried to define his spirit and determine its relationship to his body. Man, Voltaire argued, was not incomprehensible to those who really tried to understand him. But, he contended, man could not be made understandable through the doctrine of original sin.

"The misery and wretchedness of human life," Voltaire contended, "no more proves in a philosophic sense the fall of man than the misery of a cab horse proves that horses were formerly big and fat and were never subject to the whip." Voltaire agreed with Pascal's thesis that "all men desire to be happy"; but to seek happiness, as Pascal proposed, by eradicating life's joys and pleasures, seemed ridiculous and illogical. When Pascal asserted that we must love only God, Voltaire countered that we must love his creatures too. When Pascal lifted Christianity above all other religions and declared it to be holy beyond comparison, and true without question, Voltaire replied that "it was on the way to mass that men committed the mas-

sacres of St. Bartholomew; and that it was after mass and
because of the mass that so many innocent people, so many
mothers, so many children, were murdered in the crusade
against the heretics of the south of France. O Pascal! such
are the results of the endless quarrels upon the dogmas,
upon the mysteries that could have no results except quarrels. There is not one article of faith which has not given
birth to a civil war!"

Voltaire's seclusion was not without an occasional inter-
ruption. It was his custom to help young men in whom he
thought he saw signs of literary talent. Often he harbored
a protégé or two in his rooms, where he provided for their
material as well as their literary needs. One such fledgling
poet, Lefèvre, he made his secretary. Unfortunately, Lefèvre's talents never had a chance to bear fruit, for he died
very young. Today his name is remembered not for any
achievements, but because of an essay addressed to him by
Voltaire. Still smarting from the blows administered by his
adversaries, he told Lefèvre what he might expect should
he ever write a good book in France.

"The career of letters," Voltaire declared, "and particularly that of genius, is more thorny than the road to
wealth." If an author happens to be mediocre, he "will be
remorseful all his life"; if he is successful, he will have
enemies, and he "will walk on the rim of an abyss between contempt and hatred." Speaking out of bitter experience, Voltaire explained to the young poet that he
must expect difficulties from the censor—"if your way of
thought is not like his; if he is not a friend of your friends;
if he is a friend of your rival; or if he is himself your rival."
When, after at least a year's delay, the author has finally
satisfied the censor, then, Voltaire said, he would still have

to court writers, abbés, doctors and book agents to win friends for his forthcoming book. When his work finally appeared, it often did so only to fall prey to any one of several literary gazettes, which deliberately satirized a book to curry favor with the malicious reading public, hoping thereby to increase its circulation. If the author happened to write a play, then, Voltaire insisted, the situation "was even worse." Yet if by some rare chance, the drama happened to be a success, then it would be parodied in all the minor theatres. "Twenty libelous articles," Voltaire asseverated, "will prove that you should not have succeeded at all. Scholars, who understand Greek badly, and who do not read what is composed in French, will have contempt for you. . . ."

Among Voltaire's visitors was a noblewoman, the Marquise Emilie du Chatelet. She had met the poet less than a year earlier at a party in Paris. Apparently he had made more than an ordinary impression upon her, for before long she was telling her friends that his eyes had "something of velvet and an inexpressible softness." The Marquise herself had large and lovely eyes—though otherwise she was not beautiful. Her taste in clothes favored overembellishment, and failed utterly to conceal her lack of femininity. The Marquise's want of allure was happily counterbalanced, however, by rarer qualities. Even as a child she had displayed remarkable intellectual vigor. She had begun to translate the "Aeneid" into French verse before she was fifteen; and long before she knew Voltaire, she could recite from memory the entire ten cantos of the *Henriade*. She liked to dance; was a passable performer on the spinet; and as an amateur actress she had revealed more than an average talent. Keenly interested in mathematics and science, she was taking private lessons from the mathematician, Maupertuis.

The Marquise du Chatelet had been married at nineteen to an infantry officer; and at twenty-seven, when she met Voltaire, she was the mother of three children. The marriage had been one of convenience. From the outset neither the Marquis nor his wife remained true to their conjugal vows. The Marquise had what she called "a temperament of fire." When her first lover, de Guébriant, left her, she tried to take poison. Other lovers proved an effective antidote, and in time she became the mistress of the Duke of Richelieu. Her attachment to the Duke never ceased entirely. Even after their intimacy had ended, the Duke and the Marquise continued to be excellent friends —a relationship which astounded even some of the most sophisticated of their easy-going associates. "It is futile," the Marquise contended, "for people to tell me that such a thing is impossible. I have a good answer; such a thing does exist, and will exist all my life."

In some matters the Marquise was strangely decorous. She frowned on the *pas de six,* a new dance, and only slightly less formal than the minuet. The Marquise considered it vulgar, and implored the police to put an end to it, "in order," as she said, "to show the fools and immodest ones who dance it that this century does have some morals." Nor did the former mistress of Richelieu let herself commit such a *faux pas* as to come to Voltaire's rooms unescorted—at least not on her first visit. The Marquise's companion on this occasion was a lady of quality, the Duchess of Saint Pièrre.

Voltaire did his best to entertain his guests. He regaled them with chicken fricassee and recited passages from the script of his unfinished *Adelaide*. The ladies, for their part, appreciated his hospitality and even wept over some of his verses.

The poet was greatly taken with the Marquise du Chatelet. Soon he was composing verses for her in which he addressed her as his "divine Emilie" and his "beautiful Uranie." In the summer he disclosed to Cideville that he was writing an epistle on "Calumny," and was dedicating it "to a very amiable and much-calumniated woman," who, one need hardly be told, happened to be none other than Emilie. The poet told her that, since she was pretty,

> . . . *it will be your fate*
> *Respectable Emilie, to incur much hate.*
> *Almost one-half the human race*
> *Will even curse you to your face.*
> *Possessed of genius' noblest fire*
> *With fear you will each breast inspire.*
> *As you too easily confide,*
> *You will be betrayed, belied.*
> *You ne'er of virtue made parade,*
> *To hypocrites no court you ever paid;*
> *Therefore of calumny beware.*

Between poetic effusions written for Emilie and letters to Cideville extolling her charms, Voltaire still managed to find time to complete his tragedy of *Adelaide du Gues-clin*. Its plot is incredibly simple. Set in fourteenth-century France, it tells of the Duke of Vendôme and his brother, the Duke of Nemours, who are rivals in their love for Adelaide. When she seems to prefer Nemours, Vendôme, in a fit of rage, orders one of his men, Coucy, to assassinate him. Coucy pretends to obey, but actually spares Nemours. When Coucy reports to his master that he has carried out his command, the Duke becomes conscience-stricken. Overwhelmed by his sense of guilt, Vendôme becomes more and more morose. He tries to kill himself, but is stopped in time. Coucy, realizing that his master has suffered enough and is truly repentant, tells him the truth, and in the presence of Adelaide he reunites the two brothers.

The drama was performed for the first time in January, 1734. Almost from the start the audience was hostile. What seemed to be radical innovations on the part of the author frankly shocked its classical taste. The fact that Voltaire had drawn his plot from an event which had actually occurred in medieval France, and that he had introduced historic French names, was deemed dramatically unpardonable. When, in the second act, the author ventured to inject a little realism into his play by permitting Nemours to appear wounded on the stage, his arm in a sling, the spectators booed and hissed. From then on the play was doomed, and by the time it reached the last act, the audience had become so boisterous that the actors could scarcely be heard.

The failure of *Adelaide* filled Voltaire with apprehension. He knew that the animosity he had engendered with his "Temple of Taste" had never died; and that his enemies would now seek to make capital out of his misfortune. He lived in the constant fear that his "English Letters" might be discovered and he be sent to jail. To his friend d'Argental he wrote that he had "a mortal aversion to prison," adding that he was sick and that the close air would kill him. He sent frantic appeals to his friends at Rouen to warn Jore, his printer, to guard the "Letters" as he would his life. "Tell Jore," he wrote, "that if a single copy gets out, he will find himself in the Bastille, his license forfeited, and his family ruined." "There are times," he said to Cideville, "when the boldest things may be done with impunity; there are others when the simplest and most innocent act becomes dangerous and criminal." Voltaire's fears for his safety were increased by the publication in London of the English edition of the "Letters." Although this act was quite within the law, that very fact seemed to add to his peril; for his enemies, now knowing the true nature of the "English Letters," felt that the author somehow had outwitted them, and hence were more determined than ever to avenge themselves. Early in April Voltaire wrote to one of his friends, Formont, that "the Letters philosophical, political, poetical, critical, heretical and diabolical are going off in London, and with success." "But," he added, "the English are Pope-scorners, cursed of God. The Gallican Church, I fear, will be a little harder to please." He was quite right. For the authorities, having heard that the "Letters" were being surreptitiously printed at Rouen, suddenly swooped down upon that city to look for the forbidden work. They found nothing, however; and for the time being Voltaire appeared safe.

Soon afterward, he left Paris for Montjeu, where he was to be best man at the wedding of the Duke of Richelieu to the Princess de Guise. He was accompanied by the Marquise du Chatelet. Once aflame for the Duke, the Marquise apparently was now glowing for someone else. The marriage had been schemed by Voltaire, and the fact that he was now bringing it to a successful climax greatly pleased him. "I have conducted the affair like the intrigue in a comedy," he wrote to Cideville. "I have drawn up the contract, so I shall not write any verses."

But write them he did. To the bride he addressed a felicitous epistle. "A priest, an *I-do*, three Latin words," he told her, "forever fix your fate; and the village priest in the chapel of Montjeu very christian-like will require you to go to bed with Richelieu—with Richelieu the inconstant, who will swear by this holy tie to be forever faithful and good. We suspect him a little; indeed, your large, dark eyes, full of passion, are much more reassuring to us than all the oaths he makes before God." With his tongue in his cheek, Voltaire warned the Duchess of what awaited her on her return to Paris. "Have you thought, Madame, how many husbands will come to complain to Your Highness? The many cuckolds the Duke has made have put their hopes in you. They will say, when they see how attractive you are, 'Ye gods! What a pleasure is revenge!' You will feel, of course, that they are right, and that the guilty Duke must be punished. The blessed law of retaliation is the most equitable of laws. What! Your heart is not made for tit for tat? What kind of virtue is that which serves only to madden everyone! Must Richelieu be the sole possessor of your charms? And must it be said that he will not be deceived, as he so justly deserves? . . . Well, be good, if that pleases you. Let this be your chimera: With all your talents for pleasing, you must have at least one fault. In that noble and painful task of guarding what is called honor, I wish you good fortune; but that is a thing impossible."

After Voltaire had, as he said, "put the bride and groom properly to bed," he devoted himself exclusively to courting Emilie. "Lovable and brilliant nymph," he said to her in verse, "To you I consecrate all my works; it is from you I expect the prize." The Marquise remained with Voltaire at Montjeu long after the other guests had left; indeed, as far as she and the poet were concerned, this was as much their honeymoon as that of the Richelieus.

Their bliss was destined to come to an abrupt end. The storm which had been gathering so ominously over Voltaire now burst upon him with terrific fury. Someone had published a pirated edition of the "English Letters"; and together with the "Thoughts on Pascal," they were appearing all over Paris. The authorities moved swiftly. They condemned the work as "scandalous, contrary to religion, to morality, and to the respect due to authority." Every copy that could be found was confiscated. The unfortunate printer, Jore, was arrested; and though he swore his innocence, he was locked in the Bastille. As for Voltaire, the enraged authorities were determined to accord him the same treatment. To lodge him behind the bars they issued a *lettre de cachet*.

When the police arrived at Montjeu on May 11th, they found only the Duchess of Richelieu and the Marquise du Chatelet. The Duke had gone to join his regiment on the German frontier; and Voltaire had gone "to take the waters" in Lorraine, which was then beyond the jurisdiction of France.

For the time being, Voltaire remained in discreet hiding. Not even his closest friends knew his whereabouts. When the Marquise had no word from him for several weeks she became alarmed. She was sure the *lettre de cachet* must have overtaken him, and that he was suffering somewhere in a horrible dungeon. She tried to console herself with the thought that he might have escaped to

England—"his safety would make my life's tranquility."
But the terrifying spectacle of her lover in prison continued to haunt her. "To know that he, with such health
and imagination as he has, is in prison, I assure you," she
confided to a friend, "I do not find in myself constancy
enough to support the idea."

When word from the fugitive came at last, the Marquise
felt somewhat relieved. At least Voltaire was not in prison.
He had assumed what he called "a vagabond life," and
was wandering from place to place, but not daring to stay
anywhere very long. For a while he was at Cirey-sur-Blaise,
where the Marquise had offered him asylum in the ancestral castle of the du Chatelets; then he appeared in the
Swiss city of Basel, just across the Alsatian frontier; then
of a sudden we behold him in Richelieu's camp at Philips-
burg, where he watched the French making preparations
for an anticipated attack from the Austrians.

Meanwhile the Marquise du Chatelet had been exercis-
ing all her powers in an effort to mollify the authorities'
attitude towards Voltaire. In her campaign she enlisted
the help of some of Versailles' most influential women,
such persons as the Princess de Conti and the Duchess
d'Aiguillon, whose wish with certain ministers of state was
usually a command. Their efforts on Voltaire's behalf
seemed to veer toward success, and before long hints were
being dropped from Paris that if Voltaire would disavow
his objectionable book, the *lettre de cachet* might be canceled.

Voltaire was willing enough. "They say I must retract,"
he wrote to the Duchess d'Aiguillon. "Very willingly. I
will declare that Pascal is always right; that if St. Luke and
St. Mark contradict one another, it is a proof of the truth

of religion to those who know how to take such things; that another lovely proof of religion is that it is unintelligible. I will avow that all priests are gentle and disinterested; that the Jesuits are honest people; that monks are neither proud, nor given to intrigue, nor stinking; that the holy inquisition is the triumph of humanity and tolerance. In a word I will say all that is desired of me, provided they will leave me in repose, and not indulge the mania to persecute a man who has never done harm to anyone, who lives in retirement and who knows no other ambition than that of paying court to you."

"It is certain," he added, "that the edition was published in spite of me . . . and that I have done all that was humanly possible to discover the publisher." Voltaire also addressed a long letter to Police Lieutenant Hérault, begging him not "to listen to the prayers and foolish outcries of superstitious imbeciles, infected by the poison of Jansenism, and who pretend that God and the State are attacked when one mocks the convulsions of Quakers." His book, he told Hérault, had "more people approving it in Europe than it had unworthy criticism in France."

Such statements, however, were not enough. What was wanted was a clear and unconditional disavowal of the entire "English Letters"; and until Voltaire was ready to make such a repudiation, the authorities were determined to remain inflexible in their decision to punish him. In June the parliament of Paris officially condemned the "Letters"; and soon afterward the common hangman solemnly burned the offensive work in a public ceremony. When the Marquise du Chatelet heard of this, she feared Voltaire would never again be allowed to live in France. All her repressed emotions now surged up within her. "I shall retire at once to my chateau," she announced. "Men have become insupportable; so false are they, so full of prejudices."

In the meantime Voltaire had made up his mind to accept the offer of the Marquise to make her chateau at Cirey his sanctuary. It was a neglected relic of a mansion, built in the thirteenth century, and unoccupied for many years. Situated in the isolated forest lands of Champagne, it was virtually inaccessible, and had—for Voltaire—the added advantage of being only a short distance from the Belgian border. To make the place habitable Voltaire lent the Marquise forty thousand francs for "necessary repairs and sundries."

Cirey

VOLTAIRE arrived at Cirey in August. Almost at once the insidious worries of the past few months began to be forgotten; the delightful excitement engendered by his new surroundings and the anticipation of new and interesting activities overshadowed everything else. With an abundance of energy Voltaire plunged into the task of renovating what he called "the most dilapidated chateau in the world." Just as he had once directed the actors of his plays, he now supervised masons and carpenters. He worked indefatigably, laying out new garden beds and gravel paths; clambering on roofs to inspect gutters and chimney pots; drawing up plans for additional rooms to provide a study for himself and a laboratory to carry on scientific experiments. Under his direction the quiet tranquility of Cirey, which had been undisturbed for generations, now gave way to the resounding confusion of laboring men. "Every day," he told one of his neighbors, "new workmen arrive. I am the checker of all those who work.

I write their names every day into a big account book. Until someone relieves me, I cannot quit."

Amid all this activity Voltaire still found time to write. His literary labors were actually greater and more varied than ever. He was at work on a new play, *Alzire;* a history of the century of Louis XIV; a "Treatise on Metaphysics"; a series of "Discourses on Man"; and his burlesque of Joan of Arc, *La Pucelle.* For relaxation he wrote to his friends. And, as if bent on proving his maxim that "one has time for everything if one chooses to use it," he paid gallant compliments to his neighbors—especially his feminine neighbors. "I take the liberty of sending you this boar's head," he wrote to the Countess de Neuville. "This gentleman has just been assassinated to give me the opportunity of paying my court to you. I sent for a buck but none could be found. This boar was destined to give you his head. I swear to you I think very little of the head of a wild pig, and I believe it is only eaten for vanity. If I had taken nothing but a lark, I should have offered it to you just the same." In acknowledgment the Countess sent Voltaire a basket of peaches.

One evening in November the Marquise du Chatelet arrived at the chateau. She came, as Voltaire observed, "surrounded by two hundred packages." She had been traveling for a long time, with little rest, over roads that were unbelievably rough. She felt "bruised, shaken and tired." Yet by the next day she had recovered miraculously. She wasted no time on idle chit-chat, but made off at once with Voltaire on a tour of her estate, minutely inspecting every detail, scrutinizing her companion's latest innovations, suggesting dozens of others, and giving the convincing impression that in the matter of consuming energy she was every bit the equal of Voltaire.

The incredible Emilie maintained her terrific pace for days. She was at once gardener and architect. She moved things about with the force of a hurricane—and at times with almost the same effect. "She has put windows," Voltaire wrote to the Countess de Neuville, "where I put doors; she is changing the staircases into chimneys, and the chimneys into staircases; she had planted linden trees where I proposed elms; and if I have laid out a vegetable garden, she has turned it into a flower bed." But withal Voltaire found her "adorable," "a fairy in the house." "She turns rags into tapestries," he declared; "she has found the secret of furnishing Cirey with nothing." Actually, her "furnishing Cirey with nothing" took the form of installing costly terraces, balustrades and gardens; galleries and ante-chambers; rooms redecorated in yellow, blue, or silver; a lavish bathroom with a marble floor, walls of tile, and a shining porcelain tub; besides an imposing array of china images, books, pictures, mirrors, clocks, marabouts, and lacquered tables. There was even a statue of the Farnese Hercules and another of Venus.

In time, the chaos caused by Cirey's reconstruction came to an end. The workmen grew fewer and fewer, and finally disappeared altogether; and the scores of activities that went into the process of making the chateau comfortable subsided. Before long things began to assume an air of solidity and permanence.

The Marquise and her guest gradually evolved a routine from which they rarely parted. For the greater part of the day each remained in seclusion, buried in work—she in her science and mathematics, he in his writing. They joined one another for supper, after which they diverted themselves with conversation, a game of chess, or some music. Voltaire instructed Emilie in English, and she, in turn, delighted him by learning the language in three months. They read Tasso and Ariosto together, and in that way gained a fair mastery of Italian. Whenever Cirey harbored guests, the entertainment was more elaborate. On such occasions Voltaire would read from his works; sometimes he would direct a puppet show; or he would display slides on his magic lantern, a pastime of which he was incredibly fond and which never failed to excite his admiration. Sometimes, when he felt particularly exuberant, he combined all his arts, performing with tremendous enthusiasm for hours at a time. Nor was the Marquise remiss in her hospitality. Her forte in the realm of entertainment was music; when she was in good spirits she sang operas; and once, when she must have been in unusually good spirits, she sang through an entire opera.

The Marquise du Chatelet had brought her children to Cirey, but these she prudently kept in the background. Occasionally the Marquis put in a dutiful appearance at the chateau. But his presence never aroused much enthusiasm in his wife, and whenever he stayed at Cirey, she took pains to stay out of sight as much as possible. She found, she wrote to Richelieu, that her situation "was most embarrassing." As for the Marquis, he was not the man to bear ill will toward anyone; if he felt there was anything unusual in the relationship between his wife and Voltaire, he was chivalrous enough not to mention it.

Not many friends made their way from Paris to Cirey. The place was too inaccessible for all but the stoutest hearts; and its pleasures were much too placid. Those visitors who braved the hardships of travel to penetrate to

Madame du Chatelet

Cirey's wild and forlorn acres were usually relatives or intimate friends; or they were intellectuals, who cared little how cloistered from the world a place might be, as long as it offered a stimulus to their intellect. Some of the keenest minds of the eighteenth century journeyed to Cirey. Francesco Algarotti, who had written a book for young ladies on Newton, came all the way from Italy; while the noted mathematician, Johann Bernoulli, came from Switzerland. The celebrated Koenig, who had been a professor at the Hague and a librarian to the Prince of Orange, liked Cirey so much that he remained with his hosts for two whole years.

Neither Voltaire nor the Marquise brooked any interference in their accustomed routine. They were determined to do their work at all costs; and to do it, they ran their rural retreat with rules and the sound of bells, as if it were some gigantic institution housing an army, instead of a home occupied by a handful of people. The guests themselves were divided into two castes—the "cochers," who like the Marquis du Chatelet, were deemed unimportant, and the rest who were significant. All visitors to Cirey, whether they were famous intellectuals or people of the common clay, were subject to a severe discipline. No one was allowed to leave his rooms in the morning until coffee was announced, which was usually between ten and eleven o'clock, and was served in one of Voltaire's smaller rooms. An enthusiastic drinker of coffee, the poet liked to linger over its delights, while conversing with his guests. They remained with him until he rose and made a low bow—the signal for them to go. They bowed in return and left, while the poet plunged into his work, from which he rarely emerged until supper.

Things were not always serene in the paradise of Cirey. Voltaire's temper, quick and irascible, needed but a tiny spark to ignite it; and that spark was always on hand in the divine but fiery Emilie. The lovers swore they could never live alone; yet they quarreled over the most trivial incidents. A broken plate, a delay in serving supper would untap a stream of steaming accusations and counter-accusations that might flow lavishly and unabated for hours. Such eruptions might occur even in the presence of noble and distinguished guests, though on such occasions Voltaire and the Marquise discreetly insulted each other in English, which, they hoped, nobody else would understand.

In December, 1734, the Marquise du Chatelet journeyed to Paris. She went, ostensibly, to be with the Duchess of Richelieu, whose confinement was approaching. But she also went to seek relaxation and enchantment in the holiday festivities of France's gayest city. On Christmas she virtuously attended midnight mass, accompanied by her friend and teacher, Maupertuis, whom she took home with her after the ceremony. Yet the Marquise was not forgetful of the lover she had left behind at Cirey. The *lettre de cachet,* which had enabled her to lure Voltaire to Cirey, was still valid; and Emilie was haunted by the ever-present fear that at any moment it might be enforced, and she would lose her adorable prize. The mere thought of such a disaster made her redouble her efforts with the powers at Versailles. Most of the year's first weeks she passed in ministerial offices, where she pleaded with fervid eloquence on behalf of her "innocent and persecuted Voltaire." In the end her campaign was crowned with sweet and triumphant victory, and in March the odious *lettre de cachet* was canceled. Police Lieutenant Hérault, so often the transmitter of evil tidings, now changed his role to become the bearer of good news. "His Eminence and Monsieur the Keeper of the Seals," he wrote to Voltaire, "have charged me, monsieur, to inform you that you are at liberty to return to Paris whenever you think proper." Yet the Police Lieutenant could not entirely shake off the age-old habits of his stern office. With a warning shake of his finger, he reminded Voltaire that "this permission is given on condition that you will occupy yourself with matters which shall afford no complaints against you like those of the past."

Late in March Voltaire emerged from the sanctuary of Cirey. He went to Paris on business and to make arrangements for the production of *Alzire,* now completed and ready for rehearsal; also, of course, to be near the divine Emilie, who was still in attendance at the bedside of her friend, the Duchess de Richelieu. Voltaire's stay in the capital, however, was suddenly terminated. Rumors that he had written a satirical, and even a sacrilegious, poem on the blessed Maid of Orleans caused him to retreat from the capital in great haste.

His return to the refreshing solitude of Cirey marked the beginning of a period of tremendous activity, which, as usual, was as many-sided as it was energetic. He dabbled in his laboratory in what he chose to call scientific experiments. In the absence of the Marquise he watched over the chateau's housekeeping with the eye of an eagle, with a determination to get a full franc's worth for every franc he spent. He liked to seek relaxation in the chateau's sumptuous gardens, where he passed many of his leisure moments, planting and transplanting, pulling determined weeds, and composing Latin inscriptions to adorn shady retreats and flower-laden gateways. He felt invigorated.

Most of all, of course, he dedicated himself to his literary work. His "Discourses on Man," begun in the months of Cirey's turbulent rehabilitation, occupied him intermittently over a period of years, until it was finished in 1738. The seed of its inspiration had sprung from Pope's celebrated "Essay on Man"; but the fruit which that seed bore was different from its illustrious parent. The "Discourses," of which there were seven in all, were a series of semi-philosophic tracts in verse. They were neither inspired poesy nor profound philosophy; and they demonstrate once more that in these domains Voltaire was never truly great. Yet, though in the difficult spheres of metaphysics and epistemology he was only a transparent amateur, to his countrymen he was full of meaning, and at times, even inspiration. To them the subjects with which he grappled were not nebulous, philosophic phantoms; to them his lines were clear and lustrous, like some resplendent mirror in which they seemed to see the perfected image of their own ideas. Equality, liberty, happiness, moderation, pleasure, the nature of man, virtue—such were the subjects of Voltaire's seven discourses. Their tone was remarkably moderate; indeed, for a man who had to take to his heels after having written the caustic "English Letters," the "Discourses" seem at times almost saccharine. Interspersed throughout the work, however, were flashes of the critical Voltaire. Though the French were beset on every side by the harsh inequalities of a medieval despotism, and were promptly locked in the Bastille if they so much as suggested reform, Voltaire took occasion to remind his suffering countrymen that "mortals are equal—only their masks differ." When he wrote

Love the truth, but pardon error,
The mortal who goes astray is still thy brother,

he could well afford a sardonic grin, for these words, though utterly harmless in themselves, he knew would surely infuriate the pious theologians. Nor did Voltaire overlook his personal foes—particularly a jealous rival like the virtuous Rousseau. Envy, Voltaire told his enemies, was the chief obstacle to their happiness. Instead of letting jealousy consume them, why didn't they follow his own example? "Take revenge upon a rival by surpassing him," was his bland advice.

In his fifth discourse, "On the Nature of Pleasure," Voltaire reopened his assault on Pascal, upholding the classical theory of controlling the passions against the ascetic Christian theory of suppressing them. "Nature," he wrote, "calls us to God by the voice of the passions," and "the wholesome goodness of a merciful God everywhere attaches pleasure to human needs." The somber devout, Voltaire declared, damn self-love—"it is the enemy of men, conceived in hell"; yet "all love comes from heaven . . . and self-love is manifested in ourselves, in our goods, in our children, in our fellow citizens, and especially in our friends. . . . Yes, to lift us to the level of great deeds, God, through his goodness, gave us passions. Dangerous though it be, it is a celestial gift; the use of it is happy, even though abuse is fatal."

The "Treatise on Metaphysics" was in prose; but aside from that fact and the testimony of its title, the work bore little resemblance to the usual effusions of the metaphysicians. By nature, Voltaire was probably incapable of composing a systematic treatise on metaphysics; his artistic

temperament and his vivid imagination made him peren-
ially suspicious of speculative philosophy. It was, he once
asserted, "a drug that deadens the imagination"; while
metaphysics was "the art of reasoning about what we do
not know."

The "Treatise on Metaphysics" might better have been
called "What I Believe"; for such was essentially its nature.
In it Voltaire declared himself on such subjects as man,
virtue, religion, the soul, and God. The Deity he accepted
as the first cause of all phenomena of the universe, but the
miraculous he emphatically cast aside. "The universe," he
wrote, "is governed by laws which nothing can change."
They were, indeed, "as invariable as the laws of mathematics." As for the spirituality and immortality of the
soul, "all the probabilities are against such doctrines."
Organized religion, as it flourished then in Europe, aroused
Voltaire's crushing disapprobation. It was, in his scornful
eyes, "a system of exploitation and oppression, the despot's
main support and defense." Every desolator of the earth
launched his opprobrious work "with solemn acts of religion—and while the ground still smoked with carnage, he
hastened to the temple to repeat those solemn acts." Religion, Voltaire announced, was not even necessary as a
foundation for morality. "Much to be pitied are they," he
wrote, "who need the help of religion to be honest men."
Locke and Shaftesbury were moral men—as were Bayle
and Collins; yet they were all conspicuous for their skepticism. Virtue should not be judged by the yardstick of
religion, but by the service it renders to mankind—"virtue
is conduct which benefits the community; vice is conduct
which harms the community."

Most of the "Treatise on Metaphysics" was written in

1734. Because of its unorthodox pronouncements, Voltaire knew full well that publication of the "Treatise" was out of the question. The Marquise du Chatelet knew it too; and lest the temptation to the poet's vanity might prove irresistible, she personally assumed charge of the manuscript, keeping it under lock and key, carefully guarded from unfriendly eyes. She permitted it to be displayed only on special occasions; and only the most trusted friends were ever allowed to know of its existence.

The Marquise guarded another manuscript even more carefully. This was the satirical poem on the Maid of Orleans, *La Pucelle,* which Voltaire had begun several years before his flight to Cirey. He had worked on it occasionally, employing it as a pleasant diversion whenever his troubles threatened to become too burdensome. He had never envisioned it as a poem of great literary significance; it was, as he said, "a foolery," "a frivolous work," "an interlude to my occupations." Yet, as the years moved on, there had been many such interludes, and the *Pucelle* had grown to a formidable size. Like an old and trusted companion, it had assumed a warm and intimate place in the affections of its creator.

That Voltaire was concocting something scandalous about France's most celebrated virgin was a frequent rumor. He denied it vehemently; and with his customary duplicity in such matters, he put the blame for the rumors on his enemies, accusing them of spreading deliberate and malicious falsehoods against an utterly innocent man. His vanity, however, was too great to prevent him from letting his friends know about the *Pucelle.* "I want this work to give my friends amusement," he said; and to do this he kept them fully informed of the Maid's latest adventures as he continued to invent them.

Voltaire's lack of discretion in keeping the *Pucelle* secret had been the cause of constant alarm to the Marquise. She had not forgotten Police Lieutenant Hérault's well-meant suggestion that Voltaire should behave himself and give the authorities "no grounds of complaint like those in the past." The Marquise du Chatelet knew what dynamite was packed in the *Pucelle;* she knew that if it ever exploded the havoc would be greater than any yet caused by the writings of Voltaire. But the poet's pride of authorship was too great even for the divine Emilie; despite her reiterated warnings that the poem might fall into evil and dangerous hands, Voltaire gave no heed. Not until he had been obliged to make a hasty exit from Paris because of his reported composition of an infamous attack on the Maid of Orleans did he begin to share some of his mistress' anxiety; and on his return to Cirey he was quite ready to submit to her advice. From now on Emilie kept the parlous manuscript under lock and key, bringing it forth only on special occasions, when, like some rare and precious jewel, it was allowed to sparkle before an audience of favored and trusted intimates.

"I was not born to celebrate the saints," Voltaire avowed in the *Pucelle's* opening lines—and, indeed, he wasn't. The vague, mystical yearnings of the spirit which have lifted man above his prosaic world and at times propelled him to great and even noble achievements, were incomprehensible to Voltaire. Such manifestations were to him illusory or fraudulent; and in his world of reason they simply did not exist. The nobility of Joan of Arc, her simplicity, her faith in the divine—these things eluded him completely. All he could perceive in Joan was ignorance, superstition, self-delusion. Voltaire's inability to appreciate man's spiritual and emotional nature was a great weakness in him. It vitiated the greater part of his artistic expression; and it made him incapable of creating poetry that was deeply stirring. Nearly all his poems—even his love lyrics to Emilie—have a studied excellence; they teem with standard *clichés* and stereotyped rhymes; his heroines swoon in epigrams; his heroes make love, and even die, in the galloping meter of a rocking-horse.

If Voltaire was blind to the subtle and mysterious broodings of the human spirit, there were some truths he beheld with wonderful perspicacity. Ever since his unfortunate affair with the cowardly Chevalier de Rohan, Voltaire's eyes had been open to the glaring imperfections of his native land. The fanaticism and intolerance, the prejudices, inequalities and injustices which engulfed his countrymen everywhere—these he observed with penetrating clear-sightedness. He had exposed them, mildly to be sure, in *Charles XII;* he excoriated them in the "Ode to Adrienne Lecouvreur"; and he poured the concentrated acid of his scorn upon them in the "Temple of Taste" and in the "English Letters."

That attack Voltaire resumed in the *Pucelle.* Yet on this occasion he desired his onslaught to be light-hearted and jocular, in the bawdy vein, as he suggested, of Ariosto; or, one might add, of Boccaccio and Chaucer. The poem was designed as something essentially personal, and was not intended for the public eye. He wanted to see, he declared, what his imagination would produce when he gave it free rein, and when he gave no heed "to the narrow critical spirit now reigning in France." The *Pucelle* swarmed with Voltaire's pet aversions. Saints, kings and bishops were made to caper through its pages like clowns in a circus parade; while their creeds and rituals, their customs and traditions, furnished the theme for a broad and, at times, uproarious burlesque. For the story's framework Voltaire used a few historic facts and personages; but the edifice he finally created was purely one of extravagant fancy. The *Pucelle* concerned itself not primarily with the struggle of the French against the English, but rather with Joan's personal struggle against them both. "Although in visage Joan appeared the maid," wrote Voltaire,

> *Although in stays and petticoats arrayed,*
> *With boldest heroes she sustained her part;*
> *For Joan possessed a Rolland's fearless heart.*
> *For me, much better should I love by night*
> *A lamb-like beauty, to inspire delight.*
> *But soon you'll find through every glowing page*
> *That Joan of Arc could boast a lion's rage.*
> *You'll tremble at those feats she dared essay,*
> *How dauntlessly she braved the bloody fray.*
> *But greatest of her rare exploits you'll hear*
> *Was that she kept virginity—a year!*

That accomplishment was not easy. In fact, had Voltaire not taken the precaution to appoint Saint Denis, France's patron saint, to be Joan's ever-watchful guardian, her story assuredly would have had a different ending. For throughout the poem Joan finds her vaunted maidhood in constant peril. Even Charles VII, for whose cause Joan was fighting so valiantly, casts amorous glances upon her. Indeed, the king does not even believe that so beautiful a creature can be a virgin.

Turning his head toward the dauntless Joan,
Thus the king spoke in a majestic tone,
Which any might have feared but she alone;
"Joan, hear me: Joan, if thou'rt a maid, avow."
Joan answered: "Oh! great sire, give orders now
That doctors sage, with spectacles on nose,
Who, versed in female mysteries can depose,
That clerks, apothecaries, matrons tried,
Be called at once the matter to decide.
Let them scrutinize, and let them see."
By this sage answer Charles knew she must be
Inspired, and blessed with sweet virginity.
"Good," said the king, "since this you know so well,
Daughter of Heaven, I prithee, instant tell
What with my fair one passed last night in bed?
Speak free." "Why, nothing happened," Joan then
said.
Amazed, the king knelt down and cried aloud,
"A miracle!" then crossed himself and bowed.

Convinced that Joan must have descended from heaven, Charles henceforth accords her an almost reverential respect. But, unfortunately for Joan, his majesty's excellent example is not followed by many others. What with lascivious monks and the ravaging English, Joan's virtue is placed in perpetual danger. Even her faithful donkey sneaks into her bedroom one night to make eloquent declarations of love. For a brief moment his remarkable ardor is on the verge of triumph; yet, like all Joan's would-be seducers, he, too, is finally routed.

Joan's heart beats for only one man—Dunois, the Bastard and Count of Orleans. He

> *Felt with a golden shaft his heart pierced through,*
> *Which Cupid, smiling, from his quiver drew.*

But Dunois, too, must wait until Joan's fight for France is won. "Our lives are reckoned," the Maid tells Dunois,

> *'tis not yet the time;*
> *Let us naught mar of sovereign Fate's decree;*
> *My solemn faith is plighted but to thee.*
> *Thine, I protest, the virgin bud shall be.*
> *Let us wait until your vengeful arm,*
> *Your virtues, which in Britons strike alarm,*
> *Have from our soil the vile usurpers driven,*
> *Then, 'neath the laurel stretched, we'll taste*
> *love's heaven.*

Voltaire's serious writing was reserved, of course, not for the *Pucelle,* but for his dramas, his odes and epistles, his essays and histories. It was his practice to work on several manuscripts at a time; sometimes, indeed, he found himself occupied with as many as a half dozen. At the same time he was busily engaged in collecting material for still other works; though often years would elapse before such projects were actually started. His interest, for example, in the reign of Louis XIV had been kindled in his youth; for years Voltaire had assiduously tapped every possible source for material about the Grand Monarch; but it was not until now, when he was past forty, that he felt himself ready to forge his research into a solid composition. He desired the work on Louis to be in the vein of *Charles XII;* but also he wanted it to be the cultural picture of an epoch—one which dealt "less with the king

himself than with the arts which flourished in his reign."
Racine, Boileau, Corneille, Molière, Descartes, and other
such cultural giants, Voltaire felt to be more worthy of
study than "the battle of Steinkerque." "Nothing but a
name remains of those who commanded battalions and
fleets," he wrote to Thieriot; "nothing results to the
human race from a hundred battles won; but the great
men of whom I have spoken, prepared pure and durable
delights for generations unborn. A canal that connects two
seas, a picture by Poussin, a beautiful tragedy, a discovered
truth, are things a thousand times more precious than all
the annals of the court, than all the narratives of war."
"You know," he added, "that with me great men rank
first; heroes last." And lest Thieriot might not understand
just what he meant by "great men," Voltaire proceeded to
explain that he called great men, "all those who have excelled in the useful or the agreeable. The ravagers of
provinces are only heroes."

In January of 1736, *Alzire* (or "The Americans") was
produced in Paris; and for the first time in his career of
playwright Voltaire refrained from attending the opening
performance of one of his plays. His health, he intimated,
was not so good; the trip to the capital would be too great
a strain; and anyhow he preferred to stay at Cirey "to
delve into metaphysics." Yet, whatever sadness his absence
from Paris may have caused the poet, that sadness was
gratifyingly compensated by *Alzire's* magnificent success.

The scene of the play is laid in Lima, the capital of
Peru, some years after the Spanish conquest of America.
Don Gusman, a tyrannical and bigoted Spanish grandee
and governor of the province, is determined to impose the
Christian religion upon the natives, despite the sound

advice of his old and kindly father. To complicate Gusman's plans somewhat, Voltaire makes the villainous governor fall in love with Alzire, a virtuous Indian princess, and the daughter of Montèze, who had been dethroned by the Spaniards. Alzire still cherishes the memory of her former sweetheart, Zamore, a Peruvian prince, believed by all to have been killed in an attempt to save his country from the despotic Gusman. Yet, for the sake of her father, Alzire is willing to forget her lamented lover and marry the man she hates. Suddenly the supposedly dead Zamore appears. He tries to start a fresh revolt, but is captured and thrown into prison. Gusman's father intercedes on the prisoner's behalf, for Alvarez has discovered that Zamore, by some miraculous coincidence, is the very man who many years ago had saved his life. "My benefactor! My son!" he exclaims as he rushes to Gusman to obtain a pardon for the prisoner. The governor, still unaware that the jailed man happens to be his arch-enemy, has him released. For Zamore freedom becomes even more unbearable than captivity; he discovers that Montèze has become a Christian; and worse yet, his beloved Alzire has married his enemy. He tries to persuade Alzire that her marriage is void. Had she not sworn to an alien god? But his pleas are in vain. "I have promised; that's enough," says Alzire; "it matters not to what god." " 'Twas a guilty vow," Zamore expostulates,

> And binds thee not; perdition on thy oaths
> And thy false gods whom I abhor!

He hurries off with a show of great indignation, while poor, perplexed Alzire seeks the help of God:

O God of Christians, thou all-conquering power,
Whom yet I know not! O, remove the cloud
From my dark mind! If by my fatal passion
I have offended thee, pour all thy vengeance
On me! But spare Zamore! O conduct
His wandering footsteps through the dreary desert!
Is Europe alone worthy of thy care?
Art thou the partial parent of one world,
And tyrant o'er another? All deserve
Thy equal love—the victor and the vanquished
Are all the work of thy creating hand.

Alzire's lofty meditation is cut short, however, by the
police who arrest her as an accomplice of Zamore, who, it
seems, has forced his way into the presence of Gusman and
stabbed him. The Peruvian council assembles hastily and
condemns Zamore and Alzire to death. On one condition,
however, their lives may be spared: Zamore must become
a Christian. But the proud assassin prefers "death rather
than dishonor"; while Alzire makes the same choice for
herself. The elderly Don Alvarez, in complete despair,
tries to dissuade them, when Gusman, mortally wounded,
is carried into the room. His imminent death has wrought
a remarkable change in the governer; he is no longer harsh
and vengeful, but humble and polite; and in this new
spirit—and in a speech of twenty-nine lines—he pardons
everyone, while he proceeds to die.

It is hard to believe that such a weird and transparent
hodge-podge as *Alzire* should ever have been acclaimed as
great drama. Yet, thus accaimed it was not only by the
ordinary theatre-goer, who drooled all over its sentiment,
but by the critics as well, who saw in *Alzire* a piece of pro-

found philosophy. Long after the first outburst of enthusiasm had passed, Condorcet spoke of *Alzire* in hushed
tones as "an immortal monument"; while in Germany the
renowned Friedrich Schlegel put Voltaire on the same
pedestal as Racine. "The glory is indisputably Voltaire's,"
Schlegel announced, "of having succeeded in romantic
tragedy beyond any other of his countrymen." That Voltaire himself cherished a similar illusion may perhaps be
pardoned.

While *Alzire* was enchanting the Parisian multitude,
Voltaire was already at work on a new play. He called it
"The Prodigal Son," and it was to be a comedy. Yet, since
the heir to the crown of Racine deemed comedy a frivolous
pastime, quite unworthy of the glory of the French classic
tradition, he was very careful to keep his new activity a
secret. What he dreaded above all was the possibility that
some of his enemies might get wind of what he was doing,
and ruin the play's chances even before it was produced.
The story of the play had been suggested to the dramatist
by one of his lady friends, Mademoiselle Quinault, an
actress at the Théatre-Français. There were, she told Voltaire, two brothers—one a gay blade, full of deviltry, but
noble in impulse; the other, steady and plodding, but also
somewhat mean and self-interested. The two brothers fell
in love with the same girl, the noble one being prompted
by honest love, while the scheming one is attracted by the
girl's magnificent dowry. In the end, of course, the true
lover triumphs.

This threadbare plot Voltaire proceeded to weave into
five acts of rhymed, iambic couplets—for despite the fact
that he was composing a lowly comedy, he could not permit himself to become so undignified as to write a play in

prose. Though he worked only spasmodically on the piece, it made rapid progress. The realization that "The Prodigal Son" was something of a hoax, and that by it he might confound the critics as well as his enemies, fascinated Voltaire and spurred him on. Yet the fear that his enemies might prematurely discover his secret constantly overshadowed him. "If by chance," he wrote to one of his friends, "the secret of 'The Prodigal Son' escapes, swear always that I am not the author." When Thieriot accidentally found out about the comedy, Voltaire promptly pledged him to the strictest secrecy. If anyone should ever suggest that Voltaire was the author of such a piece, then Thieriot was to deny it. "Lying," Voltaire told his friend, "is a vice only when it does harm; it is a great virtue when it does good. Be, then, more virtuous than ever. It is necessary to lie like the devil; not timidly, not for a time, but boldly and always."

In February Voltaire's work was interrupted. He was ill; so ill, in fact, that he had to stay in bed. The divine Emilie, more a goddess than ever, hovered solicitously at his bedside, applying cold compresses, and soothing his fever by reciting long passages from Cicero and Pope. Unfortunately, Voltaire's progress was slow; indeed, after more than a month of Emilie's tender care, he was obliged to admit that his health "was still deplorable."

The cure which Emilie could not bring about was wrought, inadvertently, by someone else. In April a pathetic letter came from Jore. The hapless printer was still in the Bastille; but he would be released, he wrote, if Voltaire would make a written declaration admitting that he was the author of the "English Letters." The Marquise, sensing some hidden danger, strongly advised her lover against making such an admission; but the poet, who had never forgotten his own days in the Bastille, paid no attention to Emilie's advice, and sent Jore the desired statement. Its effect was remarkable. The printer was released and his license restored; and in a very short time Voltaire received a bill from Jore, demanding 1400 francs to defray the cost printing the confiscated edition of the "English Letters." Voltaire was furious. Forgetting that he was "a very ailing man," he hurried to Paris to confront "this scoundrel Jore" whose "iniquity is too crying to go unpunished."

But the printer revealed an iron determination; he wanted his money. Voltaire pleaded and cajoled; he threatened to bring suit, all in vain. Finally, in utter desperation, he offered the hard-bargaining Jore a compromise: he would pay half the amount demanded and let the whole matter drop. This offer was refused; and when Voltaire indicated that he would not pay an additional copper, Jore brought suit.

Meanwhile, Voltaire's enemies, delighted to have a chance to do him some damage, rushed to the support of the printer. Desfontaines, a cleric, and the editor of a literary paper, published a highly prejudiced account of Voltaire's business dealings with Jore, proving that Voltaire was a grasping and avaricious villain, and poor Jore his innocent victim. The libelous attack had a wide circulation; and though the poet thundered against it with all his might, and even implored the authorities to suppress it, the harm to his reputation was considerable.

When the controversy finally came before Police Lieutenant Hérault, he tried his best to make an equitable decision. The printer's claim he disallowed; but to recompense Jore for the expense he had incurred in printing the "English Letters," Voltaire was to pay him five hundred francs.

At this point Voltaire balked. He wrote long and violent letters, fulminating against Jore with venomous fury. The printer, he declared, was a liar, a cheat, and a criminal; he was the vile accomplice of Voltaire's enemies, and an extortioner. When Voltaire's friends intervened and tried to make him realize that the quarrel was too petty for the fuss he was making, he continued nonetheless in his blustering obstinacy. To give Jore five hundred francs, he protested indignantly, would be "to sign my shame—I would rather go on with the suit." Yet in the end he paid; and in July, after three months of incessant, sordid bickering the poet returned to Cirey.

His defeat—for so he construed it—rankled in his breast. Not only had his standing in the public esteem been tarnished, but he had been compelled to give away five hundred francs; and for a man who treasured money almost as much as the verses he wrote, that assuredly was very painful. For a while Voltaire was disconsolate. Neither the tranquil solace of Cirey, nor the soothing embraces of Emilie, were able to dispel the gloom and resentment which enveloped him.

But a fortnight later all traces of bitterness had vanished. A letter from Frederick, Prince Royal of Prussia, had wrought the miracle. The prince was a young man of twenty-four; aside from the fact that some day he might be king of Prussia, Frederick was unknown. Still, a prince was a prince; and Voltaire was certainly not the man to overlook an opportunity. From Frederick's letter, moreover, it was quite plain to Voltaire that the heir apparent to the throne of Prussia had some excellent qualities. He was interested, he said, in modern thought and in poetry —particularly in the superb verses of the author of *Alzire* and the *Henriade*. "The great men of modern times," Frederick wrote, "will be obliged to you if the dispute concerning the relative greatness of the Ancients and the Moderns should arise again; because you will tip the scale to their side." Voltaire, the prince added, was as great as Corneille—nay, Voltaire was even greater; for if the "great Corneille should come to life again in our days, he would see with astonishment and perhaps with envy that the Goddess of Tragedy lavishes prodigally upon you those favors of which she was so sparing to him." "Your poems," the Crown Prince continued, "possess qualities which render them respectable and worthy of the admiration and study of good men. They are a course of morality whereby we learn to think and act. Virtue is painted there in its fairest colors. The idea of true glory is there defined; and you insinuate the taste for knowledge in a manner so fine and so delicate that he who has read your works breathes the ambition of following in your footsteps." The prince continued in this glowing vein for several pages, finishing at last with the hope that "I may one day see you, whom I have admired so long and from so far."

Voltaire replied with all the grace at his command. The love of the human race, he said, had always existed in his heart; but his pleasure had been a thousand times purer when he "saw that the world holds a prince who will make men happy." Then, as if to show the prince what a great respect he had for the royal intellect, Voltaire plunged into a discussion of science, theology and the metaphysical doctrines of "the Sieur Wolff" whom Frederick had extolled as "the most celebrated philosopher of our day." Voltaire concluded with the reminder that he would "consider it a most valuable privilege to wait on your Royal Highness," adding that in whatever corner of the world he might end his life, he would constantly wish Monseigneur well, "and in so doing wish the happiness of a nation."

This initial exchange of letters soon grew into a vigorous correspondence. The epistles that traveled between Cirey and Berlin were at times astonishingly long—particularly those of Voltaire, who apparently thought it nothing at all to compose a letter of several thousand words. What the prince and the poet wrote to one another was seldom very personal; yet it was always very flattering. Thus Frederick told Voltaire that it was to him that "we owe all the virtues which create the security and charm of life." "Do not think," Frederick wrote, "that I push my skepticism to the limit. . . . I believe, for example, there is only one God, and one Voltaire; I also believe that in this century God had need of a Voltaire to render it agreeable." Voltaire for his part was just as affable, and never tired of comparing the Prince to Apollo, Alcibiades, Lycurgus and Marcus Aurelius. "Socrates means nothing to me," he exclaimed; "it is Frederick I love." "You think like Trajan," he told Frederick on another occasion; "you write like Pliny; and you use French like our best writers. . . . Under your auspices Berlin will be the Athens of Germany and perhaps of Europe." Voltaire sent Frederick his latest verses; he even went so far as to write some special ones in the prince's honor. In return, Frederick presented the poet with an expensive cane, having the head of Socrates in solid gold for a handle. Yet no matter how much poetry Voltaire sent to Berlin, the young prince always clamored for more. What he wanted particularly was the *Pucelle*. "Send me all

your works and *La Pucelle,*" he implored. The *Pucelle,*
Voltaire replied, was too dangerous to let out of his hands
—it would "lead directly to the hemlock." But Frederick
would not be side-tracked. *"La Pucelle! La Pucelle! La
Pucelle!* and again *La Pucelle!"* he chanted; "for the love
of God, or rather for the love of yourself, send it to me!"
Yet despite the prince's expostulations, the *Pucelle* continued to remain at Cirey; its custodian, the watchful
Emilie, refused to release it, even for a prince of the blood
like Frederick.

In August Voltaire wrote *Le Mondain* ("The Worldling") , and soon afterwards he sent it to Frederick. It was
a poem, light and sparkling, designed to extol life's pleasures, and to mock at those, who, like the sedate Pascal,
would eliminate them.

> *Religionists may rail in vain,*
> *I own I like this age profane.*
> *I love the pleasures of a court,*
> *I love the arts of every sort.*

Not only is luxury desirable for the pleasure it brings—
it is also economically desirable. "The superfluous," argues
the "Worldling," "is something very necessary. It has
joined the hemispheres."

> *Whilst France that pierced the Turkish lines*   ..
> *See how that fleet with canvas wings*
> *From Texel, Bordeaux, London brings*
> *All Indies' and all Ganges' stores;*
> *Sultans makes drunk with rich French wines.*

Was it a virtue, Voltaire, asks, that our ancestors ate herbs;
that they had no decent clothes; that "ease was, like

wealth, to them unknown"? Paris, he concludes, is better than Eden; for here one has "the arts that charm the human mind"—fine paintings by Poussin and Corregio; lovely statuary by Bouchardin; silver plate by St. Germain; and stately gardens of Cyprian myrtle, where "sporting waters rise from splashing fountains almost to the skies."

Frederick of Prussia found "The Mondain" to his taste. "It is," he said, "an amiable piece breathing nothing but pure joy"; and he added that he found it "a true course in morality." Unfortunately for Voltaire, Frederick's views were not those of the French authorities. Voltaire's enemies, quick to see their opportunity, promptly denounced the poem as a piece of pagan profanity for which the author should be punished. But the remoteness of Cirey made such steps somewhat difficult; and thus, for the time being, Voltaire appeared fairly safe.

As the months at Cirey went by Voltaire's activity increased tremendously in another sphere. The impression made upon him in England by "the great Sieur Newton" had been deep; and under the persuasive prompting of the Marquise it became even deeper. She herself was making an exhaustive study of the English scientist, and under her influence Voltaire devoted himself more and more to an examination of the Newtonian doctrines. His enthusiasm for the Englishman increased rapidly; and before long it seemed to dominate everything else. Voltaire lived, as he said, "between Newton and Emilie," reading and rereading the works of Sir Isaac; making his usual careful and copious notes; and eagerly discussing them with the delighted Emilie, whose enthusiasm dwarfed even his own. "There is in this world," he said, "a devil of a Newton

who has found out how much the sun weighs, and of what
color the rays are that compose light. This strange man
has turned my head."

For the time being Voltaire put aside his literary labors, and confined himself almost entirely to his laboratory. Here he worked with his customary assiduity amidst
air pumps and furnaces; peering into microscopes; examining crucibles and retorts; measuring and weighing all
kinds of substances, from minute grains of sand to a ton
of red hot iron. Nothing that money could buy was lacking
in Voltaire's laboratory—but his proudest possession by
far was his spectroscope, that mysterious, prismatic glass
by which the ingenious Newton had broken a ray of ordinary light into the brilliant colors of the rainbow. The
wonders performed by this incredible glass entranced Voltaire almost as much as his magic lantern. Whenever visitors came to Cirey he would always take them to his laboratory, where, like a child beaming over some treasured toy,
he would amaze his guests with his miracle-working prism.

Voltaire's admiration for Newton was reflected in his
letters to Frederick. It must have been contagious; for
soon the mail from Berlin began to pour its blandishments
not only on Voltaire but also on Newton. In time Frederick even caught the fever for experimentation: he sowed
radish seed in an exhausted receiver to see if it "would
germinate without air."

Not all Voltaire's friends shared his enthusiasm for science. Indeed, as the poet went deeper into his new activity,
some of them began to show alarm. Science, they feared,
might lure him from the muse, and in the end his genius
for poetry would be destroyed. "What shall you gain,"
asked Cideville, "by knowing the pathway of light and the

gravitation of Saturn?" "We must," was Voltaire's prompt reply, "have all imaginable modes of life, open all the doors of our souls to the sciences and all the sentiments; and provided they do not enter pell-mell, there is room in us for every one of them."

In October the tide of Voltaire's scientific interest receded. An incident in Paris now received his prime attention. At the Théatre-Français an audience was told that the play which it had come to see could not be produced; instead the management would offer "The Prodigal Son," a new comedy by an anonymous author. The piece was an instantaneous hit, both spectators and critics giving it vigorous applause. At once all Paris began to wonder who the author might be. Some guessed it was Piron, a leading writer of comedy and a frequent lampooner of Voltaire; others were equally certain the author was Destouches. A few spectators, perhaps more discerning than the rest, thought they perceived in the new piece the hand of Voltaire; but the poet's foes quickly demolished this hypothesis. The author of this unusual comedy, they contended, could not possilby have been Voltaire. He would never have dared to write a comedy; for this he obviously lacked the talent; and, furthermore, had not Voltaire himself announced that the author of this work was probably Gresset? No, Voltaire's foes insisted, this play was positively not by Voltaire; and the more they insisted, the more, of course, the public interest grew. Night after night, "The Prodigal Son" played to crowded houses, while at Cirey Voltaire gloated over the unwitting contribution being made by his enemies toward his success.

With "The Prodigal Son" an unqualified success, Voltaire resumed his Newtonian studies. He had conceived the idea of writing a popular version of Newton. "My dear Master Newton," he announced, "is the greatest man that ever lived," and every Frenchman, he felt, should be familiar with his wonders. "I figure, I add," he wrote to his friend, the actress Quinault; "I seek to understand what others have discovered; it is very far from a comedy or a tragedy."

Voltaire's researches were destined to be disturbed; for in the distance there was ominous rumbling. The displeasure provoked by "The Mondain" had never subsided; on the contrary, it had slowly gathered force. The poet's enemies, particularly Rousseau and Desfontaines, had sought to enhance its magnitude, and by the publication of villifying articles and the propagation of slanderous gossip they had succeeded. For a time Voltaire tried to pretend that such matters were of little concern to him. "The vapors," he wrote, "which Rousseau and Desfontaines try to raise from the filth in which they raised their heads do not reach me." Sometimes, he added, "I spit upon them— though without thinking of it."

But Voltaire's hollow rationalization deceived no one, least of all the Marquise du Chatelet. Her life with this man had been a strange mixture of storm and peace. It had started ecstatically in the setting of a country honeymoon; only to shift with incredible swiftness to weeks of horrible anguish while her lover hid from his pursuers. The tranquility which she had sought at Cirey, for him as well as for herself, had never been without a cloud. She had lived in the ever-present horror that her lover might be torn from her side, perhaps be lost to her forever. She was certain that the dreaded moment had come when trouble brewed in Paris over the *Pucelle;* and when it passed harmlessly by, her relief was immeasurable. Soon her fears returned. She tried to put them out of her mind, but she could not. It was almost as if by some unconscious, irrational precognition she realized that sooner or later Fate would strike a hard blow.

Late in December the blow fell. The aged Cardinal de Fleury had decided that "The Mondain" was contemptuous of constituted authority, and had given his consent for Voltaire's arrest. A letter from d'Argental, Voltaire's "guardian angel," warned the Marquise of her lover's imminent danger. "But for the respect felt for your house," wrote d'Argental, "M. de Voltaire would have been arrested long ago, and it is now contemplated to write to M. du Chatelet, requesting him no longer to give him asylum."

D'Argental's warning was heeded. Less than a day after its receipt Voltaire left Cirey. The Marquise accompanied him, but only as far as the neighboring village of Vassy. There Voltaire was to enter a stage-coach and be whisked away to the frontier; then the dreaded separation would no longer be a mere hallucination. As for Voltaire, bitterness overcame him. Now that the moment had come when he must part from one who had done so much for him—one whom, he said, he adored and ought to adore—the situation was horrible. "My heart is pierced," he wrote to d'Argental. "Must I let her return alone to a chateau which she has rebuilt only for me, and deprive myself of the charm of my life because I have enemies in Paris? . . . what a dreadful life! I would rather die than be eternally tormented by the dread of losing my liberty upon the most trifling complaint without form of law."

The sadness which descended upon Cirey was mitigated somewhat a few days later. A letter from Voltaire informed the Marquise that he had reached Brussels; that he was posing as a merchant by the name of Monsieur Renol; and, best of all, that his health had not suffered. Yet the Marquise was far from reassured. "When I look upon the earth covered with snow," she said, "and the weather so dismal and thick; when I think of the climate to which he is going, and his extreme sensitiveness to cold, I am ready to die of grief. I would endure his absence if I could be assured of his health."

Though the tumult of her distress gradually subsided, her cheerfulness did not return. Her old fear, now realized, alas, in gloomy separation, soon gave rise to new forebodings. She worried about her lover's health; she feared he might commit new indiscretions; that in Brussels he might have a fatal clash with Rousseau; or that he might be betrayed by his enemies and arrested. But of all her imagined dangers, worst of all was the irrepressible dread that Voltaire might never return; that he might go to England, or even to Prussia. When the Marquise du Chatelet thought of Prussia and the Prince Royal she was seized with violent apprehension. She realized at last that Frederick was a dangerous rival. All his extravagant flattery, his costly gifts, his pointed allusions to "liberty" and "tolerance"—all these now seemed just so much honey with which the prince hoped to catch the unsuspecting Voltaire.

The Marquise's agitation increased when Dutch newspapers began to suggest that "the Prince Royal of Prussia would be glad to receive Voltaire." When the Utrecht *Gazette* announced that "Monsieur de Voltaire . . . has gone forthwith to Champagne on the way to Berlin" and that "he expects to stay there some time," the Marquise's nerves were utterly shattered. Decidedly Voltaire should not go to Prussia! "I beg you on my knees to prevent it," she implored d'Argental. "He would be ruined in that country. Whole months would pass before I could get news of him. I should die of anxiety before he returned."

For the time being Voltaire did not go to Prussia. Instead, he went through Belgium to Holland. His disguise as Monsieur Renol was easily penetrated, and wherever he went he was welcomed with open arms. At Brussels *Alzire* was performed in his honor—to the obvious dissatisfaction of Rousseau; at Leyden he was introduced to Dr. Boerhaave, a noted Dutch physician; at the Hague he made arrangements for a new edition of his collected works. He finally settled in Amsterdam, where he hoped to complete the "Elements of Newton" and arrange for its publication. "I live quite like a philosopher," he wrote to d'Argental. "I study much. I see little company. I try to understand Newton; I try to make him understood."

Meanwhile the agonized Marquise deluged him with letters begging him to return. But there were letters from Frederick, too—four came at one time, with a copy of Wolff's "Metaphysics" and a batch of French verses composed by the prince himself. "Continue," Frederick exhorted the poet, "to enlighten the world, Sir. The torch of truth could not be confided to better hands. I shall admire you from afar, but yet not renounce the satisfaction of seeing you one day. This you promised, and I am determined to remind you of it some time."

Voltaire was, as he said, "dazzled by so many favors." Yet, while he allowed the Prince Royal to cherish the hope of an early meeting, Voltaire was scheming to get back to Cirey. To deceive his enemies he carefully planted rumors that he was departing for England. "I am leaving for Cambridge," he wrote Thieriot, "to complete my little study of Newtonism." "Do not forget," he told a Parisian abbé, "to tell everybody that I am in England." When, at length, he felt that the fiction was firmly established, he quietly crossed the frontier, and in March he appeared at Cirey.

Voltaire's return represented a personal triumph for the Marquise. But for her, the poet would certainly have settled in another land. "A man of letters," he asseverated, "ought to live in a free country, or make up his mind to live like a timorous slave whom other slaves, jealous of him, continually accuse to the master. In France I have nothing to expect but such persecutions; they will be my only recompense. . . . I live in continual alarm without knowing how to parry the blows dealt me every day. There is no likelihood of my ever returning to Paris, to expose myself to the furies of superstition and envy. I shall live at Cirey or in a free land." He added that he had always said that "if my father, my brother, or my son were prime minister of a despotic land, I would leave it tomorrow! Judge then what my repugnance must be on finding myself in such a state today!" But the consoling presence of the Marquise was somewhat of a compensation. "After all," he reflected to d'Argental, "she is more to me than a father, a brother, a son."

The Marquise's joy at having the poet back at Cirey stimulated her possessiveness. Henceforth, she warned him, he must be prudent; he must write no more flippant poems; he must delete all dangerous passages from his projected new edition; he must write a soothing letter to Minister de Maurepas—he must, in short, let Emilie "save him from himself."

Voltaire promised—he even wrote the desired letter to the minister; but as for the writing of flippant verses, that was something from which no one—not even the persuasive Emilie—could stop him. Shortly after his return he composed a sequel to "The Mondain" in which he tried, as he said, "to prove that luxury, magnificence, the arts, all that makes for the splendor of a state also makes for its wealth; and that those who cry out against what is called luxury are merely ill-tempered paupers." In style "The Defense of the Mondain" resembled its predecessor; but on this occasion the poet put his narrative in the form of a conversation between himself and a bigot, a "master hypocrite," and probably a Jansenist, whom he met one day while he was dining. He is predestined for a celestial life of bliss, and laughs at the poet because he knows him to be doomed to roast in hell for having suggested that Adam got wet when it rained. " 'For all these things, my son,' he remarked, 'your profane Muse will be burned hereafter, and that's the end of it.' Saying these words he poured down his thirsty gullet a delicious draught of amber-colored wine, that still had the fragrance of the grapes from which it had been pressed. A rosy color came into his face; and I said to him, 'For the love of God, Monsieur Saint, what is this wine? Where does it come from? Where did you get it?' 'It comes from Canary: it is nectar, a vintage for the elect. God gives it to us and God wishes it to be drunk.' 'And this delicious coffee, which, after five courses, your stomach is now savoring?' 'It was destined for me by the Lord.' 'Good. But before God gave it to you, wasn't it necessary that human industry should secure it from the fields of Araby?' "

From this tête-à-tête the poet drifts to a description of

the luxury of King Solomon. The ancient monarch, he tells the bigot, knew how to enjoy life. He had gold and silver, peacocks, apes and ivory. Best of all, he had a thousand wives. "What!" exclaims Monsieur Saint; "a thousand?" "So 'tis said," the poet replies. "It's a good many for a wise man. Give me only one. It is quite enough for me, who am neither a wise man—nor a king."

The "Defense of the Mondain" had no serious repercussions. To be sure, the authorities denounced it; but aside from that they did nothing, and gradually the controversy was forgotten.

Voltaire's absence from Cirey had not dimmed his ardor for science. The work on Newton was almost finished; and with the help of Emilie, the author patiently made last-minute revisions and corrections in the manuscript. Unfortunately for Voltaire his knowledge of mathematics was slight—too slight, in fact, for him to gain a full understanding of Newton. He was aware of this deficiency, however; and he strove to counteract it by tutoring himself, and by referring the problems he could not understand to authoritative mathematicians, such as Emilie, her teacher Maupertuis, and Pitot, of the Academy of Science. There must have been many of such problems; for his letters alluded increasingly to the intricacies of arcs and tangents, angles of incidence, concave mirrors, and rays of refraction. Such were the preoccupations of Voltaire's mind as his study of Newton approached completion.

For that work the author had great hopes; for in France the name of Isaac Newton was barely known. Scholars of course had heard of his discovery of gravitation and the composition of light. Yet, since Mother Church was then paying homage at the shrine of Descartes, the Newtonian doctrines were generally regarded with grave suspicion. As for the French layman, a first-hand study of Sir Isaac was clearly out of the question; for Newton had saturated his treatises with algebraic formulae and Latin profundities, making them utterly incomprehensible to the common man. Voltaire swept away the Latin and the algebra, and in clear, crisp French he tried to make understandable Newton's complicated abstractions, from his metaphysics to his researches in optics and gravitation. Voltaire had been careful, too, to anticipate the possible objections of the pious. He made it very plain to everyone that the great Sieur Newton, besides believing in gravity, also believed in God. He was, Voltaire explained, "infinitely persuaded of the existence of God"; better yet, Sir Isaac believed "in an infinite being, all-powerful, eternal, and the Creator."

With such comforting assurances to allay the fears of the devout, Voltaire felt certain that his projected book would have clear sailing. "The most imbecilic fanatic," he declared, "the most envenomed critic can find nothing objectionable in it." He was wrong. The government found it objectionable and refused to sanction its printing. "Apparently," Voltaire exclaimed, "a poor Frenchman is not allowed to say that attraction is possible and proven, that the earth is flattened at the poles, that a vacuum is demonstrated."

No, a Frenchman was not allowed to say such things. Yet Voltaire's Dutch printers were quite unconcerned over what a Frenchman could or could not say. A work by Monsieur de Voltaire, they knew, was a potential gold mine; and if that work happened to be prohibited, so much the better. Dispensing with the formality of consulting the author, the crafty Dutchman hired a hack writer

to complete the book's remaining unfinished chapters, and
early in 1738 they published it under the title of "The
Elements of Newton's Philosophy Adapted to Every Capacity."

The publication of the pirated volume burst like a
bomb on the author who realized, with shame and indignation, that he had been outmaneuvered. What incensed
him perhaps even more was the fact that the book was
replete with stupid errors. The publishers, the agitated
writer exclaimed, were "imbeciles" who had given his book
"a charlatan title." Voltaire perceived "a thousand contra-
dictions"; the book was "an anthill of mistakes"; it was
"botched and bungled." How sad it was, he lamented, to
see one's child so maltreated! The disillusioned father
made haste to disavow that child; he hoped, he said, that
he would not be blamed for the faults of the child, which
had been spoiled by its faithless and irresponsible nurse.
Voltaire's prompt disavowal, besides the fact that the work
was of a serious nature without its customary jibes at
Church and State, no doubt helped to save him from the
police. But he fared less happily with the critics; and
despite the fact that he had been polite to Descartes, and
even honestly respectful, Voltaire was assailed on all sides
as Descartes' defamer, and an enemy of God and man.

The tide of Voltaire's interest continued to flow in the
direction of science; it had swept him into fresh investiga-
tions even before the completion of his Newtonian researches. The Academy of Scence had announced a prize
for the best essay on "The Nature of Fire and Its Propagation." Although the poet knew virtually nothing about
the subject, he was hardly the man to be deterred by such
a handicap. Not only did he undertake to write a learned

discourse on fire, but he resolved to approach his theme in the true, scientific spirit of Sir Isaac. He would experiment; he would observe phenomena and record data; he would concoct hypotheses, test and verify them, and derive his conclusions.

He began his researches by purchasing elaborate and expensive equipment, which ranged from an assortment of cast-iron pots to specially made scales of gigantic size and thousands of pounds of iron. For the more arduous phases of his work, he employed a corps of rugged assistants whom he directed with his usual exuberance. Was there ever a more incongruous figure than this frail, little, vociferous man, gesticulating wildly to his sturdy, placid workmen, as he urged them on and rushed about like a madman amidst his colossal utensils? Every day he made his men weigh quantities of iron, heave it into huge furnaces, where it was heated until it became a mass of molten, bubbling liquid. Then it would have to be weighed and set aside to cool; whereupon it would be weighed all over again. Of all these processes Voltaire made meticulous notes, recording every detail of what he had observed. As was his wont, he discussed his work with the Marquise, who, as usual, rewarded him with a radiant enthusiasm. She made suggestions too; but when she read his conclusions, she found herself somewhat in disagreement. Indeed, she found her own views so divergent from his that she resolved to express them in an essay of her own.

The Marquise du Chatelet worked on her paper with the utmost secrecy. She did not want, as she said, to blush before Voltaire "for an undertaking which might displease him"; and besides she had discovered that she "combatted almost all his ideas." She was opposed to his methods, too;

the greater part of them she deemed unnecessary and somewhat foolish. In fact, she found it possible to write her own treatise without any research at all, though she did make clandestine raids on some of Voltaire's hard-earned data. To keep her activity hidden from the prying eyes of that omnipresent man was not easy; yet the intrepid Emilie solved the problem readily enough by working at night while Voltaire, worn out by the day's labors, was sleeping soundly in his room. Slumber at such times was unknown to Emilie; actually she is reported to have slept only an hour a day. She was driven by a tremendous force, which was fed constantly by the potent fuel of her enthusiasm and determination. At times her vast nervous energy almost threatened to consume her; she felt herself on the verge of an explosion; she would pace up and down her room in great agitation, waving her arms and muttering to herself; or she would rush out to plunge her arms for several minutes in ice-cold water. Yet, despite her perturbations, the Marquise was able to complete her essay in slightly more than a week, and in the early spring of 1738 she submitted it anonymously to the Academy.

Neither Voltaire nor the Marquise won a prize. What disqualified their papers was not their lack of scientific merit, for in this respect neither their essays nor any of the others radiated much lustre. The downfall of the Cirey contestants was brought about primarily because of their unorthodox philosophy. They had not accepted Descartes; and in the eyes of the judges this was manifestly not "good breeding." However, both contestants were given honorable mention, the anonymous contribution of the Marquise being ranked a place higher than that of Voltaire. When the announcement of the awards reached Cirey,

Emilie divulged her secret. "I felt," she explained, "that a rejection shared by him was an honor to me." Voltaire's own feelings were those of mingled surprise and admiration. He read her manuscript and gave it his blessing. "Its beauties," he announced, "appear great"; while to Maupertuis he wrote that "its mistakes are few in number." He was apparently more convinced than ever that his mistress possessed "a vast and powerful genius" and that she was "the Minerva of France, immortal Emilie."

Although Voltaire accepted Emilie's scientific rivalry with excellent grace, he was far from affable toward his other critics. Upon these he fell with all his vigor; and before long he found himself embroiled in a violent war of words. The first shots in the conflict were fired by his ancient foes, the Messieurs Rousseau and Desfontaines. When the pirated "Elements of Newton" appeared, Voltaire's critics swooped upon it like a flock of famished hawks. "Monsieur de Voltaire," the Abbé Desfontaines wrote in a suave and sophisticated review, "has unquestionably received from nature the talent for poetry; but is nature so prodigal of her gifts, and is there not something incompatible between the genius of philosophy and the genius for rhymes?" Then, as if bent on igniting the inflammable Voltaire, the Abbé congratulated him on abandoning poetry for philosophy at "his already advanced age."

Desfontaines' gibes quickly enkindled Voltaire, who threw off one explosive denunciation after another. Delighted by the conflagration he had started, and eager to keep it going, Desfontaines stoked it relentlessly with fresh satire and slander. Late in 1738 he outdid his own previous best effort to taunt Voltaire by printing some of the poet's love lyrics, which had been intended solely for the eyes of Emilie, but which somehow had fallen into the enemy's hands. It was of course a villainous act; but Voltaire's response was no less villainous. Under the name of the Chevalier de Mouhy, a young man then living in Paris, the poet published a vituperative pamphlet, *Le Préservatif,* in which he tore the abbé into a thousand shreds. He attacked him first as a critic; and by resorting to the dubious device of compiling within a few short pages a long list of slips and errors made by Desfontaines over a long period of time in more than a thousand pages, Voltaire created the illusion that his foe was an ignoramus who made nothing but bad mistakes. Then, as if determined to destroy the last vestige of Desfontaines' tattered reputation, Voltaire assailed his character. With remorseless malice, he dug into Desfontaines' past, accusing him of homosexual practices, of which the Abbé had unquestionably been guilty, but which had long since been mercifully forgotten.

Clearly Voltaire's action was mean and vicious. Even on the ground of extenuating circumstances it cannot be pardoned, for it was not a sudden impulse that sprang from bitter wrath, but a carefully premeditated act. Worse yet for the reputation of Voltaire, his foul blow was characteristic of him. "When I fight, I fight like the devil," he once boasted; and in his quarrels he was, indeed, a devil— a frenzied, ugly devil, cruel and blasphemous, to whom the lowest trickery was justifiable. In such moments the philosophic detachment he preached so eloquently and so gloriously deserted him completely; and by some strange and indefinable process the apostle of reason would evolve into a frantic, raving madman.

Voltaire's *Préservatif* was not the final shot in the war with Desfontaines. In a short time the abbé returned the fire with a venomous pamphlet of his own, *La Voltairo-manie*, or "The Voltaire Mania." It excoriated the poet as "the persecutor of the human race, the enemy of the living and the dead." Voltaire was a "rogue," an "impostor," who seduced the wives of his friends; he was an "ignorant fool," "a scoundrel" who "dares to carry his extravagances even to the altar." The Abbé, like his opponent, was not averse to plowing up the forgotten past; and it was for him a great delight to make pungent references to the beatings Voltaire had once received at the hands of Captain Beauregard and the Chevalier de Rohan.

The *Voltairomanie* appeared in December of 1738; and on Christmas Day a copy of it was delivered to the Marquise du Chatelet. When she read its frightening contents she was filled with a terrible apprehension. That "infamous and libelous work," she felt, must be kept concealed from Voltaire at all costs. "I should fear the worst," she confided to d'Argental, "if in his present condition, his feelings should experience a violent shock." Her fears, however, were quite unnecessary; for Voltaire, too, had received a copy of the pamphlet and was trying his best to keep it concealed from the Marquise.

Desfontaines' tract was too violent to be convincing. It was, in fact, a gross libel; and this the shrewd Voltaire was quick to perceive. He realized that Desfontaines had made himself extremely vulnerable; and that a suit in the courts would in all likelihood finish off the libelous Abbé. Accordingly, Voltaire put aside his pen and engaged lawyers to sue Desfontaines for criminal libel. The Abbé, hopelessly ensnared by his own incautious utterances, could do nothing better than to surrender; and in April, by order of the magistrate, Voltaire's foe, cornered and beaten, made a written disavowal of the *Voltairomanie,* asserting it to be "calumnious in all the charges it brought against Monsieur de Voltaire."

Voltaire's triumph was complete. Yet the aggravations which had preceded it exacted their toll. The poet, beset by fainting spells and fevers, found himself "extremely debilitated," and betook himself to bed. The Marquise compensated him with her usual tender and sympathetic care; while Prince Frederick, not to be outdone, overwhelmed the ailing man with the sweetmeats of praise and flattery. "Ah! My dear Voltaire," he wrote, "why can I not offer you a shelter where you would not have to suffer such troubles as those brought upon you by your ungrateful country?"

Why not, indeed? Long ago Frederick had made up his mind, as he said, to "possess" the "Apollo from Cirey." He wanted him for his entourage, where he could glitter like a diamond in the princely crown, and where the great man would be handy at all times to put the final touches on the prince's verses. From the outset Frederick had expressed the hope of meeting Voltaire; and to realize that hope the prince had contrived a method, which in time, he felt, would surely bring the poet to Potsdam. What, indeed, could have made the author of the *Henriade* more eager to meet the prince than a masterful appeal to the poet's vanity? From the beginning, the Prince Royal poured sweet words into the ears of Voltaire, praising his works unstintingly, deluging him, as well as the Marquise, with expensive presents, sympathizing with him in all his woes, and never failing to offer him a tranquil and pleasant sanctuary. In time even a modest man might have succumbed to the prince's blandishments—and modesty assuredly was not a Voltairean trait.

Only his deep attachment to the Marquise kept Voltaire from visiting Frederick at the time of his difficulties over the *Mondain*. When the poet returned to Cirey, Frederick's campaign to "possess" him continued with increased vigor. The prince's epistolary tone was, if anything, more flattering. Where once he had begun his letters with a simple "Sir," Frederick now addressed the Cirey Apollo as "My dear friend"; where once he had felt that Voltaire excelled the great Corneille, the prince was now convinced that a Voltaire did not exist, that actually "somewhere in France there is a select society of superior and equal geniuses who all work together under the name of Voltaire." "Your nation is ungrateful," whispered the siren voice from Potsdam. "Your country is trying to wither your laurels," it said. "Leave your ungrateful land," it entreated, "and come to a country where you will be adored." Frederick's adulation was incessant. It was the smooth lubricant of all his letters; and those letters worked like a magnet, subtle and imperceptible, pulling on the poet's inmost desires, and drawing him inexorably in the direction of Frederick.

During the next few months circumstances were to make that attraction even stronger. Early in the spring of 1738 the Marquis du Chatelet found himself obliged to make a trip to Brussels to press action in a family law suit. When legal necessity made it desirable for the Marquise to accompany her husband, Voltaire decided to go along too; his business experience—Emilie had convinced him—would be of inestimable value in helping the Marquis win his law suit. Voltaire went reluctantly to be with Emilie.

For the Marquise the journey became an exquisite delight. All through Flanders people flocked to catch a glimpse of Voltaire. When he reached Brussels, the ancient city had bedecked itself in its festive finery, and in one celebration after another it revealed its high esteem for the visiting author. In his honor there were balls and banquets, special performances at the theatre, garden parties, and even fireworks. These tributes Voltaire accepted with his customary effervescence; while the Marquise, happy in the knowledge that she was the sole possessor of this jewel called Voltaire, beamed ecstatically as she watched observers marvel at its lustre.

The Marquis' suit encountered the law's well known delay. As the hearings languished, weeks became months, and slowly summer turned to early fall. For Voltaire the trip's first enchantment had long since worn off; and although the Marquise continued to dance and frolic, the poet appeared more and more unhappy. He longed for the solitude of Cirey, where at least he could insulate himself against disconcerting attractions; where, if he chose, he could work with his full force, and without disturbing interruptions. At Brussels such work was impossible—and work to this energetic creature was almost as essential as the oxygen he breathed.

For a long time Voltaire's literary activity had been very slight. His interest in science had overshadowed everything else; and except for the *Mondain,* its sequel, the "Defense of the Mondain," and occasional additions to the *Pucelle,* Voltaire's poetic writings had been minor and casual. What was true of his verses was also true of the drama. He had worked spasmodically on a couple of tragedies, and one of them was almost completed; yet, since the production of *Alzire* several years ago, he had offered the public nothing new. However, even though Voltaire's literary productivity had reached a low point, his mind was teeming with ideas. He wanted to finish the "Age of Louis XIV"; he was anxious to issue an authorized and corrected edition of his work on Newton; and he hoped to complete his plays and get them produced.

None of these plans could be accomplished in the tumult of Brussels. Consequently, when, in September, Emilie wanted Voltaire to accompany her to Paris, he gladly acquiesced. Three years had elapsed since he had set foot in the capital; and to behold it once more with all its endearing associations filled him with pleasant warmth. The city was in a festive mood, in anticipation of the approaching marriage of Louis XV's eldest daughter to a prince of Spain. The Marquise promptly immersed herself in the swiftly moving social current. She danced and played cards; she shopped for new clothes and showy trinkets; she visited friends and renewed acquaintances; and everywhere she went she enjoyed herself immensely. Caught in this endless stream of social activity, Voltaire soon found himself overwhelmed. "I do not live," he expostulated. "I am carried, drawn from myself in whirlwinds." From the pleasant company of a few cronies he would be dragged off by the Marquise to the opera, to the theatre, and to interminable banquets and parties. He found himself taken "to see the sights, like a stranger"; he "embraced a hundred persons a day"; he "made a hundred protestations." "In Paris," he wrote Frederick, "they talk of nothing but celebrations and fireworks; they are spending a lot of money on powder and rockets." Paris had become an abyss where he lost his repose and serenity of mind. "I go, I come," he exclaimed; "I sup at the end of the city, to sup the next day at the other end."

The poet's restlessness gave way steadily to an ever-deepening gloom. An overmastering desire to fly from Paris possessed him; yet to go alone, without Emilie, seemed quite impossible. He felt fated to follow her, to be wherever she might be, and for the moment she was determined to be in the capital.

Suddenly, in October, deliverance seemed at hand. Voltaire was sick once more. The doctors, who knew little about the mysterious workings of the human temperament, bled and bathed the ailing man while they talked learnedly about his bladder and kidneys. The Marquise, for her part, suspended her pursuit of pleasure and, devoting herself almost entirely to the poet, agreed to leave Paris as soon as his health would permit. Her solicitude worked like a charm. In only a few days Voltaire was out of bed, prancing about with incredible energy while he busied himself gayly with making arrangements for a lavish supper party.

A few weeks later the couple was in its paradise of Cirey; and here at last Voltaire found happiness. After the harrowing pressure of the last few months the peacefulness of Cirey's solitude appeared almost unearthly. Each moment now seemed beautiful, a treasure to be enjoyed slowly and deliberately, like a choice delicacy. It was as if a magic wand, touching the poet's troubled spirit, had made it vanish into thin air, and had bestowed upon him the supreme and perfect contentment for which he had yearned so long.

The Marquise and Voltaire remained at Cirey for a fortnight. Then they moved to Brussels where the du Chatelet law suit had awakened at last from its slumber. The poet continued to be in high spirits, and as he settled into his new environment, he was buoyed up by a feeling of well-being, a feeling which was enhanced before long by a letter from Potsdam. Frederick, it revealed, still considered Voltaire the greatest poet of all time; and to demonstrate his conviction the prince was eager to publish the most beautiful edition of the *Henride* that one could possibly make. "Whatever the cost," Prince Frederick declared, "we shall produce a masterpiece worthy of the poem." Voltaire gladly gave the project his blessing; and when the prince royal announced that he himself would write a special introduction, Voltaire's ecstasy knew no bounds.

Frederick's publishing aspirations were matched by his literary ambitions: he yearned to be the author of a great work, one which would be no less than "a sequel of the *Henriade*." He insisted, however, that he was not motivated by self-interest—all that he wanted, it seems, was "to serve the public without expecting reward or praise." To accomplish this, the prince had planned a book to be called the *Anti-Machiavelli,* a modest little thing with which Frederick hoped "to forge the thunderbolts that will crush Caesar Borgia." Voltaire went out of his way to encourage the literary-minded prince. He felt certain, he assured him, that "if His Royal Highness deigned to write against Machiavelli, it will be Apollo crushing the serpent Python." Decidedly, the compliment was overdone; yet it pleased the prospective author and spurred him on; and by January of 1740 the opening chapters of the *Anti-Machiavelli* were delivered at Brussels. Voltaire corrected and criticized the manuscript, which in time grew into a lusty volume of twenty-six chapters. Its tone was one of high idealism, and if it could be taken at face value, it boded well for the peace and progress of Frederick's future subjects. "How monstrous, how absurd," the prince expostulated, "to render one's self illustrious through making others miserable! . . . Barbarous kings who prefer the fatal glory of conquerors to that won by kindness, clemency, and all the virtues! . . . The new conquests of a sovereign do not render the states more opulent which he already possesses; his subjects gain nothing; and he deludes himself if he imagines he will be more happy. It is not the magnitude of the country a prince governs which constitutes his glory."

It is said that when Voltaire read these lofty sentiments to the Marquise his eyes filled with tears. Frederick, he declared, was a true lover of peace and justice, a tolerant humanitarian, a friend of all the arts; he was "a philosopher prince who will make men happy." The *Anti-Machiavelli,* moreover, was a work which ought to be known to the entire world. Voltaire would, if Frederick desired, supervise its publication. The prince royal gladly gave his consent, though he felt certain Voltaire would agree with him that the name of the author had better not be revealed.

In June, 1740, Frederick became King of Prussia, and a few days after his accession he wrote to Voltaire. "My lot is changed," he said. "I have witnessed the last moments of a dying monarch, his agony, his death. On coming to the throne I had no need of that lesson to be disgusted with the vanity of human grandeur. We are not the masters of our fate, my dear Voltaire. We are borne by a whirlwind of events and we must allow ourselves to be carried with them. I beg you to see nothing in me but a zealous citizen, a somewhat skeptical philosopher, and a really faithful friend." "If I live," the king added ominously, "I shall see you, and see you this year."

Voltaire replied with all that graceful charm of which he was a master. He assured Frederick that if his lot had changed, his noble soul had not. He counseled His Majesty—or as he now called the king "His Humanity"—not to work too hard; to eat his meals regularly; and to avoid overstrain. He exhorted Frederick "in the name of the human race, to whom you have become necessary, take care of so precious a health."

In less than a fortnight Frederick answered. The "my dear friend," with which he had begun his last few letters had now been discarded for the more intimate "my dear Voltaire." There was a perceptible change, too, in his majesty's tone. He was no longer the sentimental dreamer sitting expectantly at the feet of the sage philosopher. The inexperienced youth, molded every day by hard and practical reality, was rapidly maturing. He had come to feel, since the loss of his father, that he owed himself wholly to the State. With this ever in mind he worked with infinite determination, rising at four in the morning and toiling until five in the evening. He wrote Voltaire that it was his wish to improve the State; that he had "established large granaries in all the provinces, so that each shall have enough grain on hand for at least a year and a half"; that he had founded a new college for commerce and manufacturers; and that he had laid the foundations for a new Prussian Academy. At the same time the author of the *Anti-Machiavelli* felt it necessary to strengthen the Prus-

sian Army. Could it have been an ironic accident that His
Humanity's first important offical act had called for an
increase in the forces of the state by sixteen battalions, five
squadrons of hussars, and a squadron of bodyguards?

Frederick's determination to "possess" Voltaire had
never diminished. Already the young king had inveigled
Maupertuis and Algarotti to come to Berlin by offering
them a sizable pension and an opportunity to work without molestation. He had invited other savants, too, and
offered them all sorts of extravagant inducements. But the
prize upon which he had set his heart was still Voltaire.
"Whatever happens," the king told him, "I hope to see
you,"—and "may you be joined to my flock forever." Yet
the obstacle to the fulfillment of Frederick's desire still
hovered over the poet. The grip of the Marquise du Chatelet upon Voltaire was as strong as ever. She would have
been willing to accompany the poet to Berlin, and he said
as much in his letters to Frederick. But the Prussian monarch had made up his mind that when he acquired Voltaire, he would have him by himself or not at all; besides,
Frederick had a strong aversion toward women—and Emilie was decidedly no exception. "It is you, my dear friend,
whom I desire to see," he explained; "and the divine
Emilie, with all her divinity is only the accessory of the
Newtonized Apollo." With a touch of sarcasm, he added
that to see Emilie besides Voltaire would be altogether too
dazzling. "I could not bear so much brilliance at once,"
he declared. "I should need the veil of Moses to temper
the blended rays of your divinities."

But the Marquise remained obdurate. All the persua-
siveness of a king could not budge her. If Frederick was,
as he said, so eager to meet Voltaire, then he would have

to meet the Marquise too; it was, she said with finality, either that or nothing.

When it dawned upon Frederick at last how formidable the obstinacy of the Marquise could be, he changed his tactics. He wrote that he expected to be in Flanders some time in September, and that he would come *incognito* to Brussels, where it would give him great pleasure to visit Voltaire and Emilie.

The triumph of the Marquise du Chatelet seemed complete. She had held out against her rival; she had outwitted and outmaneuvered him; and she had compelled him in the end to accept her terms. Radiant in her victory, she began at once to make elaborate preparations for the king's reception. She wanted it to be a fitting tribute to her success; but she also hoped by its imposing cordiality to overcome Frederick's dislike for women; she was determined to make him understand that she, at least, was no ordinary woman.

A few days later all her fine plans were suddenly shattered. A letter from Frederick announced that he was in bed with a fever and could not undertake the long journey from Cleves to Brussels. Wouldn't it be possible, however, he asked, for Voltaire to join him at Cleves? "Make my excuses to the Marquise," he added, "for not having the satisfaction of seeing her at Brussels." "Let us cheat the fever," he implored, "and let me at least have the pleasure of embracing you."

Emilie's first reaction was that of rage. She had been tricked, and she knew it. The king's fever—what was it but an obvious sham? It was a snare—oh, so guileful—to separate her from her lover! But, fortunately, she realized she had seen through its deceptive camouflage; and now that she understood its real purpose, she would never let Voltaire go to the king without her.

But as her wrath subsided, the Marquise realized that to try to hold Voltaire against his will would be rash. He was devoured by his desire to meet Frederick, and to thwart him, while it might be within the realm of possibility, in the end it might cause her to lose him entirely. All her emotions urged her to make no concessions; yet her reason told her plainly that she must yield. In the end she gave her reluctant consent to Voltaire's departure, after having first extracted the promise from him that he would be gone for only a few days. She addressed a brief note to Frederick, telling him, with perfect dissimulation, that she was saddened by his fever; and that she was even more saddened by the lost opportunity of paying court to him. She hoped, she said, that His Majesty would not detain the person with whom she expected to spend her life, and added, significantly, that she "had only lent him for a very few days."

Voltaire met Frederick on a bleak, cold September day in a dilapidated castle not far from Cleves. Years later the poet described the meeting in great detail and with his usual acute eye for theatrical effect. "At the gate of the court-yard I found only one soldier on guard. The Privy Councilor, Rambouet, Minister of State, was walking in the court blowing on his fingers. He wore big linen ruffles —soiled; a hat with a hole in it, and an old official periwig, of which one side hung down into his pocket, while the other hardly reached his shoulder." The Privy Councilor conducted Voltaire to the room occupied by the king. "There was no furniture but the four walls. By the light of the candle, I saw, in a dressing-room, a small trundle-bed, two feet and a half wide, on which there was a little man muffled up in a dressing gown of coarse blue cloth. It was the king, sweating and trembling under a wretched quilt, in a fit of violent fever. I bowed and made my acquaintance by feeling his pulse, as if I had been his chief physician."

The fit passed, and before long the king felt well enough to come to dinner. At the table sat the scholars Maupertuis and Algarotti, and young Count Kaiserling, besides one of the king's ministers. Frederick's fever had now vanished completely; and as the dinner progressed the men talked, as Voltaire put it, "profoundly on the Immortality of the Soul, Liberty, and the androgynes of Plato."

For three days the poet remained with Frederick and during this time they conversed on every imaginable subject. Frederick anticipated a long period of peace—his only motive in increasing his army had been, he assured Voltaire, "to make Prussia safe from attack." He had resolved to make Berlin an exemplary center of culture—the Paris of Prussia. As for himself, all that Frederick apparently desired was to dedicate himself to his subjects, and in the spirit of the *Anti-Machiavelli* render them happy and prosperous.

Both men seem to have been impressed by one another. "I saw," Voltaire wrote to Cideville, "one of the noblest men in the world, who forgets that he is a king the moment he is among friends, and so completely forgets it that he makes me forget it also. . . . His ruling passions are to be just and to please." Frederick's estimate of the poet was equally laudatory. "I have seen the Voltaire whom I was so curious to know," he declared. "He has the eloquence of Cicero, the sweetness of Pliny, the wisdom of Agrippa;

in a word he unites in himself the virtues and talents of the three greatest men of antiquity." The king added, somewhat maliciously, that "the du Chatelet is fortunate indeed to have him."

Voltaire did not return immediately to Brussels. Instead, he journeyed to the Hague, where Frederick had persuaded him to superintend the publication of a revised edition of the *Anti-Machiavelli*. He had promised also to visit Frederick before long at Remusberg, where the Prussian ruler had built an observatory and a laboratory to carry on scientific pursuits. He had also agreed to negotiate in Frederick's behalf to obtain for the king a company of French actors and ballet singers with which Frederick evidently intended to begin the conversion of Berlin into the Prussian Paris.

Late in October an ominous letter from Frederick put a sudden end to Voltaire's quest for singers and actors. "The Emperor is dead," Frederick wrote. "His death alters my pacific ideas, and I think that in June it will be rather a matter of cannon-powder, soldiers and trenches than actresses, balls and stages."

With the death of the Emperor Charles VI, all Europe turned its eyes to Vienna, where his daughter, Maria Theresa, barely out of her 'teens, had assumed the Hapsburg crown and sceptre. The great European powers had given Charles their solemn pledge to respect his daughter's territorial rights; yet, no sooner had the Emperor been laid in grave, than Europe's great nations began to cast covetous glances at the young queen's scattered domains. Each nation looked upon the others as potential aggressors, and with righteous indignation, each nation was determined to prevent such villainy. What concerned the powers above all was the unknown intention of King Frederick. Prussia, they knew, was only a secondary monarchy—still, it had a large and well drilled army, perhaps the best drilled army in all Europe. What such a military machine might do in the hands of a determined commander was indeed a vexatious problem!

Voltaire was fully aware of the stream of conjecture that was pouring with great agitation through Europe's worried chancellories. He himself was being gnawed by a hungry curiosity; for decidedly Frederick's hints about cannon-powder in June had not been lost on the poet's restless imagination. The more he reflected upon the possible hidden meaning of Frederick's letter, the more eager he became to discover the truth. It occurred to him that the French Government might also be interested in knowing the real truth—that, perhaps, it might even reward him substantially if he could obtain such information. Accordingly, Voltaire wrote to Cardinal de Fleury, now doddering in senescence, but still the political right hand man of Louis XV. Voltaire told the Cardinal of his intended visit to Remusberg, where, he said, he hoped "to pay court to a monarch who took the Cardinal de Fleury's way of thinking as his model." He went on to assure the good cleric that there were no secrets between him and the King of Prussia; that he was convinced that Frederick was truly a lover of humanity who harbored no intention of provoking a war. Yet, if King Frederick did have any plan concealed in some secret chamber of his mind, then Voltaire was certain that he was the man to find it.

The Cardinal was quick to applaud Voltaire's delicate suggestion. His letters dripped with cordiality; and where once he had roared at Voltaire with the ferocity of a tiger, he now purred like a gentle kitten. "You did me wrong," he said, "if you thought I ever wished you the least ill. . . . You are a good and honest man. . . . I have always esteemed and loved you." As for Frederick, the Cardinal bathed the Prussian monarch in fragrant admiration; the king was wise; he was reasonable; he would acquire immortal glory. The Cardinal would endeavor "not to render himself un-worthy of the good opinion which his Prussian majesty deigns to have of me." As for Europe's delicate political situation, his Prussian majesty surely must know that the King of France, the Cardinal's master, has made it "plainly evident . . . that he would faithfully keep all his engage-ments?" Could the author of the *Anti-Machiavelli* do less?

Voltaire arrived at Remusberg in late November. What he beheld there filled him with pleasant reassurance. Here, emphatically, there were no sinister omens of war. Untram-meled gayety was everywhere; and for six days the air re-sounded with merry-making. For six days the king and his guests danced and banqueted, while Voltaire recited verses and Frederick played concertos on the flute.

Meanwhile the Marquise had had virtually no news from Voltaire. She was of course privy to his diplomatic venture, an undertaking she heartily approved. Yet the dread that Frederick might still ensnare him, like Mauper-tuis and Algarotti, and so many others, would not leave her. She was not the woman, however, to stand idly by, while in the remote confines of Prussia her foes conspired to win Voltaire. She went to Paris where she, in her turn, worked assiduously to make the authorities realize what a great man Voltaire really was. She made countless trips to ministers of state, trying to make them understand what a loss it would be for France should Frederick persuade Vol-

taire to settle permanently in Berlin. In the end the states-
men agreed with the Marquise and even went so far as to
promise that the next vacant seat in the Academy would
assuredly go to Voltaire. The Marquise was much affected.
She had, she said, obtained for the poet "in three weeks all
that he had taken pains to lose in six years." She had pro-
cured for him "an honorable return to his country"; she
had opened "to him the road to the Academies." All these,
no doubt, were superb achievements; and in the full realization of their magnitude the Marquise hurried back to
Brussels to tell Voltaire about them.

But Voltaire was not in Brussels. He had gone from
Remusberg to Potsdam, and from Potsdam to Berlin. He
was still trying to penetrate into the king's inmost thoughts.
Frederick was the incarnation of affability; he laughed and
frolicked amidst the gayety of his guests; he danced and
played the flute; he talked about the arts and sciences,
about poetry and music, his plans for a greater and love-
lier Berlin, the happiness of his subjects; he talked end-
lessly about everything except the one subject which Voltaire desired so desperately to discuss. On the subject of
European politics the King of Prussia was inscrutable.

Early in December Voltaire bade farewell to Frederick.
They parted like two ambassadors, with a flourish of great
affection, but a feeling of deep suspicion. Though they
sincerely admired one another's talents, a distinct coolness
had crept into their relationship. The poet made his exit
with an insolent epigram. "In spite of your charms," he
told his majesty, "my soul is not satisfied; you are like a
coquette, subjugating all hearts, but never bestowing yourself." "Traitor," was Frederick's rapier-like retort, "it is
you who leave me to follow a coquette." Voltaire was irri-

tated by the king's over-zealous economy, which, judged
by the lavish standards of Versailles, seemed to him nothing less than shabby. Frederick, for his part, was incensed
by Voltaire's avarice. "That miser," he declared in a letter
to one of his aides, "would drink the dregs of his insatiable
desire." With sorrow the king added that Voltaire's visit
for six days would cost him five hundred and fifty crowns
a day. "That's good payment for a fool; never was the
jester of a great nobleman so well paid!"

The return to Brussels was hampered by a chain of exasperating events. The wintry roads were at times almost
impassable, and in their frozen ruts Voltaire's carriage
broke down several times; at the Hague, where the poet
had business to conduct, there were further delays; and,
as if fate were bent on annoying the poet, the vessel bearing him from the Hague became locked for almost a fortnight in an ice-jam.

Despite all these vexations, Voltaire was in good spirits.
Even the menace of the surrounding ice floes did not per-
turb him. In fact, for the first time in many months he
found it possible to work. He remained in the quiet calm
of his cabin, where, absorbed in a world of fantasy, he
worked on a play. He called it *Mahomet;* and though he
had started it long ago, and had even read parts of it to
Frederick and his court, it was not until now that he was
able to put it into final shape.

What lifted Voltaire's spirits, perhaps more than anything else, was his supreme confidence in Frederick. The
Prussian king had his bad traits—there was no doubt of
that. But at bottom the man was sincere. What he had
written in the *Anti-Machiavelli* was not just an imposing
gesture; it was a deep, an overwhelming conviction; and

it was honest. Of all this Voltaire was certain. The Prussian king, the poet wrote to the Cardinal de Fleury, was "the more sensible of your praises because he deserves them, and I believe he will continue to deserve those of all the nations of Europe." "It is to be wished," he concluded, "that the King of France and the King of Prussia should be friends." Clearly, it appeared that Frederick would respect the rights of Maria Theresa.

Late in December Voltaire arrived in Brussels. He had expected to be gone no more than two weeks; instead, his absence had been stretched into two months. The Marquise du Chatelet, distressed by Voltaire's long neglect, considered herself cruelly repaid for all that she had done for him. Her heart, she said, had been pierced by his departure. She had been sick; and she hoped she might be able to die. But Voltaire's return put a quick end to all her melancholy brooding. What did it matter if the poet had been thoughtless, if he had repaid her cruelly for all her kindness? What did it matter, indeed, if the ogre at Potsdam had cast his malevolent spell on the unfortunate poet? The King of Prussia, she exclaimed in a burst of magnanimity, may do anything he likes—"as long as he does not take from me the happiness of my life."

For the moment, however, Frederick was concerned with far different matters: striking suddenly and without warning the King of Prussia had invaded Silesia. The king's sudden act fell on Voltaire with the force of a sledge-hammer. He had been duped, sadly duped. Frederick was a far more formidable and a far more dangerous figure than Voltaire had imagined. It was clear now that the monarch's idealistic pronouncements had been nothing but roseate rhetoric. The rumors of his secret troop movements had unfortunately been true; worse yet, what Voltaire had so optimistically confided to Cardinal de Fleury had turned out to be ridiculous misinformation. The Marquise, chagrined at the realization that all her efforts for her lover at the French court would be fruitless, burst into tears. "I defy the King of Prussia," she exclaimed, "to hate me more than I have hated him during these two months past!" Her rancor was surpassed only by Voltaire's gloom and disillusionment. It seemed as if the solid earth had been swept from beneath him, and as he dangled helplessly in thin air, nothing could ever bring him back.

A letter of explanation from Frederick helped very little. He was marching, he said, with his men. The weather was fine and his health was excellent. He drank with those who wanted to drink; he ate with those who were hungry; he made himself "a Jew to the Jews, a pagan to the pagans." Such, he wrote, were his occupations. Yet, he would gladly hand them over to another, "if that phantom called Glory did not appear to me too often. It's a great folly, but a folly too difficult to banish once we dote on it."

Frederick's invasion of Silesia plunged all Europe into war. The sight of a young and inexperienced queen trying to hold off the Prussian war machine was too much of a temptation for France. To get her share of the expected spoils she joined Prussia, as did Bavaria and Saxony. Meanwhile, England, fearing a possible upset in the European balance of power, sent an army to help Austria.

Frederick and Voltaire continued to exchange letters; but their tone underwent a marked change. Their missives were still filled with pleasant compliments and with effusions of reciprocal esteem. But behind the smoke-

screen of their flattery the two men clearly revealed themselves. Each admired the other's talents, but neither was
unaware of the flaws in the other's character. Nor was
Frederick the unsophisticated youth of two or three years
ago; he had dropped his lofty visions and had emerged an
embittered cynic, a man without illusions. The world, he
was convinced, was run by "trickery, bad faith and duplicity." "One is ridiculed, one is criticized," he wrote;
"a journalist satirizes you; your neghbors tear you to
pieces; everyone wishes you to the devil, while overwhelming you with protestations of friendship. Such is the
world. . . ." As for Voltaire, his utterances were charged
with a mischievous and caustic innuendo. At times even
his flattery was barbed. "Your Majesty should put laurel
leaves in your hair like the ancient Roman generals . . .
and you need at least two laurel leaves." When Frederick
wrote verses on the field of battle, and sent them proudly
to Voltaire, the poet reminded the king of Solomon in his
glory, who, "after having experienced everything . . . said,
'All is vanity.' " When Frederick won an important victory, Voltaire commented that he had delayed congratulat-
ing the king because "I was sick in bed when Your Majesty was on horseback." With a dash of vitriol he added,
"I set only one foot on the banks of the Styx; but Sire, I
am distressed by the number of poor wretches I saw pass.
Some come from Schärding, others from Prague or Iglau.
Will you and the kings, your colleagues, never cease ravaging the earth, which, you say, you so much desire to
make happy?" At times Frederick tried to pay back his
critic in his own coin. "It is easy for you," he wrote, "to
declaim against those who support their rights and claims
by force of arms; but I remember a time when, if you had

had an army, it would have marched at once against Desfontaines, Rousseau, etc., etc." When Voltaire spoke of his
"unshakable friendship during ten years" with the Marquise du Chatelet, the cynical Frederick tittered. "Would
you have me believe," he asked, "that during all that time
you talked of nothing but philosophy to the most charming woman in France?"

Gradually Voltaire's disappointment in the author of
the *Anti-Machiavelli* resolved itself into an attitude of
philosophic resignation. Frederick, he realized, was a dangerous phenomenon. But somehow he could not quite rid
himself of the hope that some day the King of Prussia
might fulfill the promise of high and benevolent states-
manship he had so eloquently proclaimed when he was
Prince Frederick. "Time will tell," was Voltaine's one consoling thought. "After all he is only a king."

There were other matters which demanded Voltaire's
attention. The tragedy of *Mahomet* was ready for rehearsal, but the Parisian censor, noticing with distress that
it was against God and the public morals, refused to grant
the necessary license. Yet, by some strange logic, what was
blasphemous and indecent in Paris was not so in the city
of Lille. To Lille Voltaire accordingly went. It so happened that the actors he had once hired for Frederick—
only to have Frederick change his mind—were at Lille. To
remove the sting of their disappointment, which they apparently still felt, the playwright engaged them for *Mahomet*. The fact that the Parisian censor had frowned on
the play created a great interest, which, as usual, Voltaire
fully exploited. As a result, when the play opened in May,
1741, the theatre was completely sold out.

From the rise of the first curtain the applause was hearty,

and as the play progressed the audience grow more and more enthusiastic. The second act was followed by a tremendous ovation. Seated in his box, Voltaire beamed over what seemed a certain dramatic success, when a messenger was seen to hand him a note. A moment later the author rose and signaled for silence. He said he had just received a dispatch from the King of Prussia, and here it was: "They say the Austrians are in retreat and I believe it is true. Frederick." Immediately there was an outburst of frenzied delight, for the citizens of Lille were violently anti-Austrian, if not pro-Prussian. The demonstration lasted for several minutes, and it was only with difficulty that *Mahomet* was able to resume. Yet, as far as the delirious audience was concerned, the play from now on was decidedly anticlimactic. From the author's point of view, the joy of the spectators was certainly no handicap to the chances of his play; on the contrary, nearly everything in *Mahomet* seemed to strike a responsive chord. Line after line was hailed with long salvoes of applause; and when the drama at long last reached its triumphant end, it received an extravagant demonstration.

Mahomet, or to give it its full title, "Fanaticism, or Mahomet the Prophet," would without doubt have been a success even without the artificial stimulus of Voltaire's dramatic announcement. Its plot, simple and mechanical, like all of Voltaire's dramatic plots, deals with Mahomet's attempt to seize the holy city of Mecca and to assassinate its ruler Zopire. Zopire's two children, a boy and a girl, both supposedly dead, have been enslaved by Mahomet under the names of Seide and Palmire. They are unaware of their origin, and to make matters even more complicated for them, Voltaire does not let them know they are brother and sister. Mahomet, falling madly in love with his beautiful slave, desires her for one of his concubines. But Palmire, who is as virtuous as all Voltaire's young heroines, rejects the prophet's proposal. She is in love, he now discovers, with Zeide. Knowing all about the kinship of Palmire and Zeide, Mahomet makes arrangements for his revenge. He commands Zeide to assassinate Zopire, promising the youth as a reward the hand of Palmire. The diabolical Mahomet, who perhaps is even more of a villain than most villains of Voltaire, has secretly administered a slow-working poison to the unsuspecting Zeide. In the belief that he must obey his commander, Zeide carries out his chieftain's order, stabbing Zopire just as he kneels at the altar to pray for the restoration of his children. As the aged man totters he appears to recognize his slayer. "My dear Zeide!" he cries out as he expires. Wasting no time, Mahomet condemns Zeide as a murderer, and at once resumes his amorous advances toward Palmire. Yet, somehow, Zeide has managed to rally the people of Mecca; and, with sword in hand, he confronts Mahomet, determined to kill him. He falls dead at the prophet's feet by what everyone interprets as a divine miracle, but the audience knows he is the victim of the slow-working poison.

Such was the play which staggered the emotions of the drama-lovers of Lille. Its characters are made of putty; its heroes and heroines, villains, good, old men and innocent youths were the same preposterous marionettes which held forth in *Oedipus,* in *Zaire* and *Alzire.* But Voltaire's audiences wanted excitement, not depth; action, not character; sonorous rhymes and happy *mots,* not honest writing. All these *Mahomet* offered in abundance; but it also offered something more. On the surface Voltaire's tragedy appeared innocent and harmless; imbedded in it were many lines which might readily be interpreted as anti-social, anti-political, or anti-Christan. Although *Mahomet* was a bomb hurled, presumably, at fanaticism, Voltaire was careful to make its shell explode in all directions. For the French theatre-goer, it was simple to read between the lines, and to behold his pet aversions, especially the Church and the monarchy, under sly attack.

More than a year elapsed before Parisians were permitted by the authorities to see *Mahomet*. The shrewd-eyed and hard-headed clerics of Paris, unlike their sacred brethren at Lille, were quick to detect Voltaire's innuendo, and with every weapon in their arsenal they sought to prevent the play's performance in the capital. When they failed in this, they continued their attack nonetheless. At the play's opening performance in August of 1742, the holy men appeared in full force. What they heard surpassed even their basest suspicions. Not only were they convinced that *Mahomet* was a satanic mockery of the Holy Church; it was also "a bloody satire of the Christian religion"; indeed, the very name *Mahomet* was found to be a deliberate mockery "since it has three syllables—the same number as that of the adored name of Jesus Christ!" Complaints against the play were lodged at once with the Solicitor-General. That astute gentleman, having neither read nor seen the play, referred the matter to the Police Lieutenant. "I hear," he wrote, "a comedy spoken of, which, it is said, contains enormous things against religion." The Police Lieutenant, who was nobody's fool, declined to assume the responsibility of banning the play. Besides he had seen *Mahomet*, and it seemed to him somewhat far-fetched to say that the prophet "who cut the throats of the fathers and

raped their daughters" was in reality intended to be the
gentle Jesus. Instead of taking action, the Police Lieutenant sent a copy of the play to the Solicitor-General with a
letter to the effect that the drama contained nothing to
which the Church could logically take exception. Soon
afterwards the Solicitor-General condemned *Mahomet*.
His reason was as frank as it was extraordinary. "I need
not tell you," he wrote to the Police Lieutenant, "that I
have not read the play; but judging from what I hear, I
believe it is necessary to forbid its performance."

Still reluctant to take action against a piece which was
in obvious public favor, and which, moreover, had been
approved by the censor, the Police Lieutenant put the
entire matter into the hands of Cardinal Fleury. The sagacious prelate acted with promptitude. "Suggest to the
actors," he instructed the Police Lieutenant, "to assign the
sickness of one of their number as a pretext for not playing
the piece on Friday; also advise Voltaire to withdraw the
play from their hands to avoid trouble." If these measures
failed, then the Police Lieutenant was to remind the dramatist "of a certain act of the parliament by virtue of
which it is in the power of the Solicitor-General to arraign
the author of the 'English Letters.' " That, His Eminence
concluded, "will render your argument persuasive."

It did. Voltaire withdrew the play; but he did it with
bitterness. "This tragedy," he said, "is suitable rather for
English heads than French hearts. It was found too daring
in Paris because it was powerful, and dangerous because it
was truthful. . . . It is only in London that poets are allowed to be philosophers." He added that under the circumstances he wished he had "the King of Prussia for a
master and the English for fellow-citizens."

A few months later the tide of circumstances shifted, and another play, *Mérope,* brought the poet his greatest dramatic triumph. He had worked on this tragedy during odd moments in the years when he was preoccupied with Newton and science. With *Mérope,* Voltaire returned to classical antiquity. Mérope is the name of the widowed Queen of Messina, whose husband was killed in an insurrection against the throne. The queen has not heard for years from her son, Egisthe, who had been whisked out of the kingdom during the fighting. Mérope's agents have been searching for the prince for years, but to no avail— "the universe is silent." Meanwhile, Polyphonte, a man of political ambitions, proposes marriage to the queen; but anxious to preserve the throne for her son, Mérope refuses the offer. A young stranger, in chains, and accused of murder, is brought before her. In some mysterious way the queen feels herself strangely drawn to the young man; at the same time she is not unmindful of her responsibilities to the state. Evidence is produced to show that the victim of the accused slayer happens to have been her own son. Agitated by grief and terrible rage, the queen condemns the young man to death. She herself will see him die at the foot of her husband's tomb. Now that her son is dead, the despondent woman sees no reason for not marrying Polyphonte, even though she despises him. Meanwhile, a faithful old servant of the family, Narbas, who has accompanied the queen's son in his wanderings, arrives in Messina. When he sees the accused slayer, he recognizes him instantly as the queen's son. Narbas, unfortunately, cannot openly announce his discovery, since that might incite Polyphonte to murder the prince. Yet, somehow, the servant succeeds in getting word to the queen, who now finds

herself placed in the difficult position of trying to save her
son without arousing Polyphonte's suspicions. She decides
that the only way out of her dilemma is to go through with
her marriage to Polyphonte. Preparations are accordingly
made for the marriage feast; but an insurrection breaks
out in the course of which Polyphonte is killed.

Mérope won great acclamation. "The pit," said one of
the first-nighters, "not only applauded fit to break everything, but asked a thousand times that Voltaire should
appear on the stage that the people might show him their
joy and satisfaction." If we may trust the poet's word, he
tried to elude the cheering spectators by hiding in the
corridor. In the end his curiosity was apparently too
much, and he appeared in the box of his friend, the
Duchess of Villars. "The pit was mad," he subsequently explained. "They cried to the duchess to kiss me, and they
made so much noise that in the end she was obliged to do
so." In the annals of the French stage that kiss was histor-
ically significant: it marked the first time that an audience
ever shouted for the author so that it might acclaim him.

On the eve of *Mérope's* premiere Cardinal de Fleury
died; and with his death a chair in the French Academy
became vacant. The realization that he was not one of the
Forty Immortals had irked Voltaire for some time. Outwardly he had always pretended to be above the vainglory
of honors and titles; actually his infinite vanity never permitted him to reject even the smallest tribute. The fact
that *Mérope's* success had once more thrust him into
France's literary spotlight caused him to hope that this
time, certainly, he would be chosen for the coveted vacancy. He knew of course that a high accomplishment in
the realm of literature was not enough to insure a man's

election to the Academy; more important very often were his connections at the Court. The king, never very fond of Voltaire, appeared lukewarm on the subject of the poet's election; the king's mistress, who at the moment happened to be the Duchess of Chateauroux, was fond of the gay little poet and wished to see him become an Academician; as for the queen, she of course had nothing to say in such an important matter. Voltaire's chances on the surface thus appeared favorable.

Unfortunately an obstacle to Voltaire's desire stood in the way—and a formidable obstacle it was in the shape of the dauphin's tutor, Bishop Boyer of Mirepoix. As a devout man of God, His Excellency had an understandable animosity for the author of the *Henriade* and the "English Letters"; but that natural hostility had been considerably aggravated by the merciless ridicule the poet had frequently heaped upon the bishop. The dauphin's tutor was in the habit of signing himself as *"anc. de Mirepoix,"* the *anc.* standing for *ancien,* the French word for "formerly," and meaning he was formerly bishop of Mirepoix. Voltaire had mischievously converted the *anc.* to *ane,* the French word for "ass." Voltaire's jibe soon became well known and many a Frenchman took delight in speaking of Bishop Boyer as the Ass of Mirepoix.

The holy man now took his long-delayed revenge by opposing Voltaire's election to the Academy. The bishop's argument was brief and to the point: "For a profane person . . . to succeed a cardinal would be to offend God." Voltaire countered that he was "a good citizen and a true Catholic"; that he had "always been such at heart"; that "the *Henriade* from one end to the other is nothing but a eulogy of virtue which submits to Providence"; and as for the "English Letters," most of them he "had not written at all." He added that he could say all these things because he was "an honest man."

In the end the bishop prevailed; and despite Voltaire's protestations of virtue, he was not selected. Instead, some clerical nonentity was chosen. Disgusted and disappointed, the poet tried to make light of his rejection. "For a prelate to succeed a prelate," he declared, "is according to the canons of the Church"; and he added that since he did not have the honor of being a priest he thought it fitting for him to renounce the Academy. From Frederick came a letter full of extravagant commiseration. "I believe," the king wrote, "that France is now the only country in Europe where asses and idiots make their fortune."

Voltaire's disappointment was offset before long by an unexpected request from the French Government. The war which the King of Prussia had forced upon Austria, and into which France had entered so lightly, was not going too well for the French. For, having conquered Silesia with lightning swiftness, Frederick made a separate peace with Austria, leaving his astonished allies high and and dry. Freed from the Prussan menace, Maria Theresa was able to throw virtually her full strength against France, with the result that the French found their position becoming more and more precarious. Anxious to procure Frederick's help, but unwilling to approach him directly, the French Government suddenly remembered Voltaire's much advertised friendship with the King of Prussia. Why not send Voltaire to Frederick, it reasoned, and let him obtain an insight into the Prussian king's diplomatic intentions? Voltaire's misson would be masked as a purely personal, friendly call; it would thus have the virtue of being unofficial and would in no way tip France's hand. To this scheme Voltaire gave his hearty approval. He would write the King of Prussia a flattering letter; he would tell His Majesty that life in France had become insupportable; he would say that he had had a quarrel with the Ass of Mirepoix and that he was leaving France forever.

"May I see the great Frederick once more," he implored; "and may I never see that pedant of a Boyer, that Bishop of Mirepoix, who would please me far more if he were at least twenty years older." Frederick was quick to respond. With open arms he welcomed the poet; and on the last of August, 1743, Voltaire arrived in the Prussian capital.

He was greeted with lavish hospitality. As if to atone for all past misunderstandings, Frederick left nothing undone to please his famous guest. Voltaire was given abode in the royal palace with quarters adjacent to those of the king. It became the practice of His Majesty to slip into Voltaire's room before retiring and, sitting informally on Voltaire's bed, he would converse with him far into the night. Their long conversations frequently touched on the subject of politics. But the crafty Frederick was wary. Nature had given him a quickness of perception which he put to excellent use. He soon realized that Voltaire was up to some kind of duplicity. Although the king had not been able to unravel the whole scheme, he sensed that far from being a purely friendly call, Voltaire's visit had some connection with French politics. To find out more about the nature of Voltaire's plot, Frederick encouraged him to think that he looked with great esteem on the French Government, and that he might even entertain the possibility of an alliance between Prussia and France. Yet, fully aware of the utter unreliability of Frederick's assurances, Voltaire was anxious to have the king commit himself in writing. Accordingly, he carefully drew up a set of questions which he submitted to the king.

Frederick was not taken in; instead of answering Voltaire's questions directly, his replies were vague and often satirical. "Did not His Majesty fear that the Austrians might attack Silesia?" asked Voltaire. Frederick replied in verse: "We will receive them," he wrote,

> *Twiddle-dee,*
> *In the mode of Barbary,*
> *Don't you see?*

"Is it not clear," asked Voltaire, "that France displays vigor and wisdom?" "I admire the wisdom of France," Frederick replied, "but God keep me from ever imitating it." Frederick, in short, was willing enough to talk, but on paper he would not commit himself.

Voltaire's trickery was soon to be matched by a bit of trickery on the part of his host. The king's ambition to acquire Voltaire for Berlin was still as strong as ever; and now he thought he saw an excellent opportunity to gain his prize. He addressed a letter to one of his confidential agents, enclosing one from Voltaire, in which the poet had ridiculed the Bishop of Mirepoix. "Here," Frederick wrote, "is a morsel of a letter of Voltaire which I beg you in some roundabout way to get to the Bishop of Mirepoix, without either you or me appearing in the business." The king added that it was his intention "to embroil Voltaire so thoroughly in France that there will remain no course for him to take but to come to me."

But the king's stratagem misfired. Since the nature of Voltaire's visit was fully known to the French Government, the Bishop of Mirepoix for once had no just cause for complaint. Instead, the prelate informed Voltaire of what had happened. Naturally the poet was very angry. Between his duplicity and that of the king he felt there was a vast difference; his own prevarication, he was convinced, was legitimate, since it was patriotic and hurt no one, but Frederick's was outrageous since it violated the rules of friendship—and what was worse, it was intended to harm Voltaire. As for Frederick, despite the affair's unintended ending, he was greatly amused. "Voltaire," he wrote to his agent, "has unearthed . . . the little treason we have played on him. He is strongly piqued. He will get over it, I hope."

Voltaire did not get over it—at least not fully. The king's act embittered him all the more when he thought of how it might have broken up his relationship with the Marquise du Chatelet. She had been informed of the diplomatic nature of Voltaire's mission—this was the price the poet had to pay to gain her assent to his departure. He had promised her to return very soon, but because of Frederick's secretiveness with respect to his political intentions, the poet had been obliged to prolong his visit far beyond his original expectaton. Meanwhile Frederick's blandishments, his affability, his extraordinary generosity had made their impression on Voltaire. Under Frederick's genial spell, Berlin had become more and more attractive, and with it the temptation to settle there permanently had increased. The one attraction which still drew Voltaire to France was the Marquise. Yet, for the moment even her charms were overshadowed by the allurements of Frederick. Voltaire's letters to her grew fewer and fewer, and they became more and more evasive. She complained she knew nothing about his plans; she no longer "knew the man upon whom her happiness depended"; she felt he was "mad about Germany"; "he is absolutely drunk," she exploded in a tearful letter to her old friend d'Argental.

Frederick's treachery destroyed his glamor—at least for the time being. Voltaire had been on the point of staying in Berlin of his own accord; but to be tricked into staying, that was an entirely different matter, and one which filled him with horror. His antipathy for the King of Prussia was accompanied by a resurgence of his loyalty to the Marquise. It was his feeling, more than ever, that "pure friendship had rights more binding than a king's commands."

When Frederick realized that his little intrigue had failed, and that the spell of Berlin had been broken, he tried to patch up his differences with the poet. He excused himself, asked what he might do to make amends, and resumed his campaign to "possess" Voltaire. "Come, my dear Voltaire," he pleaded, "and demand anything that may be agreeable to you. I wish to please you." Voltaire might "choose an apartment or a house"; he might "arrange for the pleasure and superfluities of life"; he could make his surroundings such as he "would wish them in order to be happy." In any case, whatever Voltaire chose to do, he would "always be free and entire master of his fate." All that Frederick wanted in return, he said, "was to enlighten myself at the fire of your powerful genius"— which of course the king expected would remain in Berlin.

All the king's entreaties, however, were futile. An atti-

tude of cordiality between the two men was gradually restored—there were even some demonstrations of mutual
affection—but neither man trusted the other, and in October Voltaire returned to France.

His mission could hardly be called a success. He had
not been able to penetrate the king's mental fastness; he
had not been able to convince Frederick of any advantage
to be derived from an alliance with France; he had not
even been able to persuade the King of Prussia to send a
few battalions of troops to the aid of the hard-pressed
French.

Voltaire's lack of success did not discredit him at the
Court. In fact, before the lapse of many months Versailles
summoned him again; yet, on this occasion his services
were to be more in harmony with his special talents. It so
happened that his friend Richelieu, now risen to the post
of Versailles' First Gentleman of the Bedchamber, had
been given the task of making arrangements for a program
of festivities to celebrate the coming wedding of the Dauphin to the Infanta of Spain. Voltaire's accomplishments
as a master of ceremonies at the Duke's own wedding had
not been forgotten by Richelieu, who now asked the poet
to assume the direction of the Dauphin's festivities. Voltaire was willing enough; and in his retreat at Cirey he
made plans for a program which was to include every imaginable diversion, from feasts and balls to pageants and processions. Games, clown shows, dramas, musicals and fireworks—all were provided for. As for compensation, for
once the poet scoffed at money. What he desired, he intimated to the Duke, was something less sordid; something
which would reflect the dignity and spirit of the occasion
—something perhaps in the nature of a literary position at

the Court. Richelieu took the hint and promised to see what he could do.

The poet went to work at once on which he called "a *divertissement* for the Dauphin and the Dauphiness." It was in the nature of an extragant revue which he called the "Princess of Navarre" and whose title was intended as a delicate compliment to the Infanta. The piece was designed to be largely a feast for the eye with a lavish array of ballets, processions, music by Rameau, all done in a welter of colorful scenery and pretty costumes. To give Voltaire's decoction the vast scope the author desired, an immense stage was especially constructed in the grounds of Versailles. The titled lords and ladies who beheld the "Princess of Navarre" were greatly impressed by its sumptuous luxury, if not by its artistic qualities, which on the whole it lacked. As for Voltaire, apparently he was not misled by the value of his creation. Yet the piece had the virtue of pleasing the Court; and that, after all, had been the author's foremost purpose. "The king is grateful," Voltaire noted with satisfaction; and with even greater satisfaction he added. "The Mirepoix cannot harm me. What more do I want?"

What little more Voltaire wanted was bestowed in April, 1745, when Louis XV appointed him Historiographer of France. The appointment was made because, to quote the words of the official decree, "no one has appeared to His Majesty more worthy to receive the marks of his benevolence . . . than the Sieur Arouet de Voltaire who, by the superiority of his talents and his studied application, has made the most rapid progress in the science that he has cultivated, and of which his works, received with just applause, are the fruit." Besides being allowed to employ his title "in all papers and documents whatsoever," France's new historiographer was to receive an annual emolument of two thousand francs.

In his new capacity, which was obviously greater in implied honor than in actual significance, Voltaire performed a number of literary chores. He was the author of Louis' reply to the Empress Elizabeth of Russia, accepting her offer to act as mediator between the warring nations, and expressing the thought—surely not subscribed to by his master the king—that "kings cannot aspire to any higher glory than the happiness of their people." He also composed a note, which was sent to the Dutch, warning them against giving aid to the English in case France undertook to assist the Pretender, Charles Stuart, to regain the English crown. Besides these sober pronouncements Voltaire also wrote a number of minor verses. At the request of the Minister of War he created a poem of some three hundred lines commemorating France's recent and quite unexpected victory at Fontenoy, and laying particular stress on the reputed valor and great wisdom of King Louis.

The poet, however, was far too skeptical to be happy in his new rôle. He might fulfill the requirements of his office by writing to the English, Dutch and Russians; he might even write trifling little madrigals about Versailles' bewigged nobility; but to compose eulogiums about the doubtful greatness of a king, and to glorify war, when for most of his life he had consistently assailed war as man's most colossal folly, and had decried Europe's warring monarchs as the ravagers of the earth—to have to do such things was neither simple nor pleasant. The "Battle of Fontenoy," the poet said, had given him "a great deal more trouble to celebrate than it gave the king to win it."

Why, then, did he do it? If, as he said, "one only writes well what one writes from choice," why did he forsake the quietness of Cirey for the tinsel of Versailles and the endless, petty annoyances that engulfed it? Voltaire had desired a position at the Court, not so much for the prestige it gave him, but rather for the royal protection that went with it. If it was irksome for the poet to write about matters in which he personally disbelieved, then at least his feelings were amply assuaged by the realization that he had the king's favor, as well as that of the royal mistress, who at this moment happened to be Madame de Pompadour. He realized, of course, that the king's favor was delicate and uncertain: it might waver at any moment; or it might be withdrawn. Nor did it protect him against the machinations of people like the Bishop of Mirepoix. The king's favor, Voltaire acknowledged, was desirable, but decidedly it was not enough. The thing he yearned for was the endorsement of some towering authority, one which by its weight and awesome majesty would protect him forever from his enemies, but particularly from the persecutions of the French clergy.

Only one such personage in all Europe had within himself the power to do all that Voltaire wanted—the Pope. Yet, surely Voltaire could not expect any favors from the Vatican! Did Voltaire imagine that Rome had taken lightly his slurs on Mother Church? Or did he believe, by some strange contortion of the reason, that the Vicar of Christ could be induced to condone them?

Voltaire's belief that he could make the Pope, if not his friend, then at least a cordial sympathizer, was not a wild and extravagant dream. It was, on the contrary, a strong and profound conviction, based upon a carefully thought-out plan. To put it into effect, the poet approached d'Argenson, the Minister of Foreign Affairs. He would like, he told the Minister, some mark of papal benevolence that would do him honor, "both in this world and the next." The amazed d'Argenson retorted, somewhat banteringly, that it was hardly possible to mix political and celestial matters in such a way. Voltaire then explained that Pope Benedict XIV was the author of more than a dozen books. These Voltaire intended to read, after which he would write His Holiness and compliment him both on the style and subject matter of his writings. He had heard it said that Pope Benedict was a scholar and a kindly man, who openly prided himself on being a good fellow; and that the Pontiff was not a man to be displeased by flattery. When the time appeared ripe Voltaire wanted d'Argenson to drop a hint to His Holiness that some slight token of papal favor would be highly appreciated by the poet.

The Minister of Foreign Affairs emphatically shook his head. The Pope, he was sure, was too astute not to be able to understand the motives which prompted Voltaire's stratagem; and once having discerned their true nature, Benedict might easily forget his amiability. In such an event he might undertake to make Voltaire pay for his deception, and instead of protecting the poet from his clerical enemies, he might even go to their assistance. No—it was better by far to give up the whole scheme!

D'Argenson's rejection of Voltaire's plan failed to make the poet relinquish it. He remembered that the Marquise du Chatelet had a friend, a Mademoiselle du Thil, who in turn had a friend in the papal household, an Abbé du Tolignan. To Mademoiselle du Thil, Voltaire now addressed himself, pouring upon her his most endearing blandishments. He intimated also that, like the Mademoiselle herself, he was a profound admirer of the Holy Father, and particularly of his writings; and that he desired nothing more ardently than some small mark of papal favor. The Marquise's friend, charmed by Voltaire's beatific utterance, responded quickly. In a short time Voltaire's heartfelt desire was made known to the Abbé; and before long it was communicated to His Holiness. Benedict's response, most surprisingly, was favorable: he gave the supplicating Abbé two large medals, bearing his own portrait, to be transmitted to Voltaire.

Meanwhile, by some strange quirk of fate, Minister d'Argenson had become convinced that Voltaire's scheme, despite its utter brazenness, might perhaps be subtle enough to work. Accordingly he instructed the French envoy at Rome to ask His Holiness for two of his large medals to be given to Voltaire. Amazed by this unexpected second request, the Pontiff was nonetheless amused. How large a medal did Voltaire expect! "To Saint Peter himself," he exclaimed, "I would not give any larger ones."

The Pope's gift pleased Voltaire immensely. He took great pains to display his two medals, particularly in the presence of the sacred men of God. As for religion, he assured his companions that his friend the Pope "has an air of knowing what all that is worth." To Benedict himself he addressed his gratitude with some Latin verses in which he declared Benedict XIV to be the "ornament of Rome," the "father of the world," and one who "by his works instructs the earth and adorns it with his virtues."

The successful outcome of Voltaire's scheme soon emboldened him to seek an even greater favor. It was clear even to Voltaire that the distinction of having a pair of papal medals, large and impressive though they might be, was after all very slight. Nor was it unique, for any devout son of Mother Church, with a little influence, could easily acquire such tokens of papal grace. What the poet desired was something infinitely more personal; something no one else could have; and which, in the discerning eyes of Europe, would mark him as the possessor of the Pope's highest esteem. Accordingly he wrote a letter to the Most Holy Father, composing it in Italian, and impregnating it with extraordinary reverence, and asking Benedict's permission to dedicate *Mahomet* to him. If the author of that tragedy recalled how the theologians of Paris had poured their abuse upon it, he was careful not to mention it to the pontiff. Instead, he hoped that the Very Holy Father "would deign to permit that I place at your feet both the book and its author"; for "to whom could he more properly address a satire on the cruelty and errors of a false prophet than to the vicar and imitator of a God of peace and truth?" He added that he was "one of the humblest and one of the warmest admirers of virtue"; and that it was with sentiments of profound veneration that he prostrated himself and kissed the pontiff's "sacred feet."

Soon afterward the pontiff replied to "his dear son." He had read *Mahomet* and had been delighted by its dedication. He had been impressed, he said, by Voltaire's "goodness," which he desired to reward with a particular expression of his gratitude. "You ought not to doubt," His Holiness declared, "the singular esteem with which merit so acknowledged as yours inspires me." He added that nothing remained "but for us to grant you our Apostolic Benediction." This His Holiness bestowed upon Voltaire "on the day of Holy Mary the greater, September 19, 1745." The poet accepted his new honor by writing the Holy Father that the "lineaments of Your Holiness are not better expressed in the medals with which you have had the particular goodness to gratify me, than are those of your mind and character in the letter with which you have deigned to honor me." Henceforth he was obliged, he said, "to recognize the infallibility of Your Holiness in your literary decisions, as in other things more important."

The glow of apostolic benediction, shining with benevolent warmth upon the author of *Mahomet,* swiftly penetrated into the inner fastnesses of his opponents, and under its powerful, compelling rays it melted, irresistibly and completely, their opposition to the play. Before long an impressive edition of *Mahomet* made its appearance, having as an introduction in both Italian and French the entire correspondence between the Pope and Voltaire. Apparently even the Bishop of Mirepoix must have been impressed; for when a fresh vacancy occurred a few months later in the French Academy, Voltaire's ancient enemy made no protest against his election; and thus at last, at the age of fifty-two, after years of steady productivity and a campaign that at times was frantic and full of falsehood, Voltaire attained his coveted goal.

One person appeared quite unimpressed by the honors heaped in steady succession upon Voltaire. Far away in the rising, greater Berlin, amidst its new and resplendent buildings, its magnificent parks and shaded avenues, amid the lustre of its newly acquired celebrities in science and philosophy, the frowning countenance of Frederick cast an ever-deepening shadow. From Potsdam emanated the unmistakable signs of the monarch's growing jealousy and contempt. "Take my advice," Frederick exclaimed, "and finish the *Pucelle*. It is far better to amuse honest men than to write gazettes for blackguards." Then, reminding the poet that he had failed to send him a copy of the "Maid of Orleans," the king complained that Voltaire had lent a copy to the Duchess of Württemberg. "You must know," he wrote reproachfully, "that she had it copied during the night. Such are the people you confide in—and those who deserve your confidence, or rather those to whom you should abandon yourself completely, are the very persons you mistrust."

When Voltaire failed to show the resentment Frederick had expected, the king tried to make him jealous of Maupertuis, whom he had made not only a member of the Prussian Academy, but also its president. "The whole of Berlin," Frederick wrote, "is interested in him. He is the finest conquest I ever made in my life. As for you, you are inconstant, ungrateful, perfidious!"

Frederick's irritation over his failure to gain Voltaire permanently for Potsdam was enhanced before long by a fresh agitation. He knew that the Frenchman intended to write an account of the war with Austria, and the fear haunted him that Voltaire might actually express some uncomplimentary opinions in print. "I wish you would not write the campaign of '41," the monarch implored. Instead, why not "give the last touches to the 'Age of Louis the Great'?" After all, didn't Voltaire know that "contemporary authors are accused by all ages of falling into the bitterness of satire or the fatuity of flattery?" Unfortunately for Frederick, his excellent reasoning fell on deaf ears, for Voltaire happened to know that the king himself was then engaged in the composition of his memoirs of the Silesian campaign. Voltaire's reply to Frederick offered only scanty reassurance. "Heavens preserve me, Sire, from printing my history of the war of 1741! These are fruits which time alone can ripen. I have certainly written neither a panegyric nor a satire; but the more I love the truth, the less I should waste it." He added, with veiled significance, that "Caesar wrote his commentaries, and you are writing yours." The sting was clear, though Frederick pretended not to notice it. "So your taste for history is finally confirmed!" he wrote with feigned regret. "Well, follow this strange impulse if you must. I do not oppose it." The ovensensitive king could not, however, resist the temptation to make one more counterattack. "Good-bye, adorable historian," he declared, "good-bye to the author of the *Pucelle*, invisible prisoner of Circe; good-bye . . . to the lover of Madame du Chatelet." "Madame du Chatelet and I, Sire," was Voltaire's icy retort, "are still occupied by the same veneration for Your Majesty." He added that he was ill—very ill; he was probably drawing his last breath. As usual he seemed to take pleasure in "awaiting death patiently," having, as he said, "no regret in the world except that of not seeing the greatest man who ornaments it." But Frederick was not fooled by Voltaire's attention-getting device. Had he not himself employed a similar ruse at Voltaire's expense on the occasion of their first meeting? "As long as you die only metaphorically, I shall leave you to it," was Frederick's cold consolation. "Receive all the seven sacraments at once, if you wish; it matters little to me." Soon afterward the ironical Fates struck back at the king. He suffered a partial attack of apoplexy, and feeling certain of his approaching end, he frankly lamented the fact that he had been unable to see Voltaire before making his final departure. No sooner had the king recovered, however, than he regretted his hasty lamentation. "If I had gone below," he told Voltaire, "I should have looked for you."

Meanwhile Versailles was showing more and more an undercurrent of disturbance. Neither the royal favor nor the apostolic benediction, nor the fact that Voltaire was one of the Forty Immortals could compensate for his palpable lack of aristocratic blood. In the eyes of the Versailles *noblesse,* Voltaire was merely a pretentious upstart. When the court historiographer took his place at the table of Versailles' gentlemen-in-ordinary, his act was met with lifted eyebrows. Did not the bourgeois Arouet understand, the nobles murmured, that such things simply were not done? The thinly veiled insolence of his associates Voltaire met with feigned indifference; if his aristocratic detractors should ever become too bold with their arrogant innuendoes, a bath in his special vat of caustic satire, he knew, would swiftly annihilate them. What irritated Voltaire more than their ridiculous insolence was the oppressive burden of his office. To write to order, like a schoolboy, on subjects in which he had no interest, distressed him more and more. At the outset the honor of his office had pleased him—as it had pleased the Marquise. It still pleased the divine Emilie, and it was in no small way due to her insistence that he had not long since relinquished the post. But now it had become an irksome load, which grew heavier day by day, and which threatened in the end to stifle him completely. The odiousness of his situation prompted him at last to petition His Majesty to be allowed to give up his office. The poet's request was a remarkable reflection of his character. With mingled avarice and vanity he asked to be permitted to sell his post, but to be allowed to retain its title "as an honorary distinction." King Louis granted the desired permission.

The delicate nature of Louis' favor was to reveal itself before very long. It so happened that the poet had intoned some rhymes to Madame de Pompadour in which he had complimented the king's mistress on her relationship to the monarch. The poem had been intended solely for the madame, who apparently had been quite pleased by its flattery. Unfortunately, the worst had to happen—the verses fell into the hands of the queen. Naturally, Her Majesty was very angry. By linking the name of the king and his mistress Voltaire had not only been indiscreet, but, what was worse, he had committed an unpardonable sin against the court etiquette. Even the queen's daughters were filled with wrath by Voltaire's utter lack of delicacy. Their indignation, in fact, surpassed even that of their mother; and it was not appeased until the king, their father, had signed an order exiling Voltaire from Paris.

The king's order was not put into immediate effect, but was kept in reserve for a propitious moment, while the poet continued to remain in the capital. He put the finishing touches on a play, *Semiramis,* which he had written in honor of the Dauphine, but which he had laid aside because of the princess' untimely death. He worked also on the "Age of Louis XIV" and the account of the war of 1741, with an occasional welcome escape into the imaginative realm of the *Pucelle.* Yet his literary labors were not at their happiest, for the calmness of spirit, so essential to their best florescence, had been badly torn and battered under the incessant hammering of the court's endless activities.

One of these was destined to sweep him headlong into the pit of disaster. One night, when the Marquise du Chaletet was playing cards at the queen's table, she ran into a streak of bad luck. The Marquise, who seldom did anything halfway, persisted in trying to recoup her losses, even borrowing money when her own was gone. Despite all her frenzied efforts, her outrageous luck continued, and her losses mounted steadily. Standing at Emilie's side, Voltaire had been watching the play, his alarm increasing as the losses of his mistress went higher and higher. Finally, when they had reached the staggering total of 84,000 francs, his exasperation could no longer contain itself. "Don't you see," he said to her in English, "that you are playing with cheats?" The words had hardly been uttered when he realized that they had been understood. The atmosphere seemed frozen as the Marquise quietly rose, and on the pretext of obtaining additional funds, she and her lover hurriedly withdrew. Their peril, they realized, was very real, and in the grim hope of getting away before the inevitable axe would fall they left the palace as quickly as possible, not even bothering to take along their belongings.

Voltaire sought refuge at Sceaux, with his old and trusted friend, the Duchess of Maine, now a venerable dame of more than seventy, but as delighted as ever by intrigue and scandal and a succulent story. The aged woman welcomed Voltaire with eager arms, and while the Marquise was in Paris endeavoring to settle her gambling losses, the duchess, who needed no instruction in the arts of connivance and conspiracy, carefully concealed Voltaire from the outside world. For two months the poet remained in hiding, staying in his room during the daytime, to emerge in the evening for supper, and passing the day's remaining hours in his favorite pastime of conversation. In the solitude of his quarters, Voltaire forgot the horror of reality and, soaring into the realm of happy fancy, he busied himself with writing. What he wrote was something entirely new; neither drama nor history—but romance. Yet it was of a tone that was peculiar, if not unique. Light, satirical, sparkling with excellent badinage, it laughed at the world and its interminable follies. In particular it laughed at the author's enemies. All day long in the cloister of his study Voltaire roasted them in the slow and hellish flames of satire until, done to an appetizing turn, they were ready in the evening for the amusement of the enchanted duchess. Thus Voltaire created his philosophical romances *Barbouc, Memmon, Micromegas,* and *Zadig.*

Micromegas is said to have been inspired by Swift's Brobdingnagians and partly by Voltaire's Newtonian studies. It is a humorous slap at the conception of the orthodox heavens. Under Voltaire's direction an inhabitant from Saturn and another from Sirius undertake to convince the inhabitants of the earth of their utter insignificance and of the pettiness of their planet when contrasted to the infinite vastness of the universe.

In *Barbouc* Voltaire sought to show the alternate good and evil of mankind. Barbouc has been sent by Ituriel to make a study of conditions in Persepolis, which is in reality the city of Paris, to determine whether the metropolis should be destroyed or preserved. What Barbouc beholds fills him with mixed feelings; one day he is incensed, and is for the immediate and complete destruction of the city; the next day, lifted to the heights of rapture by

what he perceives, Barbouc is all for the city's preservation. Torn between good and evil, Barbouc reports to
Ituriel that "there are some pretty good things in abuses."
Accordingly, Barbouc's superior decides "to let the world
go, for even if everything is not right, everything is tolerable."

Zadig is an analysis of the mystery of human happiness
which, under Voltaire's scalpel, is revealed as something
pathetically rare and elusive. In essence Zadig's adventures
are those of Voltaire. Like his creator, Zadig tries to live
according to wisdom and virtue; and like his creator, he
reaps a multiude of misfortunes and disasters. Chief among
Zadig's tormentors, as one might expect, are the theologians—in particular one Yebor, who, of course, is Boyer,
the Bishop of Mirepoix. Voltaire, naturally, made the
most of his opportunity to ridicule his ancient enemy, pin-
ning him under his magnifying glass, and with an almost
sadistic pleasure, exposing the prelate's ineptitude, fanaticism and stupidity. Zadig is said to represent Voltaire's
deal for himself—what he would have liked had he been
able to live a life of pure reason. Banished, like his creator,
from his native city, Zadig "directed his course by the
stars."

> The constellations of Orion and the brilliant
> Dog Star guided him toward the port of Canopus.
> He gazed in admiration at those vast globes of
> light which appear to our eyes as so many little
> sparks, while the earth, which is in truth nothing
> but an imperceptible point in nature, appears so
> great and so noble to our fond imaginations. He
> looked upon men as they truly are, insects devour-
> ing one another on a little atom of mud. This

true picture seemed to annihilate his fortunes, by
showing him the nothingness of his own being.
. . . His soul reached up into infinity and, detached from his senses, contemplated the un-
changing order of the universe.

Of the romances written at Sceaux, the cleverest is *Memmon,* in which the leading character "conceived one day
the mad project of becoming perfectly wise." In order to
achieve this extraordinary state he decided "to be free
from all the passions." "I will never fall in love with a
woman," he declared; "for when I see a perfect beauty, I
shall say to myself 'those cheeks will be wrinkled some day,
those beautiful eyes will have red lids, that rounded breast
will be flat and pendulous; that beautiful head will become
bald. Now I will have only to see her at the present moment with the same eyes that I shall fix upon her then,
and assuredly that head will never turn mine.'" For the
sake of attaining perfect wisdom Memmon will not only
never fall in love, but he will also never get drunk; thus
he is certain he will avoid poor health, headaches and the
loss of his reason. In the hands of Voltaire, Memmon's
high resolutions have little chance of success. No sooner
does he resolve never to fall in love than he is ensnared by
some designing wench. He drinks too much wine, loses all
his property in a dice game, and to add injury to humiliation, has a dice cup thrown at him by a friend, which
causes him to lose the sight of one of his eyes. Distressed
but not disillusioned, Memmon hopes for some help from
the king, who, though apparently impressed by his story,
hands over the case to one of his subordinates. Yet, instead
of dispensing the expected justice the king's official up-
braids Memmon for having dared to ask for it. "Abandon

this affair, my friend," he advises him, "if you want to keep your remaining eye."

After the Marquise had satisfied her creditors she joined Voltaire at Sceaux. He now felt safe enough to emerge from his hideout; yet the strain and confinement of the past few months had been severe, and once more his delicate constitution gave way. He became easily upset; and his digestion, always inconstant, now betrayed him completely. Emilie tried to cheer him up. With the help of the Duchess of Maine she persuaded him to prolong his stay at Sceaux, whose gayety and diversions, she hoped, would serve as a pleasant and beneficent tonic. For a time Voltaire seemed to respond to Emilie's treatment, and he participated with apparent abandon in Sceaux's unending festivities. But it soon became apparent that the cure was only temporary: Voltaire was neither well nor happy.

In the belief that a few weeks in Paris might benefit the poet, the Marquise persuaded him to go with her to the capital. They were there only a short time, however, when Emilie decided that Cirey might be even better—and to Cirey accordingly they went.

The magic of Cirey appeared to revive Voltaire, and soon he began to be more like his old self. It was obvious that here he felt at home; and though Emilie continued to force diversions and entertainments upon him, as though these had been prescribed by a physician, it was now possible to elude them. Thus, for the greater part of the day he remained in his rooms where he concentrated on his literary projects; while the Marquise in the meantime stayed for herself, working in the main on a translation of Newton's *Principia*.

The relationship between this man and woman had now passed into its fifteenth year; and, in its relentless way, time had begun to put its mark upon Voltaire. At fifty-three he had slipped unmistakably into the first stages of age. The ardors which the passionate Emilie had once inflamed in him had now transformed themselves into the quiet glow of warm affection; imperceptibly the lover had become the friend. Of this change Voltaire himself was sadly aware. "If you wish me still to love," he wrote to his mistress, then

> *Give me back love's youthful days;*
> *Join to twilight's fading rays*
> *Dawn's resplendent heavens above.*

> *Man dies twice, 'tis very clear;*
> *Cease to love, be no one's swain,*
> *That's a death that brings great pain;*
> *Cease to live, that's no man's fear.*

To Emilie time had been more gentle. Indeed, at forty-two she appeared to be in the prime of life. Never beautiful, her mannish features had been softened by the years, and by some strange paradox of nature, they now actually seemed more attractive than when she had been in the first blush of youth. Nor had her passions diminished. They burned as hotly as ever, and mere poems, beautiful though they were, could not still them. When she perceived her lover settling gently into the state of friendship, she tried at first to love for two. But that she soon found was no remedy. For her, love was still physical, and no illusion of being loved could ever satisfy her. Her heart, she felt, "had

been led insensibly to the gentle sentiment of friendship";
but her heart, she realized, still beat with "passions which
had neither declined nor moderated."

Soon after their return to Cirey, Voltaire and the Marquise received an invitation from the former King of
Poland, Stanislas, to join him in Lorraine. There at Luneville old Stanislas went through the pretense of keeping
court. He himself had long since relinquished his royal
ambitions, and now he devoted himself, with apparent enjoyment, to the pursuit of the simpler pleasures. Interested,
like his royal colleague at Potsdam, in science, Stanislas
had converted his palace into a "hall of machines" full of
the latest scientific paraphernalia. When he wasn't peering through telescopes or microscopes, he busied himself
about the palace grounds, pottering in rock gardens, inspecting bird houses, or offering ever ready suggestions to
his workmen. His mistress, the Madame de Boufflers, by
some strange dictate of fate, had remained loyal to him,
even after the decline of his fortune, and now in the years
that still remained she was striving, with tenderness and
understanding, to fill them with happiness. To the disgust
of the old king's daughter, the Queen of France, her father
had become an admirer of Voltaire. Worse than even that,
Stanislas had been converted into an incurable skeptic—
there was a God, he felt certain, but the priests, he felt just
as certain, were not his friends.

Such a man was obviously one to Voltaire's liking. At
Luneville the poet stayed with him as much as possible;
he inspected the "hall of machines"; he peered through
telescopes and microscopes; and when the day had yielded
its full share of activities and observations, the poet and
Stanislas, who both dreaded going to bed, would glide into

an easy conversation. They would then skim through the domains of politics and religion, philosophy and letters, touching on God, tolerance, justice, the Jesuits, and insolent fellows like Mirepoix; and they would end almost invariably with the follies "of their colleagues, the members of the human race."

Voltaire settled into Luneville's benevolent hospitality with a feeling of ease and delicious comfort. His happiness didn't last very long, for discordant notes had come from Paris and the poet became alarmed. His enemies, it appeared, were up to their old tricks and were conspiring to ruin his new play, *Semiramis*. Voltaire had written to the Queen of France, imploring her help, for, as he explained, *Semiramis*, having been composed in honor of the late Dauphine, deserved no calumny. But the Queen of France remained indifferent; and when the poet saw that he could expect no help from Her Majesty, he turned to Madame de Pompadour, who promised to see what she could do. Becoming more and more alarmed by the ominous reports emanating from the capital, Voltaire decided to pay Paris a secret visit. Emilie, for once, made no effort to detain him; on the contrary, it seemed almost as if she was somewhat relieved to see him go.

He took with him his valet, Longchamp; and soon after their arrival in the capital, Voltaire appeared in the headquarters of his foes, the Café Procope. In a dark corner he sat huddled for the greater part of an evening, bespectacled and heavily bewigged, in the garb of an old priest, bowing ostensibly over his breviary, but listening eagerly to the unfolding schemes of his enemies, and restraining himself with difficulty as they tossed abuse and mockery upon his name.

The excitement proved too much, and on his return to Luneville he fell ill. No doubt his attack was real enough, though, in his love of the theatrical, he tried to make as much of it as possible. When his frightened valet wanted to rush out for help, Voltaire entreated him, with quivering voice, not to abandon him, but to remain near him and "to cast a little earth upon his body when he had breathed his last."

Voltaire recovered quickly enough, and when he returned to Luneville he lost no time in reporting the details of his latest illness to Frederick. He implored His Majesty to be gracious enough to send him "a pound of genuine Stahl's pills," adding, somewhat seductively, that "this will bring me to a state which will enable me to pay my court to you this summer." Frederick sent Voltaire the desired pills, although he took no stock in the poet's promise to come to Berlin. "The pills you ask of me," he warned, "are sufficient to purge all France and to kill your three Academies. Do you imagine that these pills are sweetmeats?" The king added that he was angry with Voltaire—really angry. Why had he gone to Luneville instead of coming to Berlin? Didn't Voltaire know that peace had been signed and that his old friend was now more anxious than ever to see him? "They say," he wrote, "that King Stanislas enchants Madame du Chatelet, and the gentleman-in-ordinary of Louis XV, that is to say, he cannot do without you both . . . and while he enjoys all sorts of pleasures, I poor fool, perhaps cursed of God, write verses." "I admire your verses passionately," Voltaire replied, "but write none myself. I limit myself to prose as a wretched historiographer should." He added, with piercing irony, that he counted "the poor people killed in the last war and always state the truth within a few thousands." "Sire," he concluded, "Your Majesty writes beautiful poetry." Yet, despite Voltaire's cutting remarks, Frederick continued to nurse the hope that some day he might yet win the poet for Potsdam. "Come," he exclaimed, "come without teeth, without ears, without eyes, without legs if you cannot come otherwise; so long as that indefinable something which makes you think and inspires you so beautifully comes with you, that will suffice."

Destiny, however, had other things in store for Voltaire. In its mysterious way it had ushered a young nobleman and officer, the handsome Marquis de Saint-Lambert, into the presence of the Marquise du Chatelet. She had been drawn to him from the first, and though he was ten years her junior, she soon felt herself passionately in love. Saint-Lambert possessed the youth which Voltaire had lost, and before long Emilie had discovered a way to still her unquenched desires. She had hoped that her affair would remain a secret, but her plans unfortunately went awry. One evening Voltaire unintentionally surprised the couple in the rooms of the Marquise engaged "in something besides verses and philosophy." Jealousy and anger rushed over him and he burst into a tirade of furious abuse. But the young Marquis was not the man to take anybody's insolence. Who was Voltaire, he demanded, to give himself airs to censure his conduct? If the Marquis' deportment had displeased anyone, then all that person had to do was to leave the chateau!

Stung by Saint-Lambert's impertinence, Voltaire ordered his valet to summon him a carriage at once—he was leaving for Paris. But the valet, familiar with Voltaire's sudden impulses, first consulted the Marquise, who told him to report to his master that no carriage was available.

Soon afterward there was a knock at Voltaire's door. Madame du Chatelet had come. Sitting at the foot of Voltaire's bed, as she had done so often before, she talked to him, first in English, then in French. But Voltaire's wrath would not be soothed. "What!" he expostulated. "You want me to believe you after what I have seen! I have exhausted my health, my fortune! I have sacrificed all for you—and you deceive me!"

He was wrong, Emilie persisted—quite wrong. She loved him; she loved only him; she would always love him. But he must realize there were other considerations, too. Had he not complained for a long time that he was ill, that his strength was waning? She was, she told him, "extremely afflicted by it," for his health "was very dear to her." "On your part," she said, "you have always shown much interest in mine; you have known and approved the regimen which suits it; you have even favored and shared it as long as it was in your power to do so." Since he himself had admitted, the Marquise now concluded, that he could not continue to take care of her except to his great harm, then ought he be offended "if one of his friends supplied his place?"

When she had finished there was a long silence. Her voice, soft and persuasive, had soothed the harassed poet. The wrath and disgust which had rushed over him so tumultuously only a few moments ago, and which had seemed so overmastering, so overwhelming, now suddenly lost their grip. Under the spell of Emilie the man became the philosopher. "You are right, madame," he said slowly, "you are always right—but since things are as they are, at least let them not pass before my eyes." They seemed good friends when the Marquise quietly withdrew at last.

Shortly after she had left there was another knock at Voltaire's door. This time the visitor was Saint-Lambert. He had come to apologize for his harsh words. But Voltaire had already forgotten all. Seizing Saint-Lambert by the hand, he declared that it was he and not the Marquis who had been in the wrong. "You are in the happy age of love and delight," he said. "Enjoy those brief moments. An old man, an invalid like me, is not made for the pleasures." The next day Voltaire, the Marquise and Saint-Lambert had supper together. They were in excellent spirits; for by the inscrutable workings of fate the very thing which should have torn them apart in angry conflict had on the contrary united them in friendship. "Saint-Lambert," Voltaire declared,

> *it is all for thee*
> *The flower grows;*
> *The rose's thorns are but for me,*
> *For thee the love.*

Late in December the Marquise and Voltaire returned to Cirey. They busied themselves as usual with their writings, and for a time contentment descended upon the chateau. Their mere proximity seemed to please them, and in such an atmosphere they could have toiled forever. But suddenly the Marquise du Chatelet was to make a hideous discovery: at the age of forty-two she had become pregnant.

At first, in the storm of her distress, she could not believe it; then when she realized that her fears were really the truth, she confided in Voltaire. Wasting no time, he

summoned Saint-Lambert to a conference with him and
the Marquise. The first question to be decided, he said,
was whether the condition of the Marquise could be concealed from the public; to which, they all agreed, the answer was plainly no. In that case what was of most importance, Voltaire declared, was the question of paternity—a
matter which seemed to be somewhat distressing to Saint-
Lambert, as well as for the Marquise. As for Voltaire, he
was ready, he submitted, to include the expected infant
"among the miscellaneous works of Madame du Chatelet,"
but that, unfortunately, would have to remain their own
little secret. Meanwhile, he felt it would be best "not to
falsify the legal axiom that he was the father whom the
nuptial relation indicates"; and that accordingly the thing
to do would be to make the Marquis du Chatelet believe
that the child was rightfully his.

At bottom this was not so easy, for the Marquis had not
had intimate relations with his wife for many a year. Yet
to the imaginative Voltaire even such an obstacle did not
appear insurmountable. He felt certain that with proper
planning everything would turn out as desired. It was decided that Emilie should write at once to her husband,
who was then some hundred miles away at Dijon. She was
to urge him to come to Cirey immediately to attend to
some business, so as to avoid a threatened lawsuit.

The Marquis came. He was delighted to find Voltaire
and Saint-Lambert, who for their part omitted nothing in
their effort to make his visit most agreeable. Nor did his
wife remain in obscurity. For the benefit of her long neglected husband she arranged all sorts of entertainment,
making sure to include what he enjoyed most—a hunting
party crowned by an elaborate banquet. In the words of

Voltaire's omnipresent valet, "the Marquis performed well his part at table, having previously gained a great appetite. . . . All the guests were in the best of humor and testified their delight in seeing Monsieur du Chatelet again." In the course of the dinner he regaled his guests "with stories of the last campaign," to which Voltaire added a few choice stories of his own, but of a far less serious nature.

Next to the exuberant Marquis sat his wife. She had prepared herself for the occasion with infinite care, with the full consciousness of the importance of her part. She paid her husband pretty little attentions who promptly responded with flattering compliments. She saw to it that he drank considerable quantities of champagne, whose magic qualities seemed to rejuvenate him most miraculously. From that night on, the couple occupied the same suite of rooms, while nothing was left undone by the conspirators to preserve the illusion of conjugal felicity. At length, when several weeks had passed, the Marquise confided to her husband that, from certain signs, she had reason to think she was going to be a mother.

The Marquis' first reaction was that of incredible amazement; then, when he realized at last that his wife was in earnest, he rushed out to announce the cause of his happiness to all his friends. Everything was done to make certain that no one would be in doubt that the Marquis was going to be a father. Swiftly the tidings flew through the neighboring countryside, and before long the happy Marquis found himself giving thanks to the congraulations of every neighbor for many miles around.

The Marquis, no doubt, would have liked to stay at Cirey; but that joy was denied him. His regiment called and he had to leave. The Marquis de Saint-Lambert also found it necessary to say good-bye; he was returning to his old haunts at Luneville, where already he was casting amorous eyes on another lady. As for Voltaire and the Marquise, they decided to spend a little time in Paris. "All four," Voltaire's valet remarked subsequently, "set out from Cirey, well content with what had passed there."

But that contentment was not to linger very long. As the time for the child's birth drew closer, the Marquise desired to return to Luneville, so that she might be near her child's real father. Voltaire went with her. He had written in the meantime to Frederick, telling him that he would have to postpone his visit. He told the king that the Marquise would have a child in the fall, and that at her age this could be very dangerous. The wily Frederick quickly suspected that neither Voltaire nor the Marquis du Chatelet was the child's father. "Listen," he wrote, "I have a whim to see you. . . . I have leisure this year, and God knows if I'll ever have it again. Madame du Chatelet will be delivered in September; you are not a midwife, she can have her child perfectly well without you; and if necessary, you can go back to Paris." "Not even Frederick, before whom they tremble," Voltaire replied, "can prevent me from carrying out a duty I consider indispensable. I am neither a maker of children nor a doctor nor a midwife, and even for Your Majesty's sake I will not leave the woman who may die in September."

As the critical time drew nearer, the Marquise du Chatelet grew despondent. She seemed to regret her fate; at the same time she poured out tender evocations of love for Saint-Lambert. "I am wretched to a degree," she confessed in a note to him, "which would frighten me if I believed in presentiments." Voltaire tried his best to cheer her up. "Madame du Chatelet is not yet delivered," he declared. "It gives her more trouble to produce a child than a book." A few days later, however, Voltaire was able to write with relief that "this evening Madame du Chatelet, being at her desk, according to her laudable custom, said, *'But I feel something!'* That something was a little girl, who came into the world forthwith. It was placed upon a volume of geometry, which happened to be lying near, and the mother has gone to bed." A few days later the infant died.

Its passing, however, was barely noticed, for the mother had suddenly developed a fever. Her husband was hurriedly summoned. She became well only to have a relapse. She lay back among the cushions, glancing at her company. What an incongruous company it was, her husband, Voltaire, Saint-Lambert—all three were there. On the fourth day the weather became very warm; she wanted a drink, an iced drink she liked very much. It made her very sick, but two days later she had recovered and apparently the crisis was over. In the evening she began to cough; she seemed to be struggling for breath, only to stop abruptly. Saint-Lambert, who was with her, thought she had fainted and tried to revive her with smelling salts, at the same time sending for her husband and Voltaire. When they came, they knew: they had lost the Marquise forever.

The Marquis, dazed and sobbing, was led out of the room, while Voltaire and Saint-Lambert stared helplessly at the bed. Then Voltaire turned toward Saint-Lambert. He seemed to want to say something, but he changed his mind and slowly left the room. He moved blindly through the halls of the palace, and when he reached the great front door, he tottered and fell insensible to the floor.

When he had recovered, he sent for Longchamp, his valet. He told him he would like the ring on her finger. "It's the ring with my picture in it," he said, "I must have it." The servant hardly knew what to say, for he was aware of the fact that Voltaire's picture had been replaced by that of Saint-Lambert. When Longchamp revealed the truth, Voltaire rose and walked toward the window. "Such are women!" he said. "I took Richelieu out of the ring. Saint-Lambert expelled me. Such is the order of nature—one nail drives out another. So go the things of the world!"

For fifteen years Voltaire had shared his life with the Marquise du Chatelet. He had been attached to her by all the bonds of friendship and gratitude. She had taken him to Cirey at a time when he stood in the shadow of the Bastille. As time moved on, however, her chateau had become much more than a comfortable sanctuary; it had evolved into a home with all the associations of content-ment, and the solidity and permanence for which the poet had longed. Yet in bringing the poet to Cirey the Marquise had not been entirely altruistic; for at heart she was a possessive woman whose desire for fame often devoured her, and who was quick to perceive in Voltaire a chance to gratify her ambitions. But if it pleased her to have the poet at her feet, she at least responded toward him with a solicitude that was sincere and affectionate. She was his mistress, but she was also his friend, understanding and appreciative, who took pride in his achievements and who knew how to cater to his egotism. Her influence on him no doubt was substantial, although it was not entirely to his best interest. She made it possible for him to work in ease and contentment; and it was with obvious satisfaction that he gave himself to his tasks. But the promise foreshadowed by the "English Letters," that he would embark upon a career of struggle against the iniquities of the Ancient Regime—that promise was not fulfilled. Instead, he had allowed himself to become sidetracked in a network of minor and insignificant bypaths. He dabbled in scientific experiments; he toyed with metaphysics; he engaged in secret diplomacy; he flattered the king and the Pope; he became an Academician. His writings, on the whole, were in the old and familiar vein—plays that were polished and cleverly constructed, but which were stereotyped and theatrical; verses that rhymed and scanned beautifully, but whose clichés anesthetized the feelings; essays on science and metaphysics which, but for their excellent and sprightly prose, were predestined to obscurity.

Yet for Voltaire the fifteen years at Cirey were of tremendous significance. He had come there as a writer of undoubted talent; when he left he had an international reputation. Although his work during this period is today considered largely insignificant, in the eyes of his contemporaries this was not the case. At the time of the Marquise's death, Voltaire was esteemed throughout Europe not only as the greatest living dramatist and poet, but also as a man of incredibly vast knowledge, a proponent of new ideas, a thinker of the highest calibre. On the threshold of sixty, Voltaire had become one of the most famous men in the world.

The removal of Emilie left Voltaire utterly disconsolate. Darkness had suddenly descended upon him; he felt old and sick; loneliness engulfed him. The thought came to him that perhaps the peacefulness of Cirey might comfort him; but he found its solitude appalling; and its memories, once so pleasant, filled him with dread. In the tumult of his anguish he began to accuse himself. How foolish he had been—how utterly foolish to have taken the whole affair so lightly! "Alas," he confided to his old friend, the Marquise du Deffand, "we had turned that event into a joke. . . . If anything could augment the horror of my condition, it would be to have taken with gayety an adventure whose outcome will poison the remainder of my miserable life."

There was no solace for the poet at Cirey and he stayed only long enough to put his affairs in order. After a fortnight he left for Paris, where he planned to make his abode in quarters he had rented from the Marquis in the du Chatelet town house. With Voltaire came his servant Longchamp, whose duties were now more those of a nurse than those of a valet. Voltaire's emotions had been badly shaken, and as Longchamp ministered to his needs, the valet noticed, with fear and alarm, how his master was succumbing to the strain. There were moments when Voltaire appeared to be losing his mind. He began to have hallucinations. He would imagine he saw Emilie before him and he would call out to her. One night when he couldn't sleep, the poet got out of bed, and while groping about the room in the dark, stumbled over a pile of books. He was too weak to rise, and when Longchamp came to him at last, he found his master speechless and almost frozen.

Yet Voltaire was not the man to become a permanent victim of his grief. Though his sensitivity was great, it was counterbalanced admirably by his sense of the practical. As the horror of the first dreadful moments receded mercifully into the background, only his loneliness remained—and soon even this was to pass, when his niece, the widowed Madame Denis, came to live with him. Gradually his overwrought emotions gave way before a determination to work. He wanted to work with every ounce of his being, relentlessly, for the rest of his life. It was not easy at first. He found himself staring at his desk, passing whole hours without writing a single line. Only one thought possessed him day and night. Yet, under the pressure of his determination, that thought began to disintegrate, like a river's ice floes in the spring, and before long his creative thoughts began to move once more.

Voltaire's sorrow had not subdued his enemies; on the contrary they took full advantage of his momentary weakness and, led by Piron and Crebillon, two rival playwrights, they conspired vigorously to ruin his reputation as a dramatist. With Voltaire out of the way they hoped to have clear sailing for their own compositions. As for Voltaire, he lost no time in trying to repay his enemies in ther own coin by rewriting some of the plays of Crebillon. He hoped that his own versions would be superior to those of his rival, and so loudly applauded by the public, that Crebillon would be obliged to hide his head in shame. Voltaire's efforts, however, were not very successful; and instead of silencing his foes once for all, they merely incited them to more aggressive action. They ridiculed him in a steady stream of burlesques and parodies; they tried to destroy his remaining influence with Madame de Pompadour; finally they induced some of his best actors to desert him. When this happened they were certain they had brought him to his knees.

Voltaire refused to capitulate. He rented the Marquis' entire house and transformed its largest room into a little theatre. Here he produced his favorite plays, acting in them himself, and employing for his cast a group of amateurs recruited mostly from working people. One of them, Lekain, possessed extraordinary talent, and this the trained eye of Voltaire was quick to notice. He encouraged Lekain in every way, advising him, coaching time, and at times helping him with money. Then one day he assisted him in getting a part in the professional theatre. From then on Lekain marched from one triumph to another, until with the passage of time he became acclaimed as one of France's greatest actors.

Voltaire's little theatre was the first of its kind in France. He had intended it as an answer to his enemies and for the pleasure of his friends. Yet its fame spread swiftly, and before long the clamor for admission became so great that its creator found it necessary to issue tickets. The tremendous success of Voltaire's private theatre was not lost on Versailles, where Madame de Pompadour "after long hesitation" produced *Alzire*. She acted the titular part herself, and hoped that Voltaire would be able to watch her—but the poet found himself "regretfully unable to be present."

Frederick The Great

THE DEATH of the Marquise du Chatelet had removed the main obstacle to Frederick's desire to acquire Voltaire. No sooner was she in her grave than seductive notes began to arrive from Berlin. The king wanted Voltaire—and he wanted him forthwith. "I respected the friendship which bound you to Madame du Chatelet," he explained, "but after her, I am one of your oldest friends." Voltaire tried to put Frederick off with vague promises; he couldn't come now; he wasn't very well; and before he could leave France he would have to have the king's permission, since officially he was still a member of Louis' household. When Voltaire continued to procrastinate, Frederick undertook to scold him. "You will never lack excuses," he exclaimed; "an imagination as keen as yours is inexhaustible." Yet Frederick was careful to repeat his invitation; and this time the poet accepted: he would be in Berlin by early summer. "I cannot be in your Heaven, Sire," he wrote, "before the first days of July." At the same time he was careful to make Frederick agree to pay for his traveling expenses.

Late in June Voltaire reached Compiègne, where he hoped to receive Louis' permisson for his projected visit. "I am at Compiègne," he wrote Frederick, "only to ask the greatest king of the south for permission to throw myself at the feet of the greatest king of the north." The reception accorded Voltaire by "the greatest king of the south" was not very cordial. "You can set out whenever you wish," Louis told Voltaire and turned his back.

Voltaire arrived in Berlin on the tenth of July. The Carrousel, a festive event of considerable importance, was to be celebrated in a few days. In anticipation of it the Berliners had gone to great length to give their city the proper festive appearance. What Voltaire beheld, he said, "was at once a spectacle of the time of Louis XIV, and a Chinese festival of lanterns. Forty-six thousand little lanterns lighted the ground. Three thousand soldiers under arms lined all the avenues, and the amphitheatre was enclosed by four immense grandstands." Soon after his arrival in Prussia Voltaire visited the amphitheatre. Here he saw army maneuvers of various kinds. "Four 'quadrilles,' or rather four little armies of Romans, Carthaginians, Persians and Greeks entered the lists, and maneuvered to the sound of martial music." When the displays were over, the judges picked the winners, while one of the royal princesses who, Voltaire declared, "looked like Venus awarding the golden apple," distributed the prizes.

Impressive as all this pageantry seemed to the Frenchman, he was touched more deeply by an incident which was personal. It happened in the amphitheatre shortly before the arrival of Frederick. As Voltaire was walking to one of the royal boxes someone in the crowd recognized him, and before long his name appeared to be on everyone's lips. Aware of the commotion he was causing, Voltaire continued his march through the arena. One of the spectators, observing the great man's evident self-satisfaction, remarked that "he wore a modest countenance, but joy painted itself in his eyes."

Frederick made generous arrangements for Voltaire's comfort. The poet was given a suite of rooms in the royal palace both at Potsdam and Berlin; and soon after his arrival he was made a Court Chamberlain with an annual pension of four thousand dollars, in addition to being awarded the Prussian Order of Merit. Frederick relaxed his wonted thrift even further by offering Voltaire's niece, Madame Denis, a pension of eight hundred dollars for life, if she came to Berlin to keep house for her uncle. However, Madame Denis did not accept the offer; much as she liked money, to leave Paris for its Prussian imitation seemed to her quite unthinkable.

Despite Frederick's manifestations of generosity, the monarch had not changed his opinion of Voltaire's character. Indeed, he was now more certain than ever that the French poet was a thorough scoundrel. Less than a year earlier Frederick had confided to one of his courtly scientists that he considered it "a pity that a soul as cowardly as his (Voltaire's) should be linked to such a wonderful genius. He has the caressing ways and the maliciousness of a monkey." Yet the monkey apparently had some redeeming qualities, of which his mastery of the French muse was by no means the least important. "Good things may be learned from a scoundrel," Frederick declared. "I want to know his French; what do I care about his character!"

The king's remark, so cynical and yet so forthright, was the basis of his entire attitude toward Voltaire. Frederick's devotion to the French muse had become an irresistible passion. Like most well-educated Germans of his class, the King of Prussia preferred to speak in French, employing German only to address his servants. To him, as to most of his contemporaries, western culture had reached its richest bloom in France, and French literature, especially that of the golden age of Louis XIV, represented its loveliest flower. But Frederick was not satisfied with mere appreciation; in him smoldered the desire to create; he yearned to write like Racine and Corneille; he wanted to express himself in odes and madrigals that would rank with the very best. To attain his lofty goal Frederick naturally needed help—and as his eye scanned the literary firmament it inevitably came upon Voltaire. As the acknowledged heir of France's classic tradition, the little Frenchman seemed admirably fitted to give the Prussian monarch the guidance he so much desired. A little help from the great man, Frederick felt, would soon bring color and correctness to his ailing verses. Yes, indeed! Frederick was positive that he could learn good things from a scoundrel; and should that scoundrel ever threaten to get out of hand, a prompt cuff from the King of Prussia—a frown on the royal countenance or a threat to stop the poet's pension—and the rogue would soon behave!

As for Voltaire, he, too, was under no illusions. His motives in coming to Berlin were perhaps not as clear as those which had prompted Frederick to invite him. The poet was obviously disgusted with Paris; he was tired of the petty jealousies and the constant bickering; and he was keenly disappointed by the apparent coolness manifested toward him by the French Government. Instead of appreciating him at what he considered to be his full worth, those in authority preferred to ignore him, or even to persecute him. Everything, he felt, was to be feared in Paris as long as he lived; while in Prussia he hoped he could be forever tranquil. Nor could a shrewd man like Voltaire overlook the fact that by going to Potsdam as the guest of the King of Prussia, he was sure to make an impression upon the entire world. On the other hand, he was fully aware of the nature of his position. He knew that his annual pension was not a gift but a salary; it was hard cash paid by one whose thrift bordered on penury, and who would certainly insist on getting his full money's worth. Voltaire realized that he had bartered his freedom for servitude, and that at bottom he was nothing more than a well-paid menial. Voltaire understood clearly with what sort of a man he was dealing. He had not forgotten his Prussian majesty's utter lack of scruples. Frederick's claws had scratched him before, and certainly there was no reason to imagine that they would not do it again.

Life at Potsdam moved along with the regularity of a clock. A worshiper at the shrine of precision, Frederick arranged his life in homage to his idol. There was a certain time for every act, and to perform it at any other time was apparently unthinkable. The king rose at five; at seven he dressed for the day; at ten he met his cabinet; at eleven he reviewed the change of the guard; at twelve-thirty he dined with ministers and ambassadors. Not until five did he become a man of leisure, and even then he continued to live by his timetable. At five His Majesty gave his full attention to the French muse, endeavoring, with an earnestness that was almost comic, to fathom the secret of her charm and to lure her into his own creations. At seven there was a concert at which Frederick played the flute to the accompaniment of his musicians or a quintette of singers, a man, a woman and three eunuchs. The crowning event of the monarch's busy day came in the evening at nine when Frederick joined his boon companions at supper.

The king had surrounded himself with a small group of men—mostly foreigners—whose task was to entertain or instruct him, as his mood would dictate. They were for the most part second-rate men. Algarotti, an Italian, had composed an insignificant book on Newton; d'Arget was the king's secretary and somewhat of a philanderer; d'Argens was an amiable writer with an academic turn of mind; Chasot was a retired major, heavily in debt, but with the distinction of having saved Frederick from capture at the battle of Mollwitz; Pöllnitz was a disintegrating baron who had changed his religion at least a half-dozen times; La Mettrie was a doctor and a writer, as well as an eccentric atheist, who, in Voltaire's opinion, was "very amusing for the first fifteen minutes, but mortally wearisome thereafter."

Such were Frederick's chosen associates. Every evening at the royal supper-parties they were his guests, and while they partook of the monarch's excellent food and champagne, they would exchange epigrams, discuss the Jewish religion, the advantages of platonic love, or the irrefutability of materialism. The king would turn to Algarotti and discourse with him upon the significance of the scientific method; or he would smile upon La Mettrie, who would promptly plunge into a philosophical lecture, only to cross himself on upsetting the salt. Or else the king, unable to curb his inner sadism, would amuse himself by cutting off Pöllnitz's pension, and then slyly suggesting that if the unfortunate butt of the royal humor would forsake his Lutheranism and become a Catholic, his generous Majesty would make him a Silesian Abbot. The monarch had tried to establish the fiction that at his suppers there was no rank—they were all equals and they were friends. However, Frederick could never forget that he was the King of Prussia; and though he tried valiantly to unbend, his stiffness at times was all too obvious, with the result that he was far from popular. One or another of the king's intimates was constantly seeking to get out of his clutches. Chasot and d'Arget did manage to get back to Paris. D'Argens tried to follow their example; he made off several times for France, but having no money, he always returned to his royal master. As for the physician La Mettrie, he made his escape quite unexpectedly—by dying one evening after having devoured a huge paté of eagle, pork, pheasant, and ginger. "Jesus, Mary and Joseph!" he gasped as death put its icy hand upon him. "Ah," said the priest who had been summoned, "at last you have returned to these consoling names." When Frederick was told what the priest had said, he shrugged his shoulders. "I am glad," he remarked, "for the repose of his soul."

Among the persons who made up Frederick's strange and incongruous company, one stood out head and shoulders above the rest—the mathematician Maupertuis, once the teacher of the Marquise du Chatelet but since 1745 the President of the Prussian Academy of Sciences. Maupertuis was not a great mathematician, though his talents were by no means slight. He had led a small expedition to Lapland and by his observations had been able to affirm

Newton's doctrine of the earth's flatness at the poles. Impressed by Maupertuis' accomplishment, as well as by his tremendous display of interest in scientific matters, Frederick had invited him to Berlin where His Majesty hoped he would help to elevate Prussian science to the high place it deserved. The king's choice had not been bad. Maupertuis, who in his younger days had been something of a skeptic, was still able to scintillate occasionally, an attainment which pleased the monarch, who soon found himself calling his President a "man of the intellect." Unfortunately, Maupertuis was over-ambitious. As long as the king's smile beamed upon him he was content; but with the arrival of Voltaire the royal refulgence began to shine in another direction. Not that Frederick had lost any of his admiration for the President. No, for him the king had only the highest regard. But in the presence of the incomparable Voltaire, who could pay attention to Maupertuis? Who could listen to discourses on mathematics when the author of *La Pucelle* was warbling poetry? Decidedly the presence of Voltaire made Maupertuis shrink to insignificance, for the poet towered over the mathematician as Maupertuis towered over d'Arget, Chasot and the rest. In time this became obvious even to Maupertuis, and when it did, he forgot all about his ideal of remaining cool and detached in all things, and became instead a sad and anxious man, consumed by a cancerous jealousy.

If Voltaire had come to Potsdam hoping, as he intimated, to "find a port after thirty years of storm," he was destined to be disappointed. The jealousy and backbiting from which he had fled soon reappeared, not only in the person of the envious Maupertuis, but in the king himself. Voltaire had hoped—somewhat skeptically, it is true—that his "marriage to the King of Prussia" would be happy. Unfortunately, when two egotists such as Voltaire and Frederick, each with a supreme contempt for one another, set up house together, each at the other's expense, there can be only one result—disaster. For a time two such persons may control their inmost feelings, but sooner or later there will come the inevitable explosion and their union will collapse. The difficulties in the relationship between the king and the poet were aggravated by the fact that it was at bottom one of master and servant. Despite his shining chamberlain's key and his Order of Merit, Voltaire was still a paid hireling; while Frederick, despite his efforts to be friendly and informal, was still Voltaire's employer, whose merest whim was law.

Before long there were unmistakable signs of a growing hostility. "When one has sucked the orange, one throws away the peel," somebody told Voltaire that the king had said, when he was asked how much longer he expected to harbor the poet; while Voltaire, impatient at having to correct the king's verses, exclaimed, "Does the man expect me to go on washing his dirty linen forever?" "The monster," Voltaire wrote to Madame Denis, "opens all our mail." "The monkey," Frederick complained, "shows my private letters to his friends." Less than four months after his arrival in Berlin Voltaire told his niece that at Potsdam "there is such a thing as pleasure . . . *but—!* The king's suppers are delicious. We talk reason, wit, science; liberty reigns at the table; he is the soul of all that. . . . My life is free and occupied; *but—but!*" "How happy I should be here," he burst out on another occasion, "but for one thing, His Majesty is utterly heartless!" In the meantime

Frederick was busy writing a verse in which he excoriated Voltaire for his avarice.

It was, indeed, Voltaire's love of money which produced the first serious quarrel. Shortly after settling in the Prussian capital, the poet became involved in a series of dubious financial transactions. The King of Prussia had put a strict ban on such speculation; yet the temptation to make some easy money proved too strong for Voltaire. He took the plunge, and to keep his illegal activity in the dark, he engaged a Jewish money-lender as his go-between. Unfortunately, Voltaire quarreled with his agent, who, very likely, was no more scrupulous than the poet; there was an acrimonious law suit in which both parties deluged one another with charges and counter-charges; and though in the end the Frenchman won his suit—largely on a technical point—he emerged from the courtroom with anything but an impeccable character. It is almost certain—though the evidence is inadequate—that in order to win his case Voltaire committed forgery.

When Frederick heard of the affair he flew into a rage. He summoned his secretary d'Arget. "Write him," the king ordered, "to be gone from my domains within twenty-four hours." Yet before the order could be carried out, Frederick had cooled off and changed his mind—he could not give up his poet so soon. He punished him, instead, with a stern rebuke. "You have caused a frightful turmoil throughout the entire city," he declared. "The affair . . . is so well known that grievous complaints have been forwarded to me concerning it." He went on to say that he had been glad to receive Voltaire in his house; that he esteemed his intellect, his talents, his knowledge; that he had thought a man of the poet's age would be glad to seek refuge in a tranquil haven. "I kept the peace in my house until your arrival," Frederick exclaimed; "and I notify you that if you have a passion to intrigue and cabal you have come to the wrong man."

Meanwhile life at Potsdam proceeded on its usual course. It was a simple life, austere and retired, rigidly regulated, and devoid of the pleasures usually associated with courtly living. "How do you pass the time here?" someone once asked one of the royal princes. "We conjugate the verb 'to be bored,' " was the answer. But that verb was not in Voltaire's vocabulary. Closeted in his study, with its windows overlooking the palace gardens, with its yellowish walls, adorned with the gaudy shapes of flowers, fruits and birds, the tireless man worked for most of the day; while on the nearby parade-grounds tall and fierce-looking soldiers goose-stepped to the roll of the drum. "Potsdam," Voltaire informed his niece, "is full of moustaches and helmets of grenadiers; thank God I do not see them. I work peacefully in my rooms."

In particular he labored on the "Age of Louis XIV," which he had started in his youth in the chateau of the old Marquis de Villars. The work had grown to three well-filled volumes and was almost ready for the printer. Like the "History of Charles XII," Voltaire's Louis XIV was an attempt to portray not an individual but a culture. "Former historians," the author wrote, "too often resembled the tyrants of whom they speak. They sacrificed the race to a single man." It so happened that Voltaire believed, as did most of his educated contemporaries, that the age of Louis XIV was the most civilized in recorded history. He was deeply impressed by its order, its polish and grandeur; by the government's encouragement of manufacturing and commerce; and by the tremendous intellectual and literary activity. Yet the author of the "English Letters" could hardly have been expected to overlook the evils that dimmed much of the era's lustre. He recognized the fact that there had been too many wars of aggression; that the government had been profligate and rash in its expenditures; and that the country had been overtaxed and the people exploited. His method, as in the case of Charles XII, anticipated the procedures of modern historical research; he tapped original, unpublished sources; assiduously checked and rechecked them; weeded out the legendary from the factual; and tried—though he did not altogether succeed—to write in the vein of a scholar rather than in that of a patriot. For this he expected to be criticized. "Some good French patriots," he said, "who have read the book will raise a noble clamor against me, for having praised Marlborough and Eugene; and some good churchmen will damn me for having turned into ridicule our Jansenism and Molinism."

In spite of Voltaire's efforts to work peacefully in his rooms, and avoid all possible trouble, it soon became obvious that at Potsdam trouble could not be easily avoided. The ominous rumblings beneath the surface were plainly audible. Certainly they must have been heard by Maupertuis; but instead of trying to conciliate Voltaire, the President was rash enough to antagonize him. When Voltaire became entangled in the meshes of his law suit, Maupertuis intrigued vigorously against him. While he was doing his utmost to bring about a complete rupture between the poet and the king, the President tried at the same time to improve his own standing with Frederick by publishing a book of "Letters," in which he treated a number of miscellaneous scientific subjects. The volume was dull and insignificant, not to say stupid. Among other things the verifier of one of the Newtonian doctrines contended "that a gigantic hole should be bored through the center of the earth for scientific experiment thereat"; and "that to prolong life for hundreds of years the pores should be closed by applying a kind of varnish to the body."

Voltaire read Maupertuis' work. Not long afterward at one of the king's supper-parties he addressed its author.

"Your book," he remarked, "has given me great pleasure —though there are some obscurities in it, which we will discuss together."

"Obscurities!" Maupertuis exploded; "it might very well have obscurities for *you!*"

For a moment Voltaire stared at the President, as if he were mentally measuring him. "You have my esteem, mon Président," he said. "You want war. You shall have it."

In the war that followed Maupertuis had the distinction of firing the first shot. He did it by giving his official approbation to La Beaumelle, a disreputable man of letters, who in one of his writings had suggested that Voltaire was "a buffoon and a dwarf" on whom the King of Prussia was wasting his money. When Voltaire indignantly protested, Maupertuis dismissed the matter with an airy gesture.

Voltaire's opportunity for a counter-attack came in the spring of 1752. Some years previously the President had discovered—so he believed—a mathematical law, the "principle of least action." Actually the principle was important, as its subsequent history was to show; but unfortunately Maupertuis had not expressed it correctly; and within a short time another mathematician was able to

make a far more valid enunciation. To this Maupertuis
paid no attention: he continued to take full credit for the
"principle of least action," which by now, he was able to
report, was one of the main reasons for believing in God.
Shortly after Voltaire's arrival in Prussia another mathematician, Koenig, composed a brief and dignified essay in
which he attacked both the validity and the originality of
Maupertuis' law, and offered in substantiation of his argument an unpublished letter from Leibnitz in which the
law had been correctly expressed. Maupertuis, enraged by
what he considered an affront, promptly declared Leibnitz's letter to be a forgery unworthy of any consideration.
When Koenig tried to remonstrate, Maupertuis decided to
silence him once and forever. He convened a meeting of
the Academy of Science, of which Koenig happened to be
a member, and proposed that it should solemnly denounce
Koenig as a rogue and a forger, and the letter of Leibnitz
imaginary and fraudulent. The members of the Academy
were cowed; their pensions depended almost wholly on
the President's good will; accordingly they passed sentence
upon the unfortunate Koenig with only one dissenting
vote.

Voltaire observed the feud between Koenig and his ac-
cuser with a perfervid interest. Its outcome filled him with
horror and indignation. "Never," he exclaimed, "was there
such a thing as a criminal suit in an academy of sciences."
At the same time he saw that his opportunity had come.
Plainly, Maupertuis had blundered. He had erred in trying to claim credit for a discovery he had not really made;
he had erred in maintaining that the Leibnitz letter was
false; and he had erred when, by virtue of his office, he
coerced the Academicians to take disciplinary action in an

affair which ought to have been judged on its scientific merits alone. Voltaire realized, with pleasant anticipation, that if he struck now he could easily annihilate this "turkey-cock who thought himself an eagle." There was only one factor to deter him. An attack on Maupertuis was certain to displease the king, for to Frederick the President was the embodiment of all the hopes and plans for the advancement of Prussian science. Any criticism of the Academy or its President would inevitably provoke the sensitive Frederick. But these considerations Voltaire brushed aside; he would take the risk; he would give Maupertuis the war he had wanted; and if the king joined the fray, he would take him on, too.

As a precaution Voltaire withdrew all his cash from Berlin and deposited it far from the Prussian arm, with the Duke of Württemberg. "I am quietly putting my affairs in order," he wrote in an ominous note to his niece. Then, on September 18, 1752, he struck. On that day there appeared in the papers a brief article entitled "A Reply of an Academician of Berlin to an Academician of Paris." It was an analysis of Koenig's case against Maupertuis. Frederick, however, was not misled by the author's anonymity. Only one person could have written with such remorseless logic and with such crushing power—and that person was Frederick's court chamberlain, with a royal pension of four thousand dollars a year, and the Order of Merit on his breast! The enraged monarch lost no time. Seizing his pen, he rushed to the aid of the dazed Maupertuis. In a pamphlet bearing the royal coat-of-arms on the title page, the king branded the author of "The Reply of an Academician of Berlin" as a "witless creator of libels," a "shameless impostor," and a "miserable writer"; while his article was "dull and coarse," and its publication "a malicious, cowardly, infamous act," a "frightful brigandage."

The presence of the royal insignia made it obvious that the king intended to stand by his President. "The eagle, the sceptre and the crown," Voltaire declared, "are very much astonished to find themselves there." To Madame Denis he wrote that "coquettes, kings and poets are accustomed to be flattered. Frederick is a combination of all three. How can truth pierce that triple wall of vanity?"

The king's act stung Voltaire; yet it also pleased him. He had nothing to regret; from now on his course was clear—he would "fight like a devil"; work as much havoc as possible; and then he would leave Prussia and its despotic monarch forever. "I have no sceptre," he said to his niece, "but I have a pen."

That pen he now put to use. He loaded it with his sharpest raillery and turned it gleefully upon Maupertuis. He called his blast the "Diatribe of Doctor Akakia." Just as the President had doubted the authenticity of the Leibnitz letter, so Voltaire now pretended to believe that Maupertuis, whom he represented as Doctor Akakia, could not possibly have composed his "Letters"—"he would certainly not have fallen into certain little errors which are pardonable only in a youth." With fiendish delight Voltaire pounced on Maupertuis' "Letters," exploring some of their eccentric suggestions, and coating them with ridicule. Nor was Frederick's favorite Academy overlooked. At one of its learned meetings "two physicians produced each one a sick man smeared with resinous wax, and two surgeons pricked the legs and arms of these sick men with long needles; whereupon the patients, who before were scarcely able to move, began to cry and run about with all their strength; and the Secretary noted this in the minutes." Subsequently all the town's workmen presented themselves "for the purpose of making a hole to reach the very center of the earth," while "the Perpetual Secretary arranged a meeting between the workmen and the builders of the tower of Babel." Finally, after having hanged the President on the gibbet of his satire and watched him kick and dangle, Voltaire gave him the *coup de grace*: "When in an author, the sum of errors equals the sum of absurdities," he said, "then nothingness is the equivalent of his existence."

Though Voltaire's prime purpose had been to smother Maupertuis with ridicule and thus destroy his reputation, utterly and forever, within the bubbling stream of his mockery there flowed a perceptible undercurrent. Beneath the farce there was an implied appeal to scientific principles. To Voltaire metaphysics had no place in geometry, and to justify the existence of God by mathematics, as Maupertuis had done, was an absurdity. Throughout the "Diatribe" there was a persistent attack on pseudo-science; on the unwarranted assumptions and vague generalizations made by so-called men of learning. What Voltaire desired, in other words, was the proper use of the experimental method.

With the completion of the "Diatribe of Doctor Akakia," Voltaire was faced with the problem of getting it published. The king had forbidden any further criticism of Maupertuis; and to expect Frederick to make an exception in the case of a work so cruel and remorseless as the "Diatribe" was obviously out of the question. However, the creator of Doctor Akakia showed the manuscript to Frederick, who laughed till tears came to his eyes—but he forbade Voltaire to publish it. Voltaire of course made his customary promises; indeed, to prove his good intentions he tossed the manuscript into the fire. But, a few days later, under a license obtained from the king for another work, the forbidden Akakia appeared in print.

The king's wrath, of course, was enormous, though he managed to control it. He confiscated the entire edition of the work and had it privately destroyed; he gave Voltaire a tongue-lashing; and he felt certain that would be the end of the matter. To Maupertuis he wrote a soothing note. "Do not let anything upset you, my dear Maupertuis," he said; "the business of the libels is finished. I have spoken so plainly to the man, I have washed his head so thoroughly that I do not think he will repeat the offense. I have frightened him on the side of the purse, and it has had all the effect I expected. I have declared to him plumply that my house is to be a sanctuary, and not a retreat for brigands and scoundrels to distil poisons therein."

Frederick's reassurance came somewhat late. The cruel pen of Voltaire had been too much for Maupertuis, who, overpowered by rage and shattered nerves, had to take to his bed. "A little too much self-esteem," Frederick remarked, "has made him susceptible to the maneuvers of a monkey whom he should scorn now that he has been whipped."

The monkey had been whipped. Yet surely Frederick must have realized that whipping was not enough. Or was it possible, after two years of close association with Voltaire, that the King of Prussia had not the slightest grasp of the man with whom he was dealing? Could it be that it never occurred to the master of the Prussian state that a genius was no ordinary man? That he might have a spirit and a will which would bow to no one, not even an all-powerful autocrat?

Frederick's supreme egotism had led him blindly into the pitfall of underestimating his man! Voltaire, anticipating the confiscation of the forbidden tract, had taken the precaution of sending a number of copies out of Prussia. Before the month was up all Germany was swarming with Dr. Akakias; Dutch presses were pouring forth thousands of copies; while in Paris the demand exceeded the supply.

Voltaire's act ignited the dynamite, hoarded so long in Frederick's soul. When the king heard that all Europe was rocking with laughter over the man he had selected as president of his beloved Academy, he blew up in a terrific explosion. All Akakias were seized; the printer was arrested; and Voltaire was imprisoned in his rooms, with a gigantic grenadier on guard.

"Your effrontery amazes me," the king fulminated in a note to the prisoner. "You persist in it instead of owning yourself guilty—do not imagine that you can make people believe that black is white—when one takes no notice, it is because one prefers to see nothing—but if you carry this business any further, I shall have everything printed, and the world will see that if your works deserve statues, your conduct deserves chains!" He added that "the printer has been questioned, and has confessed all."

"Ah, *mon Dieu*, Sire, in my condition!" Voltaire scribbled on Frederick's note and returned it to His Majesty. He was, of course, dying once more. He was, he wailed, a victim of dysentery, scurvy, erysipelas, and constant attacks of fever—and he had no teeth. As for the publication of the prohibited work, he, of course, knew nothing about it; it must have been a malicious trick of one of his enemies, who must have made a copy of the manuscript before it was burned. "What!" he ejaculated in righteous indignation. "You would judge me without a hearing! I ask for justice and death."

Voltaire remained a prisoner a week, during which, as usual, he sought the consolation of his creative spirit. For most of the time he worked on his writings, as if nothing at all had occurred. After a few days Frederick was ready to relent—but only on condition that his prisoner would sign a written pledge. He was to promise that so long as His Majesty did him the favor to lodge him at the palace, he would "write against no one; neither against the government of France, nor against other sovereigns, nor against illustrious men of letters"; furthermore, he was to govern himself "in a manner becoming a man of letters, who has the honor to be a chamberlain of His Majesty, and who lives with respectable people." Voltaire refused to sign the king's statement; instead he scribbled some submissive generalities on it; and then he sent it back.

Frederick replied by having the offensive pamphlet burned by the public executioner. To make sure that everyone would understand what he was capable of doing when aroused, Frederick caused the work to be burned in three separate places. His act was gratifying to Maupertuis, who explained triumphantly to his friends that it was received "with the great applause of all respectable people," who had "come in carriage from every direction." The same evening the monarch wrote his President a charming letter in which he sent him some "of the ashes of that 'Diatribe' as a cooling powder."

As for Voltaire, he was well aware, as he said to his niece, "that the orange has been squeezed." Unlike the ruler of Prussia, he did "not possess one hundred and fifty thousand soldiers." "I cannot pretend to make war," he said. "My only plan is to desert honorably; to take care of my health; and to forget this three years' nightmare." He was compiling, he added, "a little Dictionary for the Use of Kings." In it,"*my friend* means *my slave. My dear friend* means *you are absolutely nothing to me.* By *I will make you happy* understand *I will bear with you as long as I need you. Sup with me tonight* means *I shall make fun of you this evening. . . .*"

Soon afterward the embittered poet returned his gold chamberlain's key, his cross and ribbon of the Prussian Order of Merit. On the envelope containing the articles he jotted a little quatrain, saying that he had received them with tenderness, was returning them with sadness, as a jealous lover in ill humor returns the portrait of his mistress.

One might suppose that this was the end, and that the curtain would now discreetly descend on the tragi-comedy. But Frederick could not bring himself to the point of admitting that the marriage was over. He sent back the honors Voltaire had surrendered, and actually went so far as to ask the poet's forgiveness, and to invite him to supper. But Voltaire's mind was made up—he was determined to leave Prussia once and for all. Several months elapsed before Frederick gave his reluctant consent; there was a final burst of fêtes and suppers and a desperate effort to restore the vanished gayety; but in the meantime Voltaire was busy with arrangements to go to the waters of Plombières; and then, on March 26, 1753, the two men parted forever.

The tempest had spent itself; but it was not over. On his way to Plombières Voltaire stopped at Leipzig, where in spite of his glowing promises to Frederick, he made arrangements for another edition of "Akakia." When Maupertuis heard of this latest outrage, he couldn't contain his wrath: he wrote to Voltaire, reminding him of his canings in France, and threatened to administer one himself if there were any more Doctor Akakias. Thereupon the relentless Voltaire issued yet another edition of the infamous pamphlet, appended an unauthorized version of the President's letter, and added that if this dangerous and brutal man attempted to carry out his threat, he would be met with the contents of a chamber pot. For Maupertuis this was the last straw. Sick in body and mind, his reputation irretrievably gone, he betook himself to Switzerland, where he passed the rest of his unhappy life reading the Genevan Bible.

Meanwhile the smoldering grudge within Frederick burst out anew. He had suddenly remembered that Voltaire had gone off with the chamberlain's key and the insignia of the Order of Merit; worse yet, the scoundrel had taken with him a copy of some of Frederick's privately printed verses. It now occurred to Frederick that because of their somewhat bawdy temper, their publication would be most embarrassing; and he realized, with alarm and apprehension, that as long as a copy remained in the hands of Voltaire there was no certainty of keeping the verses confidential. Accordingly Frederick decided upon a drastic step: he ordered the Prussian Resident at Frankfurt, where Voltaire was to meet his niece, to detain the poet until he surrendered the desired articles.

A series of weird events followed. For more than a

month Voltaire and Madame Denis remained prisoners; their belongings were confiscated; Frederick's representative got drunk and tried to seduce Madame Denis. On his release, Voltaire became hysterical and tried to attack the amorous Prussian, an act which one of the bystanders fortunately frustrated. In the meantime Frederick wrote reassuring letters to the Resident, complimenting him for having "executed the royal order in a way that His Majesty is satisfied." "The lies and calumnies of Voltaire," he concluded, "will find credence neither here nor elsewhere." To make his prediction a certainty Frederick wrote a poem in which he "unmasked Voltaire at last." The man whom the monarch had once addressed endearingly as Socrates he now described as "the unworthy favorite of the nine sisters"; he was "detested at Paris, burned in Berlin, cursed at Rome"; and he was "a cheat and an impudent deceiver."

Meanwhile Prussian diplomacy had been put to work. At Versailles hints were dropped that His Prussian Majesty would certainly be displeased if Monsieur de Voltaire should be allowed to re-enter France, an opinion in which Voltaire's enemies at the Court heartily concurred. When the matter was brought before Louis, he gave it his wholehearted approval. Madame de Pompadour alone objected, but when the King of France persisted in his hostility to Voltaire, her opposition wavered. Early in August, 1753, the king signed the order which formally banished his former historiographer from France. "He will wander from country to country," Frederick prophesied with obvious delight.

For several months Voltaire hesitated. He tried, as usual, to soften the king with flattery; but Louis' determination was of iron and, for once, it was impervious to sweet compliments. Voltaire hoped that his friends might come to his aid, and that their efforts might cause the king to relent. The poet's most powerful friends, Richelieu and the brothers d'Argenson, did, indeed, try to exercise their influence in their friend's behalf, but it soon became apparent that Louis despised him even more than did the vindictive Frederick, and that nowhere in France would Voltaire be safe. For almost a year he went from one place to another, hoping vainly that Louis might at last give in. He spent some months in Alsace, and for a while even harbored the idea of settling there permanently; but the Alsatian Jesuits, horrified by such a prospect, agitated against him and quickly made him change his mind. In June, 1754, he cloistered himself in a Benedictine monastery, where he appears to have spent most of his time in the company of a learned monk, Dom Calmet. He preferred the friar's company, he said, to that of kings. All that he desired was some books, a warm cell, and if he could have a thick soup, a little mutton, and some eggs, he would "prefer that happy, healthy frugality to royal fare." From his Benedictine retreat Voltaire went to Plombières, where he met his niece and some of his friends. Torn between his desire to return to France and his longing to settle in some permanent abode, Voltaire hovered in uncertainty. He thought for a time that he would like to spend his remaining years in Pennsylvania; but he was weary of travel, and the prospect of a long and arduous trip over the Atlantic dismayed him. Finally he made up his mind: he crossed the Swiss border and went to the Republic of Geneva.

He arrived in Geneva on the 12th of December, 1754, accompanied by his niece and his secretary Collini. Before very long he rented a winter house not far from Lausanne; at the same time he purchased a summer home at Saint Jean, close to Geneva. Shortly afterward he acquired a place in the neighboring Kingdom of Sardinia, and still another across the Swiss border, in France. Although Voltaire's properties were all under different flags, they were, as he said, "in one neighborhood" within easy reach of each other. In this way he hoped to dodge any possible persecutors, "to creep," as he put it, "from den to den, escaping from kings and from armies." "I am like the Old Man of the Mountain," he said. "With my four estates, I am upon my four paws."

Switzerland

VOLTAIRE was now sixty years old, though actually he looked much older. He was thin and pale, and his face was that of a mummy, with a skin that was dry and creased with wrinkles. He was quite bald and because he caught cold so easily he usually wore a cap under his heavy wig. He had lost his teeth and his lower jaw sagged revealingly. Yet his eyes had not lost their sharp, uncanny lustre; and combined with the impish grin that hung suggestively upon the corner of his lips, he looked at times strangely like a monkey.

Perhaps that grin was ominous, or perhaps it merely reflected Voltaire's inmost thoughts and feelings. For at sixty the poet was free, free from the clutches of tyrants; free from all the annoyances, large and small, that tend to make successful living difficult. At sixty Voltaire was free to do as he pleased. Under the impact of his freedom, his spirit soared, and his health improved. Whenever he felt the symptoms of an oncoming relapse, he would remind himself that three or four princes would gain by his death.

"Then," he said, "I take courage from pure malice and I conspire against them with rhubarb and sobriety."

The acquisition of his new properties filled Voltaire with excitement. His estate at Saint Jean, with its beautiful view of Lake Geneva and the majestic Alps, filled him with ecstatic wonder. "Fifteen windows command the lake," he once exclaimed. "A hundred gardens are below my garden; the blue mirror of the lake bathes them. I see all Savoy beyond this little sea, and beyond Savoy the Alps which rise into an amphitheatre, and upon which the rays of the sun form a thousand accidental effects of light. There is not a more beautiful view in the world." Voltaire called his home at Saint Jean *Les Délices*, "The Delights." With Madame Denis he turned to the task of making it habitable—a task he apparently enjoyed. "We are occupied," he wrote to a friend, "in making rooms for our friends and our chickens; we have ordered coaches and barrows; we plant onions and orange trees, carrots and tulips. We are short of everything, but Carthage must be built."

Life at *Les Délices* was far different from that which the poet had experienced in the sylvan retreat of Cirey. For Madame Denis was neither a philosopher nor a writer. She was unable to be alone with her thoughts. She was, she frankly admitted, a Parisienne, and even when she found herself transplanted to the shores of Lake Geneva, she could not renounce what she called "the vanities of the world." It was all very well for her uncle to rhapsodize over the scenic grandeurs, but as for her, what she wanted was "a fine house, lovely gardens, and plenty of company." Like Emilie before her, Madame Denis had her way with Voltaire. The man who had laughed at kings, who had outmaneuvered bishops, and even the Pope, was no match for his niece. In her hands he was as pliant as a reed, and whatever her heart desired, the uncle found before very long that he, too, desired it.

Voltaire's income now was immense—a hundred thousand livres it has been estimated. He could afford, if he chose, to live like a nabob; and with his love of comfort and refinement, he needed very little prodding to spend his money. Gradually the "vanities of the world," which the plump Madame Denis coveted so much, and which he himself admired no little, made their way to *Les Délices*. There was a French chef, a staff of servants, gardeners, a postillon, a secretary, and even a fireworks expert; there were libraries and picture galleries, expensive knickknacks and rare plants and shrubs; there was a private theatre in which Voltaire produced comedies and tragedies, in which he and Madame Denis frequently acted, along with some of the best actors from Paris. There were also a couple of extraordinary pets—a monkey and a bear. The monkey was the poet's favorite, and with him he would often pretend to discuss philosophy and other learned subjects. He called the animal Luke, but one day, after it had bitten his hand, he named it for the King of Prussia. As for the bear, he became Voltaire's public executioner. Once, on hearing that a priest had composed a work in which he justified the Massacre of St. Bartholomew, the poet exclaimed, "Send me that book, and I will put it in my bear's cage!"

In their new home Voltaire and his niece entertained on a grand scale. Visitors came to them from every part of the world, and their mansion was almost always full. At times, indeed, *Les Délices* harbored as many as a score of guests and prospective visitors had to be put on a waiting list.

Whenever a guest arrived, Voltaire tried to accord him a personal welcome. Heavily bewigged and impeccably attired, he would appear at the great front door, bowing solemnly to his guest, and flattering him with his most gracious compliments.

Meanwhile, Madame Denis, cast in the double role of hostess and housekeeper, supervised the domestic machine. She did it with extraordinary vigor and a skill that was superb. She seemed to be everywhere at once! She would appear in the bedrooms to see if the beds had been properly made; a moment later she might be in the kitchen tasting soups and sauces; or she might be examining her culinary stores, or out in the garden scrutinizing the plants and vegetables. In the crowded salon of *Les Délices*, Madame Denis was ubiquitous, moving about as if on invisible wheels, glancing lightly upon a score of persons, mingling flattery with reflection, only to burst into a torrent of hearty laughter while her large and buxom figure quivered like jelly. After a while she would drop a gentle curtsey and suddenly vanish, only to reappear later, costumed as a Roman or a Turk, while she interpreted a part in one of her uncle's favorite dramas.

Pleasant as was Voltaire's new mode of life, to spend his remaining years as a retired country gentleman was hardly a tempting prospect to a man whose happiness had always depended upon work. Though he received his visitors with great felicity, when it came to his work he tolerated no interruptions. Even in his darkest hours at Potsdam Voltaire had continued to write. There he completed the "Age of Louis XIV," the exasperating "Doctor Akakia" and a number of minor works, besides starting a "Philosophical Dictionary," and a study which he was to call an

Voltaire's Chateau at Ferney

"Essay on Manners and Mind of Nations" (*Essai sur les Moeurs et l'Esprit des Nations*). While he was in Alsace he wrote a new play, "The Orphan of China," and a history, "The Annals of the Empire Since Charlemagne." This work, which he composed at the request of the Duchess of Saxe-Coburg, has the unique distinction among all his prose writings of being almost completely dull.

In August, 1755, "The Orphan of China" was played at Paris. There had been some doubts whether the meticulous censor would approve the piece. The queen, it seems, "had heard there were some questionable passages in it"; but after a few deletions "The Orphan of China" was deemed sufficiently moral for even such a strict and devout person as the Queen of France. The play's setting was in the Imperial Palace at Pekin, where the ladies of the court, some learned mandarins, the infant prince and his attendants, were huddled in terror while Genghis Khan and his hordes were sacking the city. While the ancient Chinese civilization was toppling before everyone's frightened eyes, one of the mandarins swore to save the infant prince at all costs. To this end he surrendered his own child to the invaders, hoodwinking them into the belief that the child was in reality the son of the slain emperor. But the empress, shocked by such a sacrifice, revealed the truth to Genghis and implored his mercy, a request to which, strangely enough, he acceded.

The play, written with Voltaire's best artistry, was a great hit. In his enforced absence from Paris, the author sent his secretary Collini to report on what happened. He kept his master fully informed, and on Voltaire's authority made arrangements for the publication of the play in book form. For his excellent work Collini was allowed to keep the entire proceeds derived from the sale of the rights to the book.

While Voltaire's new play was attracting the Parisian crowds, a small parcel was delivered one day at *Les Délices*. It contained a booklet, the "Essay on Inequality," and with it there was a letter from its author, Jean-Jacques Rousseau. Then in his early forties, Rousseau had until quite recently toiled in comparative obscurity. In 1750 he had leaped into fame by winning the first prize offered by the Academy of Dijon for the best essay on the theme "whether or not the progress of the sciences and the arts has corrupted or improved morals." As a youth Rousseau had read the "English Letters" and had been, as he intimated, warmed by their message. Though Rousseau still professed an ardent admiration for the author of that book, he was temperamentally almost the antithesis of Voltaire. Emotional, deeply sensitive, pathetically sombre, Rousseau was a dreamer. His dreams, freed from the dead weight of reality, swept far beyond the horizon, where they envisaged a new society in which man was to be truly happy. Despising the world in which he lived, Rousseau condemned and opposed it. Man's salvation, he believed, lay in his return to the simple life. "Everything," he asserted, "is good as it comes from the hands of the Author of Nature; but everything degenerates in the hands of man." Rousseau felt that man had been "originally good" and that civilization had corrupted him. With an insolence that rose at times to the heights of exquisite poetry, the Apostle of Nature thundered against the false gods of his times—Science, Philosophy and Convenience. Rousseau derived his convictions from his heart, and though he was tortured in his own spirit, he held that in importance and dignity nothing could ever surpass the human soul. With a temper that was strangely modern, Rousseau espoused the cause of the "common man" whose rights he championed with tremendous fervor, and who, he was certain, was the most important creature in the world.

In contrast to the intuitive Rousseau, Voltaire put his faith in reason. He believed in the benefits of human progress, and, as he had once declared in *Le Mondain,* he even liked luxury and comfort. To the Advocate of Reason the mysticism of Rousseau seemed strange and nebulous; while his nostalgia for a return to a more primitive and simpler society seemed absurd.

"I have received, sir," Voltaire wrote Rousseau, "your book against the human race. I thank you for it. You will please men to whom you frankly tell their faults, but you will not correct them. It is impossible to paint in bolder colors the horrors of human society, from which our ignorance and our weakness lead us to expect so much consolation. Never has anyone employed so much wit in trying to make us witless; the reading of your book makes us want to creep on all fours." Then, with mingled mockery and seriousness, Voltaire went on to say that since he was now more than sixty years old, he had lost the habit of creeping on all fours; and that, unfortunately, he felt it was impossible for him to take it up again. "I leave that natural attitude to those who are more worthy of it than you or I. Neither can I embark to go and live with the savages of Canada: first, because the ailments with which I am afflicted retain me by the side of the greatest doctor of Europe, and I could not find the same attentions among the Missouri Indians; secondly, because war has been carried into those countries, and by the example of our civilized peoples has made the savages almost as wicked as we."

It is doubtful whether the humorless Rousseau understood Voltaire's sarcasm. At any rate, he took great pains to address a long letter to his satirical critic in which he thanked him profusely. "In sending you the outline of my sad thoughts," he wrote, "I never believed I was making you a gift worthy of your merit, but I meant to acquit myself of a duty, and to render you the homage that we all owe to you, as the Chief. Sensitive, moreover, to the honor you do my country (Geneva), I share the gratitude of my compatriots; and I hope it will be greatly increased, when they have profited by the instruction you can give them."

Rousseau then proceeded to explain his views in detail. Man, he declared, must revert to the life of the "noble savage"; only thus can he be happy; for "only Nature is good."

Shortly afterward Nature herself struck a grim and fatal blow. On November 1st, 1755, Lisbon was shaken by a terrible earthquake. The day happened to be All Saints' Day, and when the first shock occurred the greater part of the people of Lisbon were worshipping in church. Within a few minutes the entire city lay in ruins; more than thirty thousand were dead, and thousands more were dying.

When the news of the disaster reached Voltaire he burst into tears. For weeks its spectre haunted him and he could speak of little else. Rousseau's views, which only a short time ago had seemed silly, now became appalling, as did those of optimists like Leibnitz and Pope, who had asserted that "all is well." "If Pope had been at Lisbon," Voltaire reflected, "would he have dared to say, 'All is well'?" "It will cause people no little embarrassment," he wrote to a friend at Lyons, "to divine how the laws of nature bring about such frightful disasters *in the best of all possible worlds;* a hundred thousand ants, our neighbors crushed at one blow in our ant-heap, and half of them doubtless in inexpressible anguish, in the midst of debris; families ruined to the end of Europe, the wealth of a hundred merchants from your country swallowed up in Lisbon's ruins. What a game of chance it is, the game of human life!"

The horror and despair which had mounted in his spirit Voltaire released in a "Poem on the Disaster of Lisbon." In it he questioned the philosophical optimism of Pope and Leibnitz and the general view that nature is benevolent. If all is well, Voltaire asked, "if this earthquake was necessary, why could it not have burst forth in the midst of an uninhabited desert? To say that the suffering of some brings joy to others is mockery! What solace is it to the dying man to know that from his decaying body a thousand worms will come to life?" When optimists cry that all is well, then, said Voltaire, "the universe gives them the lie. Your own heart refutes the error. What sad, what perplexing truths! A God, you say, came to console our afflicted race; he visited the earth and changed it not! One sophist says he could not; another says he did not choose to, but will at some future time; and even while they argue Lisbon crumbles into ruins. . . . All is well! . . . No, no! . . . One day all will be well—that is our hope. All is well today . . . this is illusion!"

If Voltaire had hoped that reasoning might convince Rousseau of the weakness of his theories, then he completely misunderstood his man. By nature Rousseau was almost impervious to intellectual appeal. Voltaire's poem, he exclaimed, "sharpens all my pains, excites me to mur-

muring, and reduces me to despair." In a long and eloquent letter the Apostle of Nature reiterated his views. God, he repeated, is perfect; consequently everything that occurs must be for the best. This world "really is, because it must be, the best of all possible worlds." Although Voltaire's poem had ended on a faint note of hope, Rousseau failed to be impressed. "I have suffered too much in this life," he cried out, "not to expect another. All the subtleties of metaphysics will not make me doubt for a moment the immortality of the soul and a beneficent Providence. I feel it, I believe it, I wish it, I hope it, I will defend it with my last breath."

Voltaire made no effort to reply. Perhaps he thought that any further discussion might be useless; or perhaps he was too preoccupied with other matters. At any rate he turned his attention to other activities. "I have become a gardener, a vine dresser, and a workman," he announced with pride. "I must do in a small way what the King of Poland has done in the grand style. I must plant, uproot, build houses . . . while he dreams of palaces."

In the meantime Voltaire's intellectual interests had swung into a new direction. In Paris a small group of liberal-minded savants, who called themselves the *Philosophes,* had banded together to advance the cause of Reason and Humanity. Among them was d'Alembert, a brilliant and witty mathematician; Condillac, a psychologist; Turgot, a grave and distinguished statesman; Buffon, a student of natural history; and the scintillating Diderot, cynical, genial, and indefatigable.

Under Diderot's leadership and that of d'Alembert the *Philosophes* had undertaken the publication of an Encyclopedia. It was to be a monumental work, containing a com-

plete survey of human activity, its politics and science, its
art, commerce and philosophy, and it was to offer in permanent form an account of the advance of civilization.
What was immensely more important, however, was the
spirit which had prompted this remarkable venture. For
at bottom the Encyclopedists sought not merely to record
facts, but also to raise questions; they were concerned not
primarily with the enunciation of learned profundities,
but rather with the enlightenment of the ordinary man
and woman. Other writers before them had spoken more
learnedly and more accurately; but none of their prede-
cessors had endeavored to reach so many readers; and none
had written with their zeal and passion, their love of humanity, and their determination to awaken France from
its political and intellectual slumber.

Under the banners of reason and humanity, the *Philosophes* waged a furious intellectual war. Their weapons
were wit, learning and raillery. These they concentrated,
brilliantly and relentlessly, on the forces of the old regime,
but in particular on their most powerful citadels, the State
and the Church. Naturally the authorities struck back,
employing their traditional weapons of censorship, imprisonment and exile. Few *Philosophes* escaped unscathed. All
of them had had some of their works suppressed; and
nearly all had been lodged in the Bastille. Yet, as time
went on, it became clear that the fibre of these men was
tough; that jails and persecution would not intimidate
them; that the public of Paris was rallying more and more
to their side; and that to destroy them, the forces of reaction would have to strain themselves to the utmost.

In the midst of the conflict Voltaire entered the fray.
By temperament and training he was of course admirably

suited for such a struggle. His "English Letters" had been aimed at the same foe, and though for a score of years he had done little to fulfill their promise, reason and humanity had been his constant watchword. It had been discernible in his philosophic treatises; it had been woven into the themes of many of his plays; and it had propelled him to the defense of Koenig in his conflict with the high-handed Maupertuis. All the weapons employed by the *Philosophes* were in Voltaire's armory; and in their deadly use he knew no master. Unlike most of his battle-companions, Voltaire was ideally situated. With his huge fortune, he could afford to embark upon campaigns that were impossible to a man of ordinary means; and with his four estates located in the heart of Europe, each in a different land—"with my left flank in the Jura, my right on the Alps"—Voltaire was fortunately free from the clutches of the enemy.

To his new sphere of interest Voltaire brought all his energy. He was old; he was sick; but his activity had never been greater. "As long as I have a breath of life," he wrote to d'Alembert, "I am at the service of the illustrious authors of the Encyclopedia. I consider myself greatly honored to be able to contribute even feebly to the greatest and handsomest monument of the nation and of literature. I pay my sincerest compliments to all who are working on it." Indefatigably he worked, soliciting articles for the Encyclopedia, and contributing a series of his own. He offered to write on Taste, Genius, History, Facility, Falsity, Fire, Finesse, Force, Feebleness, Frenchmen and Fornication.

From the outset Voltaire realized that the battle for enlightenment could be waged successfully only if the philosophers banded together for mutual protection. To this end he gradually assumed the role of party whip, a position which required tact and restraint as well as boldness and imagination. He defended his "brethren, the *Philosophes*" against the attacks of Fréron and Rousseau; he sought to enlist the sympathy and protection of his influential friends; and he strove to preserve harmony among the philosophers themselves, for, though they fought a common foe, they were not without their petty jealousies among themselves, and their internecine quarrels were seemingly without end.

"The philosophers," Voltaire remarked, "are a small flock who must be kept from the slaughter. They have their failings like other men; they do not always write excellent works; but if they could all write against the common enemy it would be a fine thing for the human race. The monsters called Jansenists and Molinists, after biting each other, are now joined in barking at the poor partisans of reason and humanity. These should at least protect one another from their fangs."

The attack of the *Philosophes* covered a wide area. The abuses of the financial system, the maladministration of justice, the restraints upon trade and commerce, the indolence of a parasitic *noblesse*, the profligacy of a reckless court—upon these they fell with all their fury. But there was one source of iniquity which drew their concentrated wrath; which they attacked with every means, fair and foul; and which they were determined to crush once and forever. This was the Church. "Crush the infamous thing!" —"*Ecrasez l'infame!*"—became Voltaire's personal battle-cry. Like Cato of old, who so despised Carthage that he ended every one of his speeches in the Roman Senate—no

matter what the subject—with the words "Carthage must
be destroyed!" Voltaire inserted his battle-cry into every
letter. He wrote it out in full; he abbreviated it; he put it
at the beginning, or in the middle, or at the end; he
scribbled it on odd bits of paper; he jotted it on manuscripts. Given pen and paper—no matter what it was—
somewhere, certainly, he was bound to *"écrasez l'infame."*
"I want you to crush *l'infame;* that is the main point," he
wrote to one friend. "I am always interested in the success
of the French drama," he wrote to another, "but much
more so in the brethren (the *Philosophes*) and in the destruction of *l'inf."* His health, he announced, "is terrible,
écr. l'inf." Does "comic opera," he asked, "still sustain the
glory of France? *Ecr. l'inf."* How lovely it would be, he
reflected, if one could have "musical chimes that should
end with *"Ecrasez l'infame!"*

The struggle for reason and humanity had little respect
for the sanctity of national frontiers. While Voltaire and
the philosophers addressed themselves chiefly to the enemy
within France, they struck at fanaticism and injustice
wherever these showed their fangs. When a Genevan
youth, convicted of fornication, was persecuted for refusing to genuflect before the members of the City Council,
Voltaire defended him. When the English, stung by their
naval loss at Majorca in 1756, sentenced their Admiral
Byng to death, Voltaire rushed to his help. Reinforced by
letters from the Duke of Richelieu, which clearly vindi-
cated the unfortunate man, Voltaire tried valiantly to save
him. The poet was, he said, "commanded by honor, equity
and humanity," and he felt certain that "the judges will
render justice." Unfortunately they did not, and Byng
was executed. "In this country," Voltaire acidly observed,

"it is found advisable from time to time to kill one admiral to encourage others."

In the meantime the Apostle of Reason had not forgotten Jean-Jacques Rousseau. This, indeed, would have been quite impossible, for the Apostle of Nature was not the kind of man one could readily forget. He had been waiting for a long time for Voltaire to make some sort of a reply to his criticism of the views expressed in the "Poem on the Disaster of Lisbon." When the months went by and no answer came, Rousseau shook his head in amazement. "A man who could take my letter as he has done," he said, "deserves the title of philosopher."

Meanwhile events were being shaped which were destined to break Voltaire's silence. At the poet's suggestion d'Alembert had composed an article on Geneva and had published it in the Encyclopedia. Its tone on the whole was complimentary. It even went so far as to extol the Geneva clergymen for their liberalism. "Hell," it said, "is not believed in at all by several ministers of Geneva." It went on to say that some of the pastors "rejected all that is called mystery" and believed that the first principle of a true religion "must be to propose nothing for belief that is offensive to reason." What d'Alembert had intended as praise was not seen in that light by Geneva's men of God. They felt that they had been made to appear guilty of Socinianism, a heresy which some were privately willing to admit might have its merits, but which publicly they declared abhorrent.

What was almost as despicable in the minds of the irritated pastors was d'Alembert's plea that for the edification of Genevan taste the city should establish a theatre. Though the suggestion came from the pen of d'Alembert, to the Genevans the cloven hoof of Voltaire showed itself very plainly. It was evident to anyone who took the pains to look; and it was particularly evident to Rousseau. Though Jean-Jacques had at one time written a play, he had long since renounced the dramatic art, which he had come to see was the devil's handiwork. To make his views clear in the matter, Rousseau addressed a 200-page letter to d'Alembert. Let the theatre remain in Paris where it belonged, he argued. "Geneva knew it not. How sad the change, if the honest people of Geneva . . . should waste at the theatre the money needed for their children's bread!" All plays, he went on to say, were immoral, even the best of Racine and Molière, as were all persons connected with their presentation. The theatre, he conceded, "is the sublimest art of civilization," but "it is also the most dangerous because it excites the passions. . . . It makes vice triumph, virtue ridiculous."

Rousseau's attitude toward Voltaire personally was still cordial, a feeling which was not reciprocated by the dramatist. "Has Rousseau become a Church father?" he burst out. "This madman who might have been something under the guidance of his brethren of the Encyclopedia takes it into his head to make his own sect. After writing a bad play he writes against the stage. He finds four or five staves of Diogenes' tub and gets within them to bark at his friends." In a less agitated tone Voltaire undertook to defend the theatre. "What is the true drama?" he wrote. "It is the art of teaching virtue and good manners by action and dialogue." "I have had the pleasure of seeing at my country house *Alzire* performed—the tragedy wherein Christianity and the rights of man triumph equally. I have seen Mérope's maternal love bring tears without the aid of the love of gallantry. Such subjects move the rudest soul as they do the most sublime; and if the common people were in the habit of witnessing such spectacles of human worth there would be fewer souls gross and obdurate."

But Voltaire's words fell on deaf ears. There would be no theatre to sully the holy ground of Calvin's Geneva. Thanks to Rousseau, it was possible for Pastor Sarasin to say that the Apostle of Nature had won the gratitude of all those who "could think wholesomely and who were not given to the love of frivolity and pleasure." Meanwhile the author of *Alzire* and *Mérope* had to content himself with productions in his private theatre at *Les Délices*.

In the meantime Voltaire had completed the *Essai sur les Moeurs et l'Esprit des Nations* ("Manners and Mind of Nations"). The work comprised several large volumes and surveyed the entire development of man to the age of Louis XIV. In harmony with Voltaire's conception of history, the *Essai sur les Moeurs* described the march of civilization in its broadest scope, stressing the progress of the arts and sciences, and including a consideration of the oriental nations. Voltaire's object was not to compose a catalogue of facts, but rather to discover those factors which would serve man in shaping a better future. But the book had yet another purpose. It was aimed in reality at another historical work, Bossuet's "Universal History." That book interpreted history as the unfolding of God's will according to which, among other things, Rome fell because it was the providential design to establish Christianity. Voltaire's view was different. To him history was to be explained only in terms of natural causes, and the fall of Rome was to be traced to human conduct, human passion, human reason.

But this was not all. To Voltaire it appeared that there was one influence in the entire course of human events which had been persistently bad. This was religion. Voltaire's view that religious belief had retarded the progress of mankind pervaded the entire essay. "Voltaire," the astute Montesquieu observed, "writes history to glorify his own convent, like any Benedictine monk." As far as the *Essai sur les Moeurs* is concerned, the charge was fully justified. For in it Voltaire was more often the propagandist rather than the dispassionate historian.

The reply which Rousseau had expected when he criticized Voltaire's views on the Lisbon disaster came at last in 1759. Its name was "Candide, or Optimism." Its author was *le Docteur Ralph,* a pseudonym which deceived no one, since almost every sentence glistened with the brilliance that was peculiarly Voltaire's. To the eye *Candide* is a romance of a racy and flippant sort; yet beneath the clowning it contains the essence of Voltaire's philosophy. At bottom it was an attack on the optimism of Leibnitz and Rousseau; on the belief that "all is well"; and on the doctrine that this "is the best of all possible worlds."

The plot is simple. An ingenuous youth, Candide, grows up in the Westphalian home of the Baron Thunder-ten-Tronckh, where he is tutored in philosophy by Dr. Pangloss, whose specialty is "metaphysico-theologo-cosmolonigologie," and who, like the great Leibnitz, believes that "all is well in this best of all possible worlds." Dr. Pangloss has proved this, for has he not found that "noses have been made to wear spectacles, therefore we have spectacles; legs have been made for stockings, therefore we have stockings; pigs were made to be eaten, and therefore we have pork all the year round"? Candide's admiration for his tutor is boundless—"he is the greatest philosopher of the province, consequently of all mankind."

One day Candide falls desperately in love with the Baron's daughter, the gracious Cunegonde; but the unsympathetic father makes short shrift of the youth's amorous hopes by chasing him out of the house. Accompanied by Dr. Pangloss the young man wanders from place to place, always certain that, in this best of all possible worlds, he will in the end be reunited with Cunegonde. His wanderings take him all over the globe, to Paraguay and to China, and wherever he goes he runs into trouble. He is conscripted into the army of the Bulgars—which is strangely like that of the Prussians; he contracts a venereal disease; he is almost killed by an earthquake. He meets a fanatical anabaptist to whom he confesses that he had not heard that the Pope was Antichrist. The anabaptist's wife "put her head out of the window and, perceiving a man who doubted the Pope was Antichrist, poured on his head a full . . . Oh Heavens! to what excesses are ladies carried by their religious zeal."

No matter where Candide goes, no matter what evils befall him, he is never shaken from his belief that "all is well." Buoyed up by the hope that some day he will win his beloved Cunegonde, he bears his afflictions with singular fortitude. Finally, after years of tortuous wandering, Candide recovers his sweetheart. When he beholds Cunegonde, he recoils with horror; time has left its inevitable mark, and the once lovely Cunegonde has become "bleary-eyed, flat-breasted, with wrinkles round her eyes, and red, chapped arms."

Candide is a compendium of all the evil, all the wretchedness, all the cruelties and degradations that beset the

human race; yet on every page there is the malicious, sardonic grin of the author. As the naive Candide is propelled
from one ridiculous situation to another, as he is ham-
mered remorselessly to the pillory of mockery, Voltaire's
laughter becomes thunderous. Yet the laughter is a mask;
behind it there is an intense earnestness. Not until the
story's end does its full meaning become clear; only then
are Candide's adventures thrown into sharp focus; and as
the blur of hilarious farce vanishes, one suddenly perceives the grim, the unforgettable sadness. After all the
years of ardent groping, the disillusioned Candide has
learned one thing. "What I know," he says, "is that we
must cultivate our garden." That is Candide's final word.

Among the people of Geneva *Candide* aroused great
agitation. They knew very well that Voltaire had written
the book. He denied it, it is true. "I have at length read
Candide," he wrote to a pastor. "People must have lost
their senses to attribute to me that pack of nonsense."
Perhaps it was just as well that he lied, for on March
second the Council of Geneva condemned the book to be
burned.

The satire of *Candide* was not lost on Jean-Jacques Rousseau. Its harshness repelled him. It was loathsome; it was
evil. In the depth of his spirit he felt that he had been
maligned. It was not the first attack; he saw that clearly
now. Voltaire's whole attitude, from their first exchange
of letters, had been harsh and cynical. In the tumult of
his agitation Rousseau felt perplexed; gradually his bewilderment gave way to despair, until in the end it overwhelmed him. In his tormented mind he saw in Voltaire
the embodiment of everything he loathed. "I would hate
him more if I despised him less," he wrote to a friend. As

time went on his hatred grew fiercer, until finally it consumed him.

"I don't like you, sir," he erupted. "You have hurt me,
your disciple and enthusiast, in things which were the
nearest to my heart; you have alienated from me the affections of fellow citizens in payment for the applause that
I have so lavishly given you among them. You are the one
who will force me to die in a foreign land, deprived of the
consolation of the dying, and to be thrown, not otherwise
honored, on the dump, while all the honors that a man
can expect will attend you in my native land. I hate you,
then, since you have so desired; but I hate you as a man
still more worthy of loving you if you had so desired."

As for Voltaire, he despised Rousseau's ideas more than
he despised Rousseau. He realized, too, that Rousseau was
ill, a distracted and tortured soul. When Voltaire had
settled at *Les Délices,* he had offered Jean-Jacques a quiet
retreat, where he might recover his health and peace of
mind "under his native skies and liberty." But aside from
that Voltaire made no serious effort to soothe or conciliate
Rousseau. When Voltaire heard that Jean-Jacques had
been trying to stir up Geneva against him, his antagonism
became relentless. He hovered over his victim like an
immense wasp, stinging him and quickly soaring away,
only to return and sting him again and again. He called
Rousseau every name in the lexicon of vituperation. He
was "a madman," "a bastard Diogenes," "a Judas who had
betrayed the Apostles." Rousseau's treatise on education,
Emile, he contemptuously dismissed as "a hodge-podge of
silly wet nurse in four volumes"; while his "Social Contract" was "an unsocial contract, remarkable only for a few
insults coarsely said to kings by the citizen of the town of

Geneva." So a philosopher's feud grew into deep hatred.

What really rankled in Voltaire's breast was the obvious fact that Rousseau had talent, and that he was wasting that talent on silly trivialities, instead of devoting them to the cause of the enlightenment. "He is the greatest madman in the world," Voltaire exclaimed upon reading a letter Rousseau had written to the Archbishop of Paris. "If he had been content to attack *l'infame,*" Voltaire declared to one of his friends, "he would have found defenders everywhere." As it was, "his conduct puts philosophy to shame."

Shortly after Voltaire had settled in Switzerland Europe plunged into war. It was in essence the same struggle which Frederick had started several years previously when he had seized the province of Silesia from Austria. For, even though that conflict had ended, the peace which followed had never been more than a breathing spell. In 1756 the war erupted once more, and within two years the Prussian king was thrust into the crisis of his career. Attacked simultaneously on all sides by the armies of France, Russia and Austria, the Prussian battalions were gradually being ground to bits; defeat followed defeat; strategic retreats failed to stem the onrushing tide; Berlin itself was invaded by the Russians; and more than once the despairing Frederick was on the brink of suicide.

An unexpected outcome of the war was the resumption of the correspondence between Frederick and Voltaire. The poet, having heard of Frederick's dejection, wrote the king a sympathetic note. The monarch gratefully acknowledged Voltaire's letter and stated that his despair had passed. The king's letter was soon followed by others, and before long letters between the two men were going back and forth. At first the old wounds still hurt. "For twenty years you were my idol," Voltaire wrote. "But your occupation as a hero, and your rank as a king did not make your heart very tender; it is a pity, for that heart was made to be human. . . ." "There can be no doubt," Frederick asseverated, "you did me the greatest wrongs. No philosopher would ever have tolerated your conduct." "You did me harm enough," Voltaire shot back. "You have embroiled me forever with the King of France; you have made me lose my office and my pensions; at Frankfort you ill-treated me and an innocent woman, a respected woman, who was dragged through the mud and cast into prison, and afterwards, when honoring me with your letters, you mar the pleasantness of this consolation with bitter reproaches." One would think that two such men, mutually so antagonistic, would cease their exchanges once and for all. But they didn't. In time their old grievances were extinguished and they were ready to forgive and forget everything, even the wrongs of Maupertuis and the vilifications of *Akakia*. In the course of time their letters resumed some of their former tone; the blandishments, the cordiality, the deft and sugary compliments returned, and before long Frederick was once more submitting verses for the scrutinizing eye of the greatest poet in the world. But the relationship between the two men was no longer that of old; they were neither master and servant, nor author and pupil, but two independent beings, each a power in his own sphere.

As Voltaire settled into his role of country squire he found himself very happy. At times it seemed to him almost incredible that he was actually free from the insidious worries which had plagued him so persistently in Paris and

Berlin. He feared monarchs and bishops, he confessed, and he would never go to Paris or Berlin. "I shall live and die in peace," he said, "if it please destiny, the sovereign queen of the world." Though he was not romantic, he thrilled to the scenic beauty of his new surroundings. What could equal the natural splendor of the lake and the Alps? Here even the air he breathed seemed freer than anywhere else. "I owe my life to the course I have taken," he wrote to Madame du Deffand. "If I dared, I would believe myself wise, so happy am I. I have lived only since the day I chose my retreat."

Voltaire's happiness reflected itself in an increased and ever-widening activity. He still believed, as he had ever since early manhood, that the time given to pleasure left the mind empty, while the hours devoted to study left the mind replete. The more he advanced in life, the more he found work necessary; it was, indeed, essential to his very existence. "It becomes," he said, "in the long run the greatest of pleasures and makes up for the illusions one has lost." Even on the threshold of seventy, he seemed to defy the usual dictates of time. His energy was boundless, and his zeal for activity was inexhaustible. There were periods when he worked from eighteen to twenty hours a day. He detested sleep and got along with as little as possible. When he was in the throes of composition, he shut his mind to everything else, and with a concentration that was amazing and enormous, he even forgot to take nourishment, a practice which caused his dutiful secretary no end of concern.

As the number of Voltaire's properties increased, he found himself absorbed in rebuilding and beautifying them. He became a mason, a carpenter, and a gardener. "The poor Parisians," he reflected, "do not know what a pleasure it is to cultivate one's garden; only Candide and we are right." As he grew older his garden attracted him more and more. It was very beautiful and very large with lavish plantings of flowers and clumps of shrubbery and evergreens. As he wandered in its enchantment he often found the philosophic solace which other things denied him. In it kings, courts and the follies of mankind were forgotten. "Fountains, flowers and shrubbery console," he wrote to an aging countess; "men do not always console."

Voltaire had an insatiable desire for space, and to gratify it he kept adding more and more land to his domains. But whatever he had must needs be put to use. How could an Arouet, even if he happened to be a poet, even think of anything else? The lands that he owned were tilled and cultivated with the same assiduity he bestowed upon his alexandrines. When Voltaire found, to his dismay, that the soil was poor and that nothing would grow, he transported huge quantities of loam and fertilizer. When this threatened to become too expensive, he hit upon the idea of penning cows at night on the poorer lands. He was convinced of the great merits of his scheme and advocated its use on a large scale. "A sovereign," he explained, "could thus change the nature of a vast tract of land by having cavalry camp upon it and consume forage drawn from the neighborhood." He added that whole regiments would be needed, but that "in the long run another tract of good land would be won from nature."

Not only was it Voltaire's ambition, as he said, "to make two blades of wheat grow where only one had grown before"; he hoped also to demonstrate in a practical way how farming could be turned to profit. Perhaps he was motivated in this by the same spirit which had once prompted him to conduct experiments on the nature of fire and on the Newtonian doctrines. Or was he, perhaps, moved by his persistently practical nature, which made it essential for him always to seek his full money's worth? Whatever may have been the force behind his motives, he found himself before long the owner of a model farm. He invested in the finest poultry and live stock. He raised silkworms, and for them he planted avenues of mulberry trees as far as the eye could reach. He had a large peach orchard and an excellent vineyard, as well as a fine kitchen and fruit garden. He had an apiary of more than four hundred colonies of bees. Not content to be an idle bystander, he reserved a plot of land which he called "Voltaire's field," and which he alone was allowed to till. He had the best and most up-to-date equipment. He had chicken coops, and barns and stables which, in a time when personal cleanliness was deemed a silly affectation, were almost impeccable. Voltaire was fastidious about such matters and took great pleasure in conducting his guests through his barns and stables. "I am only a peasant," he would say as he urged them to drink the purest milk in the world from cows "that dwelt in clean chateaux."

The poet's interest in animal husbandry prompted him to undertake the breeding of fine horses. With his customary display of enthusiasm he obtained a mare and a stallion, but despite all his encouragement, the animals failed to produce an offspring. When he made inquiries he found that the horses were too old, a fact which amused him and which became the butt of many a lusty joke. When the news of Voltaire's experience reached the Marquis de Voyer, the steward of the royal stables at Versailles, he presented him with a fine young stallion. "My seraglio is ready," Voltaire wrote, "nothing is wanting but the sultan you have promised me."

The lack of agricultural experience made itself felt in still another way. To gratify his fondness for trees, Voltaire planted thousands of saplings, elm, plane, hornbeam, chestnut and walnut. But most of his early plantings died because of the harsh winds and the impoverished soil, or because they were pulled up by peasants who saw no sense in the planting of trees. Yet Voltaire persisted: those that died he replaced, and when some of these perished, they too were replaced. He planted some twenty thousand trees. Four times he bordered the main highway with walnut and chestnut trees only to lose most of them. Yet he was undaunted. "I would plant today even if I were sure to die tomorrow. Others would enjoy them," he declared.

On the whole the results of Voltaire's agricultural endeavors were not very encouraging. He had been lured for a while by the theories of the physiocrats who held the powers of nature to be the only source of public wealth, and which stressed the necessity of non-interference with the laws of nature in so far as these bore on the relationships of society and industry. But Voltaire's practical experience as a farmer soon deflated any confidence he might have had in such theories. He found that, aside from the dairy business and the raising of wheat, his farm bore him no profits. The soil was too poor. Worse yet, he could get no efficient help, as most of the native sons were swarming to Geneva, where the city's rising industry was paying excellent wages. Confronted by such harsh facts, Voltaire returned to the economic theories of Colbert. He now believed in state subsidies to industry and in protective tariffs.

In 1765 Voltaire moved to his estate at Ferney. He had
grown weary of the thick air of sanctity which hovered
over Geneva and which at times penetrated even to *Les
Délices*. Ferney was a tiny hamlet of some forty or fifty
inhabitants, and about four miles from Geneva, but beyond its jurisdiction. Voltaire had acquired the property
some years earlier. Its condition at the time was old and
decrepit, and to put it into a suitable state he had spared
neither effort nor money. It was not a "palace," he wrote
—though it had fourteen bedrooms. It was only "a commo-
dious country house, with lands adjacent which produce
much hay, wheat and oats." It was also renowned for its
wonderful oaks, which, Voltaire said, were "as straight as
pines, which touch the sky, and which would render great
service to our navy, if we had one."

With the acquisition of Ferney Voltaire came into possession of a feudal title. He was now a full-fledged *Seigneur,*
"with all the rights and privileges thereunto appertain-
ing." He was on the whole quite unimpressed by his new
rank, and instead of being called *Seigneur,* he preferred to
be known by homelier titles he had himself devised, such
as "the little Swiss," "the old owl of Ferney," "the wood-
chuck of the Alps," "the old man of the mountain," or
"Friar Voltaire, unworthy Capuchin."

As at *Les Délices* Voltaire's Ferney home was constantly
besieged by visitors. They came from far and near, out of
honest admiration, or devoured by curiosity, to catch a
glimpse of Europe's most famous man. They represented
all walks of life, and many of them were themselves renowned. Among them was Marmontel, an author of some
distinction; d'Alembert, the brilliant *Philosophe;* Charles
James Fox, then a young man, but destined to play an

important part in English politics; James Boswell, Johnson's celebrated *alter ego;* and that talented jack-of-all-trades and specialist in amour, Casanova. To his guests, particularly to such whose qualities he esteemed, Voltaire was the most genial of hosts. He was fastidious about his personal appearance. Usually he wore a large waistcoat which stretched almost to his knees, and below which his thin little grey-stockinged legs protruded like two flimsy little sticks. He was heavily bewigged, and even indoors he topped his hair with a little cap of black velvet. When especially distinguished guests came to Ferney, or on Sundays, the author of *Candide* liked to splurge. On such occasions he put on a long coat, handsomely embroidered, vest and breeches of the same style, but the vest with tremendous flaps, galooned in gold, with huge sleeves and lace extending almost to the tips of his fingers. Thus, he told his guests, one has a noble appearance and is fit for the society of his colleagues. There was never any gastronomic failing at his house, for the master of Ferney was meticulous in such matters. Though he himself had long observed a diet that was almost Spartan in simplicity, the sight of good food and drink was still a delight to his epicurean heart. Voltaire wined and dined his guests in a grand manner, and when they were surfeited with food and beverage, he eased their digestion with mirth-provoking lines from *La Pucelle* or readings from *Ariosto,* or with the latest bawdy stories about Calvinian Geneva. The old man beguiled his guests with innumerable attentions, and once they were with him, they were generally reluctant to leave. D'Alembert came to Ferney intending to remain for only a few days before proceeding to Italy; instead, he stayed two entire months and never completed his trip.

When Casanova arrived at Ferney, he found Voltaire just rising from dinner.

"At last," the visitor exclaimed, "the happiest moment of my life has arrived. At length I behold my great teacher. For the last twenty years, sir, I have attended your school."

"Do me this honor twenty years longer," the old man replied, "and then do not fail to bring me the money for your tuition."

"I promise," said Casanova. "It shall not be withheld. But do you also promise that you will expect me?"

"I promise," Voltaire retorted, "and would sooner die than break my promise."

To Casanova Voltaire showed the letters he had received during his lifetime. It was a vast accumulation which he kept tied up in little bundles and which he stored in a special room.

"This," Voltaire explained, "is my correspondence. You see here nearly fifty thousand letters which I have answered."

"Do you keep copies of your answers?"

"Of a great many of them. I keep a secretary for that purpose."

"I know booksellers who would give you a high price for these treasures."

"Be on guard with the booksellers, should you ever publish a work. But perhaps you have already published something?"

"I will begin when I am older," replied the future author of the Memoirs.

Despite his cynicism and worldliness, despite his sophistry and the remarkable flexibility of his morals, Casanova was not in agreement with Voltaire's views on the Church.

"If you were to succeed in abolishing superstition," he asked, "what would you substitute for it?"

"I like that!" the old man shot back. "When I deliver the world from a monster that devours it, I am asked what I will put in its place."

A very different visitor was the earnest and punctilious Boswell. Before presenting himself to Voltaire he had taken the precaution to obtain several letters of introduction, including one from "a Swiss colonel at the Hague." He was apparently impressed by his reception and carefully recorded in his notes that he had been "received by two or three footmen." Unfortunately, the old man of the mountain wasn't well, and when the Englishman was ushered into the poet's presence, Voltaire could do no more than "sit erect upon his chair and simper when he spoke." "He was not in spirits, nor I either," Boswell remarked, as he wrote a letter "in the finest humor and full of wit" to Madame Denis, to beg for another interview.

The young man came back the next day and in the evening there followed a long conversation with Voltaire. "I placed myself before him," he wrote. "I touched the keys in unison with his imagination. I wish you had heard the Music." Now and then Voltaire would break into English, and when he did, Boswell observed, "he was animated with the soul of a Briton. He had bold flights. . . . He swore bloodily as was the fashion when he was in England. . . ." He called Dr. Johnson a "superstitious dog." To mollify the rising tempest in Voltaire's spirit, Boswell told him what Johnson had said of the King of Prussia. "He writes," the Englishman had once remarked, "just as you may suppose Voltaire's footboy to do when he has been his amanuensis." Pleased by the Doctor's sage observation, Voltaire now expressed the thought that Dr. Johnson was "a very honest fellow."

Like Casanova, Boswell piloted the conversation to the subject of religion. "At last we came upon Religion," he wrote. "Then did he rage . . . and if ever two men disputed with vehemence we did. . . . For a certain portion of time there was a fair opposition between Voltaire and Boswell." Yet before long Voltaire's corrosive ridicule of the Infamous Thing proved too much for the solemn visitor. "He went too far," Boswell felt—though he persisted in asking questions. What about immortality? he wanted to know. "I know nothing about it," Voltaire retorted. He spoke lightly of "that pretty thing called Soul," though Voltaire conceded that for his part he was "but a very ignorant fellow." "But must we not believe, Sir, in the Master of the Universe?" the Englishman pleaded. Wearied at length by Boswell's insistent questioning, Voltaire shammed a sudden attack of vertigo. He fell helplessly into his chair and closed his eyes; yet when, some moments later, he hopefully reopened them, the young man was still there. The next morning Voltaire sent word that he was ill; he stayed in his room until the Englishman had gone.

There were times when Voltaire wearied of the steady stream of callers. He was tired of being "the innkeeper of Europe," particularly when so many travelers, "unlike Don Quixote, who mistook inns for chateaux," persisted in mistaking Voltaire's chateau for an inn. His usual device in turning away an undesired stranger was to send word that he was ill—that he was, as a matter of fact, at death's door. On one occasion an unknown Englishman called. He was received with Voltaire's customary excuse. The next

Portrait of Madame Denis
(Attributed to Duplessis)

day the stranger returned, and again Voltaire was dying. "And if," he added to his servant, "the persistent fellow comes back, tell him I am dead and even buried." He retreated until the man went away.

Such maneuvering was not always successful. When an unknown caller was told that Voltaire was "not at home," the visitor insisted that he had heard his voice. "Tell him then," the voice shot back from the adjacent room, "that I am sick." "I shall take his pulse, I am of the profession," retorted the stranger. "Say that I am dead," continued Voltaire. "I will bury him. It will not be the first time, for I am a doctor." "This is a very obstinate man, let him enter." The stranger appeared. "You must take me for a curious beast," Voltaire said. "Yes, indeed, monsieur—for a phoenix." "Very well, then; know that it will cost you twelve sous to see me." "Here are twenty-four," said the stranger, "and I will be back tomorrow." This was too much even for Voltaire. His iron front collapsed and he bade his obstinate visitor to make himself comfortable.

Madame Denis continued to be in charge of Voltaire's household, a position she filled with the help of a multitude of servants. Yet the relationship between the plump little woman and her uncle was not always serene. Her integrity was not of the highest order. A consummate liar, she was not a bit hesitant in deceiving her uncle. She had a number of lovers, first the Marquis de Ximénès and then La Harpe. Both affairs were accompanied by the loss and publication of some of Voltaire's manuscripts. The second betrayal was too much even for a doting uncle, and Voltaire bundled his niece off to Paris. He felt it was "lamentable that neither her reason nor her ordinary amiability can assuage in her soul those violent tempests of passion."

In his dejection he planned to sell Ferney, to change his whole mode of living, to retreat to the hills and become a hermit. Nonetheless, he didn't have the heart to cut his niece's allowance; he continued to give her twenty thousand francs a year even while she was gone.

As for Madame Denis, in the beginning she was delighted to be back in the capital and to be carried along by its fast and delightful currents. She would never return to Ferney—of that she was certain! If her uncle wanted her, then he would have to come to Paris. She knew he was fond of her, and she was quite sure that if she handled him tactfully, she could induce him to return to his native city. But Voltaire was impermeable. When her effort failed, she took another course. She would come back to Ferney; she knew her uncle needed her; she knew he loved her; had he not been torn by grief when they parted? And she loved him too. Had she not for thirty-seven years been an affectionate daughter? And had she not left him "with death in her soul"? The very memory of her leave-taking "was poison to her spirit." Yes; she would come back. Not only would she come back, but she would even consent to having fewer attendants. All that she desired, now that she was determined to economize, was a personal maid and a Parisian valet "in white shirt and cuffs"; and also a coachman and two horses. If her uncle insisted, she added, she would set up a separate household.

At first Madame Denis' protestations made little headway. Voltaire tried valiantly to get along without his self-indulgent niece. Yet, as the months went by, he began to miss her. He found, curiously enough, that all her thefts and her deceptions, her violent emotional outbursts, all her faults and vices, could not counterbalance the loneliness of an aging man. He regretted having sent her away, and after a separation of twenty months, he asked her to return. "They say old men are hard," he reflected. "I am unfortunately as tender-hearted as if I were twenty years old."

Besides Voltaire and his niece there were several other more or less intimate members of the domestic circle. One of them was Marie Corneille, a relative of the distinguished dramatist. When Voltaire heard that the Corneille family was in dire financial straits, he offered to take Marie into his home. "It is only right," he remarked, "that an old soldier of the great Corneille should be useful to the grandchild of his general." The old man treated her with the care and tenderness he might have bestowed upon a child of his own. Toward her the springs of his generosity overflowed. He gave her an excellent education, and to provide her with an adequate dowry, he wrote an elaborate commentary to an edition of Corneille. When Marie married, nothing else would do but that she and her husband should set up house in the chateau at Ferney.

Another recipient of Voltaire's generosity was Father Adam. Associated with the Jesuits until their suppression in 1762, Father Adam was old and friendless, and somewhat the worse from the treatment a harsh destiny had accorded him. Voltaire had befriended him not long after his own banishment from Paris, and when he settled in Switzerland, the poet offered him sanctuary in his home. It did not take the old man long to become deeply attached to his benefactor. Indeed, so deep was his affection that he could not resist the hope that his benevolent host might yet be saved for Life Eternal. He believed in the depth of his heart that some day Voltaire would return to the teach-

ings of Holy Church, and to expedite the poet's conversion
he offered long and fervent prayers. As for Voltaire, he
was far more impressed by the reverend father's extraordinary talent for chess. He played frequently with the priest
and as the game proceeded he teased him relentlessly with
un-Christian pleasantries. But the venerable Jesuit usually
obtained his sweet revenge by winning the game. Now and
then the incessant beatings administered by the priest
would get under the poet's skin, and he would renounce
the game forever. "To spend two hours," he would say, "in
moving little pieces of wood! A scene could be written in
that time." Yet, gradually, the hope of avenging his defeat
would tempt him, and his resolution was forgotten. "Adam,
where art thou?" he would call, as he summoned the white-
haired man for another session of the ancient game.

Meanwhile Voltaire's pen had not been idle. From it
there flowed, incessantly and irrepressibly, the sparkling
stream of his thoughts. They swept through endless pages,
and in hundreds of rippling sentences, they poured into
the vast sea of his prose and verse. Never, not even in his
happiest days at Cirey, did he write with such prolific ease.
Though he was far from Paris, even in his remote corner
close to the Alps, he still dominated the Parisian theatre;
and while his critics intrigued with consummate shrewdness to break his spell, the old man was still their master.
"I receive a hundred thrusts and I give back two hundred
—and I laugh," he said as he struck against his foes.

To dispose of Fréron, a literary critic approved by the
Court, Voltaire composed a comedy in which he made one
Frelon (the wasp), the target for his ridicule. The play,
which was announced as the work of an English clergyman,
was called "The Scotch Girl" (*L'Ecossaise*). Produced in

the summer of 1760, it was an immediate hit, and despite
the warm weather it played to crowded houses. The scene
of Voltaire's comedy was a London coffee house, replete
with boisterous talk of stocks and bonds, business and politics. In it appeared Frelon, a Grub Street hack, "always
eager to manufacture infamy at a *pistole* a paragraph."
Fréron tried bravely to pretend that his enemy's critical
shafts had not hurt him. "The 'epigrams' of spider, viper,
scoundrel, rascal," with which the play had bombarded
him, he intimated, "were the work of a man of low taste,
whose chief supporters were the *Philosophes*." "The poor
man," Voltaire commented on hearing this, "is so wounded
he cannot laugh." In time Fréron's wounds healed, though
the memory of their pain lingered. Whenever the critic
forgot himself so much as to give any of Paris' leading
actors a bad notice, they promptly revived "The Scotch
Girl"—and invariably Frelon mended his ways.

The unfortunate Fréron was not the only one to feel
the Old Owl's claws. Another victim was the redoubtable
Le Franc, Marquis de Pompignan, and Voltaire's successor
as Royal Historiographer. Though he was a man of only
slight literary ability, Le Franc had recently been made a
member of the French Academy, to succeed Maupertuis,
now gone to another world. The honor of being among the
Forty Immortals apparently went to the new member's
head. For in his acceptance speech, Le Franc was rash
enough to attack the literature and philosophy of his era.
Naturally the author of *Candide* needed no interpreter to
tell him that Le Franc's attack had been aimed at him;
nor did he need an invitation to reply. He lashed out at
the Marquis with a pamphlet entitled "The Whens" (*Les
Quands*), because each one of its paragraphs began with

the word *when*. It forcefully reminded the Marquis that:

"*When* one happens to be rich, one ought not to taunt men of letters with their poverty.

"*When* one succeeds a bizarre writer (Maupertuis) ... one ought not to propose him as the model for religious writers. One ought to keep silent, or use more art or restraint.

"*When* one is hardly a man of letters and not at all a philosopher, it is not becoming to say that our nation has only a false literature and a vain philosophy.

"*When* one has the honor to be admitted into a respectable company of literary men, one need not make one's opening speech a satire against them."

After the "Whens" came a salvo of "Fors" and "Ah! Ah's!" "*Ah! Ah!* Moses le Franc de Pompignan, you wished, then, to make all literature tremble! There was one day a braggart who gave some kicks to a poor devil, who received them with respect; but a strong man came up who kicked the braggart. Then the poor devil turned, and said to the braggart, '*Ah! Ah!*' monsieur, you did not tell me you were a coward; and he kicked the braggart in his turn, with which the neighborhood was marvelously content. *Ah! Ah!*"

Voltaire's outburst was a signal to the *Philosophes*, who now rushed into the fray, their guns blazing at the befuddled Marquis. The free-thinking Abbé Morellet fired off a volley of "Ifs," after which the air crackled with resounding "Yesses," "Noes," "Whats," "Whos," and "Whys." "Why," ran a riddle, "did Jeremiah weep so much?" "Because as a prophet he foresaw that some day Le Franc would translate him." Pompignan struggled like a man in a bog, but to no avail; the more he strove to extricate himself, the deeper he sank; until finally he submerged to the tune of a frivolous popular song, "The Village of Pompignan,"

> Can it be Pompignan I see
> Before mine eyes?
> And its great Marquis?
> So witty and so wise,
> As he most frankly testifies?
> Long live the king, and Simon the Wise!
> His favorite! His favorite!

The same year that witnessed "The Scotch Girl" saw a more serious attempt at dramatic achievement, with *Tancrède*, a tragedy. A decree, forbidding spectators henceforth to be seated on the stage, made it possible for an author to offer a much grander spectacle than heretofore; and of this opportunity Voltaire made the fullest use. Setting the play in Sicily in the days of chivalry, he presented a council room with knights ranged in a huge semi-circle, and discussing the troubled affairs of their country. The theme of the drama, which as usual was quite simple, recounted the story of a knight, returning from an unjust exile, and entering the lists, where he triumphed over his foes—after which he turned to the task of defeating the enemies of his country, which had treated him so shabbily. *Tancrède*, produced in September, 1760, was an immediate success. Its romantic, patriotic appeal provoked more tears than anything Voltaire had yet written. Even the caustic Fréron was constrained to admit that *Tancrède* possessed all "the simplicity and beauty of the classic, above all the

Odyssey," though he felt—quite rightly—that the quality of the author's verse had deteriorated.

Tancrède's triumph was due not merely to its enchanting theme, but also to the excellence of its two leading actors, Lekain and Mademoiselle Clairon. Voltaire realized this and to express his gratitude he wrote a poetic "Epistle to Mademoiselle Clairon." Some time afterward, when the actress embarked on a campaign to alleviate the harsh treatment accorded by the State and Church authorities to the acting profession, the dramatist came to her support. "Actors," he wrote, "are paid wages by the king, and excommunicated by the church: they are ordered by the king to play every evening, and forbidden to play at all by the ritual. If they do not play, they are put into prison; if they play, they are cast into sewers. We delight to live with them, and object to being buried with them; we admit them to our tables and close our cemeteries against them. It must be admitted that we are a very reasonable and a very consistent people."

Shortly before the presentation of *Tancrède* Voltaire published "The History of the Russian Empire under Peter the Great." The subject had not been his own choice, but had been suggested to him by Peter's daughter, the Empress Elizabeth. Yet for Voltaire the topic was not devoid of interest. As a youth in Paris—just prior to his introduction to the Bastille—he had seen the Russian monarch walking in the streets of Paris. The strange contrast between the obviously foreign Peter, with his rough and alien manners and the very proper French *noblesse,* was obvious at once to Voltaire. Subsequently, when he wrote about Charles XII of Sweden, his researches inevitably brought him into contact with Russian affairs. The study of Peter, however, involved more than the usual difficulties encountered by the writer of history. It was not easy to draw a frank and honest picture of a man called great by all the Russians—particularly when that picture had been ordered by the great man's daughter. True, the Russian government was lavish in its help. Voltaire could have all the maps he wanted, all the documents he needed; but the maps, he found, were often quite fantastic, while the documents were frequently unreliable. As for the author, for once he himself was filled with doubts. "I doubt," he wrote to Madame du Deffand, "if Peter will be as amusing as the 'Life of Charles XII,' for Peter was only extraordinarily wise, while Charles was extraordinarily foolish." Yet, when the book was finished, it was a commendable piece of writing. Voltaire found, in essence, that "the Russians ought certainly to regard Peter as the greatest of men. From the Baltic sea to the frontiers of China he was a hero. But ought he to be a hero to ourselves? Was he comparable in valor to our Condés and Villars; and in knowledge, intellect, morals, was he comparable with a crowd of men among whom we live today? No. But he was a king, and a badly instructed king; and he did what perhaps a thousand sovereigns in his place would not have done. . . . He was an architect who built in brick, and who elsewhere would have built in marble." With such an estimate, so delicately balanced between praise and censure, not even the Empress could find fault; in fact, so delighted was Elizabeth that she sent the author her portrait set in diamonds.

A very different work was the "Philosophical Dictionary." Its foundations had been laid in Potsdam, where it occurred to Voltaire that the learned disquisitions which passed back and forth over the royal supper table merited permanent preservation in a book. The "Philosophical Dictionary," said its author, "can be read only really by enlightened people; the ordinary man is not made for such knowledge." The remark was probably nothing more than a subtle attention-getting device, for where is the person who would imagine himself to be only ordinary? If Voltaire really was in earnest, then nobody believed him. For, when the "Philosophical Dictionary" appeared in 1764, it was promptly gobbled up by an eager public. People read it, whether they were enlightened or not—whether they understood it or not. They were enchanted by its pointed, mocking sentences, which laughed and danced so lightly through its pages; they were enamored of its humor; and they were delighted by its daring. Voltaire, chuckling with fiendish joy, delved into Adultery, Atheism, into Fraud, Kissing and Nakedness. It explored the Limits of the Human Mind, the meaning of Love, the sadness of Tears. There was even a short essay on "Why?" "Why," it asked, "does one hardly ever do the tenth part of good one might do?" "Why in half of Europe do girls pray to God in Latin which they do not understand?" "Why does so much evil exist . . . ?" "Why do we exist? Why is there anything?"

Voltaire was careful not to sign his name to the book, and though only one man could possibly have written it, that man stoutly denied it. There were Hebrew quotations in it, weren't there? and what did he know about Hebrew? He protested to all his friends that he had not written it. "I have heard the abominable dictionary spoken of," he wrote to d'Alembert. "It is a work of Satan." "It has terrified me," he declared; "but the climax of my affliction is that some Christians are so little worthy of that beautiful name as to suspect me of being the author of a work so anti-Christian." "Alas!" he added, "I have scarcely been able to get a copy of it."

His duplicity, if not commendable, was at least a protection which served him well. For to the shrewd eyes of the authorities, the poison lurking in the sentences of the "Philosophical Dictionary" was obvious; and in March of 1765 the Parliament of Paris ordered the book burned by the public hangman. A month later the Pope hurled his solemn curses and anathema upon it; and soon after that, Protestant Geneva followed suit. Meanwhile, of course, the book was in great demand, and it ran from one surreptitious edition to the next. "I have always offered one prayer to God," Voltaire subsequently wrote. "This is it: 'May God render my enemies very ridiculous!' God has answered me."

The dramas and histories, and the numerous essays Voltaire contributed to the Encyclopedia, the letters, the odes and epistles—all these formed only a part of the writings which came from his indefatigable pen. He had recognized from that outset that in his campaign for Reason and Humanity the Encyclopedia, while admirable and desirable, was an insufficient weapon. Its cost was far too great to make it available to the multitude. Accordingly Voltaire set himself the task of unleashing upon Europe a deluge of small pamphlets wherein he expounded his views, and blasted away against cruelty, injustice, superstition and intolerance. Nothing that was absurd escaped his mockery; and his writings were broadcast everywhere. From his citadel overlooking Lake Geneva he sent them out in bulk to every part of the world; he wrapped packages with paper on which his attacks were printed; he slipped his tracts into the trunks and traveling bags of his guests; and no matter where he went, he was sure to leave a trail of pamphlets. And while these writings were the journalism of a genius, they were also the weapons of war. This the authorities realized; every page they read contained a blazing indictment of their antiquated system; and they resorted to the usual punitive measures. They confiscated the outrageous writings, and had them solemnly destroyed by the common hangman. Meanwhile, secure in his fastness across the border, their author, whose name never appeared on any of his bellicose tracts, grinned sardonically as he composed more pamphlets. "As for my puny self," he declared, "I make war up to the last moment."

And war it was. For the authorities recognized the strength of their opponents. Alarmed and apprehensive, they introduced stringent counter-measures. Circumstances, unfortunately, played into their hands when an attempt was made on the life of the king. Though the would-be assassin was a fanatical Jansenist, and consequently a sworn enemy of virtually everything Voltaire and the *Philosophes* upheld, a royal decree was issued whereby "all persons convicted of having composed and printed writings tending to attack religion, to excite the minds of the people, to impair royal authority, and disturb the order and tranqulity of the state shall be punished with death, as well as the printers, agents and others who shall have spread them abroad."

A reign of terror followed. Authors were branded and imprisoned; printers were sent to the galleys; the Encyclopedia was suppressed; and books were seized and burned in the public square.

Meanwhile the diabolical Fates were at work. In Toulouse there lived a family by the name of Calas. They were Huguenots. One of their sons, Marc-Antoine, a morbid and sensitive youth, had dreamed of becoming a lawyer, but because of his faith the profession was closed to him. One night, while the Calases were upstairs at supper, Marc-Antoine hanged himself in his father's dry goods store. When the youth's body was found, a fanatical mob accused the suicide's aged father, Jean Calas, of having killed his son in order to prevent his conversion to Catholicism. Tried before a prejudiced and bigoted court, the aged man was found guilty by a vote of eight to five and sentenced to torture and death.

The sentence imposed upon Jean Calas was incredibly brutal. By it the old man was to "undergo the question ordinary and extraordinary." Wearing only a hair shirt, he was to be conducted in a cart from the prison to the cathedral, where, on his knees, and with a wax taper in his hand, he was to beg in all humility for the pardon and mercy of God, the king and the state; then he was to be led to the Place Saint-George, where on a scaffold in full view to all, the executioner was to break his arms, thighs and loins; after which he was to be bound to the wheel, "his face towards the sky, living, if it pleased God, in pain and repentance of his crimes." Finally, the body was to be flung into a fire and the ashes scattered to the wind.

On the tenth of March, 1762, the sentence was carried out. First came the torture of the question, then the penance. Accompanied by two Jesuit priests and a magistrate, the aged man was brought to the scaffold, where he was bound to a huge wooden cross. Then with an iron bar the executioner proceeded to break the condemned man's limbs one by one, pausing after each stroke while the magistrate urged him to confess. "There is fire which will burn your body to ashes," he shrieked. "Speak the truth." It was too late; merciful death had sealed his lips.

Yet this was not all. The two daughters of Jean Calas were forced into a convent; his two sons were banished forever; and all the Calas property was confiscated by the crown.

When Voltaire heard of the affair he felt that Jean Calas must have been guilty: the parliament of Toulouse would certainly never murder an innocent man. "Even in France," he declared, "it is improbable that the Calas judges should without any motive break an innocent man on the wheel." Before long, doubts began to assail him. A merchant, who with him. The suicide's brother, Pierre, now a refugee in had been in Toulouse at the time of the tragedy, talked Geneva, told him what had really happened. "I found," Voltaire declared, "a simple and ingenuous youth, with a gentle and very interesting countenance, who, as he talked to me, made vain efforts to restrain his tears." Yet Voltaire wanted to be sure of his ground: to find out whether Pièrre always told the same story, the poet hired a detective to follow him. To satisfy himself about Pièrre's integrity, he wrote to friends of the family. More and more the evidence pointed to the horrible truth. To d'Alembert he wrote: "The city of Toulouse, greatly exceeding Geneva in folly and fanaticism, made a martyr of this young man. No one thought of finding out whether he had hanged himself, which is highly probable. They buried him with pomp in the cathedral; some of the parliament assisted with bare feet at the ceremony; the new saint was invoked;

after which, the criminal court broke the father on the wheel by a majority of eight votes to five. The judgment was the more Christian since there was no evidence against the accused. . . . We are become the horror and scorn of Europe."

These were crushing words, but they were deeply serious. They sprang from his inmost feelings and in them was bound an overmastering determination to establish justice. It was not easy to reopen the case; for the magistrates of Toulouse kept their records under lock and key; and to prove there had been a miscarriage of justice access to the records was essential. "Why do you bother about such things?" a friendly pastor asked him. "Let the dead bury their dead. "I found an Israelite in the desert," Voltaire replied, "an Israelite covered in blood; suffer me to pour a little wine and oil into his wounds; you are the Levite, leave me to play the Samaritan."

Implacably Voltaire proceeded. The utter hopelessness of rehabilitating the Calas family only served to spur him on. Soon the fire which burned in his soul flamed over Europe. He wrote pamphlet after pamphlet, seeking to mobilize public opinion against the infamous court; he poured indictments upon the judges, the royal court, and the fanatics who approved the action of the magistrates. Every friend he had Voltaire harnessed to the cause: Richelieu, the Duke of Villars, Madame de Pompadour, Frederick of Prussia, Elizabeth of Russia—all were made to serve. Meanwhile subscriptions poured in from all over Europe—in England the list was headed by the Queen, followed by the Archbishop of Canterbury and seventy-nine lords. "There is one influence," Voltaire said, "great enough to obtain from the Chancellor or the King an order to send a copy of the record—*the cry of the public!*"

Eventually, after three years, the cry of the public could no longer be denied. The King of France, bowing before a master he had never known, ordered a new trial in Paris, and the Parliament of Toulouse to produce the records. The denouement, when it came, came swiftly. Forty metropolitan judges unanimously declared Jean Calas to have been innocent. The Calas property was to be restored. Against the magistrates no action was taken; but one of them, David de Beaudrigue, the most fanatical of them all, died a raving madman.

The decision of the Parisian judges was universally applauded. "It was the finest fifth act the stage has ever presented," declared the jubilant Voltaire. Congratulations from all over Europe rained down upon Ferney. To all his other titles, the Old Man of the Mountain had now added one more: he had become the Man of Justice. "A philosopher is not to pity the unhappy—he is to be of use to them," he said.

Even before the triumphant end of the Calas affair Voltaire was occupied with another. The case concerned a young Protestant girl, Elizabeth Sirven, a pitiable, half-witted creature. One night she wandered from her home and a few days later her dead body was found floating in a well in a nearby town. The same fanaticism which had victimized Jean Calas now put its fateful hand upon the Sirven family. A warrant was issued by the local magistrates ordering the arrest of the entire family, which, however, succeeded in escaping over the Swiss border before the writ could be executed. Meanwhile Sirven and his wife were tried in their absence and convicted of murder. Their property was confiscated; Sirven was condemned to be broken on the wheel and his wife to be hanged. The daughters, convicted as accomplices, were condemned to witness the execution of their parents and then to be banished. Meanwhile, since the condemned people were not available, they were to be hanged in effigy. What Voltaire had done for the Calas family he now did for the Sirvens. This time the mills of justice ground even more slowly, for it required ten years to bring about a retrial. In the end the triumph was perhaps even greater than in the Calas affair. Not only were the Sirvens completely exonerated and indemnified, but by a strange stroke of ironical fate, the court which made the decision happened to be that of Toulouse.

The fight for justice brought the defender of Calas and the Sirvens universal acclaim. Victims of oppression turned to him for help. But sometimes even he could not help; some victims he could not vindicate. Montbailli was broken on the wheel as a parricide, though he was innocent; the young Chevalier de la Barre was tortured and burned at the stake for alleged blasphemy; Count de Lally was executed by an irate government for having allowed himself to be defeated by Clive in India; and there were many others. Yes, the promise of the "English Letters" was at last fulfilled. It had taken a long time. When it came it came in superabundance; it overflowed everything far and wide; it could not be stemmed; for the currents that it started were deep, far-reaching, irrepressible. In their turbulent sweep even Frederick's skepticism dissolved. "The nations," he said, "will write in their annals that Voltaire was the promoter of that revolution in the human mind which took place in the nineteenth century! Who would have said in the twelfth century that the light which lighted the world would come from a little village called Ferney?"

The light that was to shine from Ferney was not yet fully lit. There were iniquities and injustices within an hour's walk. In Geneva there were ominous rumblings. There, there were civil disorders coupled to political unrest. The underprivileged who furnished the city's cheap and servile labor, but who had no voice in the government, were demanding suffrage and representation. They were resisted by the town's aristocracy and the clash which ensued brought on the "War of Geneva." Voltaire not only encouraged the underprivileged but gave them active support. When they fled from the city he established them at Ferney and at Versoix, a hamlet on the Lake, but outside of Genevan jurisdiction. On his estate at Tournay he converted his treasured theatre into a factory for the production of silk. Here he gave employment to the refugees, and before long he was sending sample stockings, accompanied by flattering compliments, to the Duchess of Choiseul, the wife of the French Minister of Foreign Affairs, and to other prominent women, in the hope that they would not only honor him by wearing them, but also help him to promote their sales. "Deign to wear them, madame, one single time," he wrote. "Then show your legs to whomsoever you wish, and if they don't confess that my silk is stronger and more beautiful than that of Provence and Italy, I renounce my trade."

Among the refugees who came from Geneva were a multitude of watchmakers, whose skilled craftsmanship was renowned even then. Voltaire tried to settle these people at Versoix, but when the town's facilities proved inadequate, he brought most of them to Ferney. Houses

were built as rapidly as possible, and to start the watchmakers at their old trade, Voltaire advanced them sixty
thousand louis. The houses were deeded to the tenants,
who agreed to pay Voltaire a rent of six per cent during
his life, and after his death a rent of three per cent to
Madame Denis. Voltaire himself bought the gold and silver and the jewels required by the workers, and under his
direction, energetic yet sympathetic, a thriving watch business rapidly evolved. Within six weeks the first watches
were ready. They were as handsome and as accurate as any
to be had in Geneva, and they had the added advantage
of being much cheaper. The first half dozen were sold,
amid a fanfare of publicity, to the Duke of Choiseul.

Voltaire's talent for getting attention served him well in
his new venture. Few letters he wrote ever left Ferney
without containing some glowing tribute to its watches.
Whether the letter concerned itself with poetry or politics,
or with the infamies of priests and bishops—it made little
difference—somewhere it was sure to speak of Ferney's incomparable watches and stockings. To influential persons
everywhere Voltaire sent complimentary samples of his
merchandise. The Countess d'Argental received a beautiful watch encrusted with diamonds, as did the Countess
Dubarry, the king's new mistress. The imagination the
poet had hitherto reserved for his dramas and histories, he
now directed into the composition of advertising circulars.
In them he extolled the advantages of owning a watch
made at the Royal Manufactory of Ferney—for so the new
enterprise was called—and which was ready to sell exemplary timepieces of "plain silver from three louis to re-
peaters at forty-two louis." With every circular that left
Ferney there went a personal sales letter from Voltaire.

One of the first to patronize the new industry was Catherine II of Russia. "Send me watches, to the value of some thousand rubles. I will take them all," she wrote. Voltaire sent her 8,000 rubles' worth. Then, fearing that Her Majesty might not know what to do with so many watches, he wrote her apologetically that he had scolded "those poor artists for abusing her goodness." "I take the liberty above all," he wrote, "to pray you, madame, not to pay all at once the sum of 39,238 livres, which is the total of the two invoices. Though my colonists should have to wait a year for half the amount, I should regard them as fortunate." He concluded with the suggestion that, should Her Majesty be satisfied with the goods and the prices, he would be pleased to execute her further orders.

As for Catherine, she was quick to assure Voltaire that the expense would not ruin her. "I would be very unfortunate," she wrote, "if I were so reduced as not to have little sums of money wherever and whenever I want them." The empress meant what she said, and within a few weeks she paid her account in full. On behalf of the watchmakers Voltaire thanked her profusely. He added that he could not recall whether he had spoken to her of a pendulum clock now being made at Ferney. "If you wish one, you shall have it immediately," he assured her. All that was required was that Her Majesty should name the price— and Voltaire "would answer for it that she shall be well served, and cheaply too." Then, as if it were a casual afterthought, he wondered if Catherine would help him establish a market for Ferney timepieces in China.

Within a few years watches valued at more than a half million francs were being exported from Ferney to every part of the world. The greater part of the profits derived from their sale went to the watchmakers themselves. True, Voltaire never consulted his workers when he made his decisions, but whatever he decided was nearly always prompted by what he deemed to be their best interests. Now and then, when there was a bad debt, as on the occasion of the marriage of the Dauphin to Marie Antoinette, then by some strange paradox, one of the most avaricious of men would also be one of the most generous, and insist on bearing such a loss himself.

The correspondence between Ferney and St. Petersburg was not always of a purely business nature. Catherine, who had succeeded to the Russian throne when her husband died with mysterious suddenness, was, like Frederick, a strange alloy of good and evil. She had every vice and every virtue; she was egotistical yet disinterested; she was the most benevolent of mortals, yet also one of the most ruthless. She possessed wit and charm; she was clever; yet she was treacherous, malicious, and she had a furious temper. By birth a German princess, she had come to Russia to be the wife of Peter, the heir to the imperial crown. The early years of her marriage had not been happy; and to escape their unpleasant thralldom, she sought refuge in sentimental stories. It so happened that one of Voltaire's works fell into her hands, and ever since, she declared, she had been under the greatest obligation to the author. "I have," she wrote him, "not ceased to read them, and I have desired no books which were not as well written as yours, or as instructive." Voltaire, she averred, was the "creator of her taste." If she had any knowledge at all, then "it was to you that I owe it." Voltaire's admiration for Catherine glowed no less brightly than hers for him. "Your Imperial Majesty," he said with an adulation he had once reserved for Frederick, "has found a glory unknown to all other sovereigns." When he offered her some verses he had composed in her honor, Catherine's delight knew no bounds. "My head is as hard as my name is inharmonious," she replied. "I have never written verses, but I adore nonetheless those of others." As an expression of her appreciation she sent the poet a snuff box with her portrait on it, surrounded with diamonds, a robe of Russian sable, and a digest of the laws of her realm. In return Voltaire dedicated the next edition of the "Essay on Morals" to "the very high and august princess, Catherine II, Empress of all the Russias, Protectress of the Arts and Sciences, worthy by her understanding to judge ancient nations as she is worthy to govern her own." Three thousand copies of the work were printed in St. Petersburg and within a week they were all sold.

As Ferney evolved from a little hamlet of half a hundred peasants into a colony of more than a thousand inhabitants, it was only natural that there should be economic problems. Though everybody labored diligently and lived modestly, at the end of the year there was pitifully little to show for one's effort. An archaic system of taxation, complicated and unjustly applied, deprived the worker of more than three-quarters of his earnings. He paid taxes on virtually everything, and he was subject at all times to special assessments, such as those levied on the occasion of a prince's marriage or the accession of a ruler. He paid a head tax and a salt tax; he paid a tax on property, even though he owned none; he paid a tithe to the Church, whose clergy, however, were exempt. As he went from one place to another he had to pass through numerous tol!

gates, where again he was required to pay a tax.

At first Voltaire's interest in the tax problem was purely selfish. As the owner of vast acreages, situated in several states, he found his taxes extraordinarily high. His operations as a farmer were hampered on all sides by stringent tariff regulations. He could not, for example, sell wheat in Geneva except by yearly application—while in the meantime smugglers on the city's borderlands were doing a thriving business. He had purchased Ferney in the name of Madame Denis, the widow of an officer of the king, and had thereby been able to obtain some of the exemptions usually enjoyed only by the nobles of the neighborhood. Yet what he had been able to save in this manner was more than offset by the heavy tax he had been obliged to pay when he leased the estate at Tournay.

In time his interest in the tax problem became more generalized, for he had come to realize that the burdens which put such a strain on his own resources bore much more crushingly on the less fortunate worker. When this became clear, he became absorbed in the study of economics. He entered into a long correspondence with the economist Moreau; he read Gallani's "Dialogues on Corn" and became exuberant over Abbé Morellet's "Dictionary of Commerce." To lighten the burden of the salt tax he proposed that Ferney should be allowed to run its own salt monopoly, whereby the required tax money could be obtained, while the salt would be considerably cheaper to the consumer than under the existing scheme. The merits of his plan were apparently recognized in high governmental circles, but beyond that nothing happened.

More and more Voltaire found himself in sympathy with the tax grievances of the peasants and the middle classes.

He supported the farmers and the artisans in their struggles against the tax collectors and the privileged lords of the neighborhood. His biting pen snapped at the iniquities and imbecilities of the existing tax system; and in a burlesque, "The Man with Forty Crowns," he satirized the financial troubles of France as well as the economic panaceas that were being used to solve the difficulties. "What will happen," the Man of Forty Crowns asked a geometer, "if the people of France should take a fancy to have twice as many children?" "It would come to pass," was the reply, "either that everyone would have his income cut down or the land would have to produce double, or that there would be twice as many paupers, or that there would be twice as much gain by foreign commerce, or that half the people would have to go to America, or that one-half the nation would eat the other half." When the Man of Forty Crowns desired to know why the monks lived in ease and comfort, while he had to struggle for a living, he was told that the monks prayed to God to save the souls of such wretched persons as himself. "Very well," the naive man suggested, "I will pray to God for them. Let us share." When an official had reduced an entire community to abject poverty, he received the personal commendation of the Minister of Finance. "Well done, you good and faithful servant," the Minister exclaimed. "Because you have been faithful, I will make you a tax collector." Then, turning his back on the new appointee, the Minister muttered, "We shall have to make these sacred and profane leeches disgorge! It is time to relieve the people, who without our care and our justice would never have anything to live upon except in the other world."

As might be expected, "The Man of Forty Crowns" was

very popular with a public that suffered from the injustices it so remorselessly ridiculed. Before long the work joined the distinguished company of the "English Letters," *Candide* and the "Philosophical Dictionary." Condemned by the Parliament of Paris, it was burned by the common hangman; and like its illustrious companions, it was eagerly read and furtively discussed.

For the next few years Voltaire worked tirelessly to advance the welfare of the colonists. "Give me a chance," he wrote to Richelieu, "and I am the man to build a city." His mind, which was accustomed to soaring in the higher altitude of fancy, was now held down by a mass of heavy detail and routine. There were houses to be built; merchandise to be made; markets to be established. There were swamps to be drained; fields to be tilled; and food provided for all. There was a school to be built, a hospital and a reservoir. And there was the ever-present spectre of insufficient money, for despite Voltaire's large personal fortune, the successful operation of Ferney required more than he could afford. He petitioned the authorities for "some privileges for my children," and was able, after a long struggle, to obtain economic concessions for them. But he dug into his own pocket too; and whenever any of his colonists needed money he lent it to them, and to people of the neighboring communities, without a cent of interest.

Yet there were moments when his spirit was heavy. He was over seventy and he realized the hour glass was running low. His doubts tormented him. Had he been wise, he wondered, to have begun such an ambitious project in his advanced age? A man of letters, he felt, should never have founded a community in which a half million francs' worth of trade was transacted every year. Ferney required his constant presence, his unrelenting effort. He had transformed a wilderness into a thriving, contented village; he had a thousand people to guide. All that was very fine—yet he dared not absent himself lest everything would relapse into the nothingness whence he had drawn it. When he thought how inextricably interwoven the interests of his villagers were with his continued activity in their behalf, he felt overwhelmed. The magnitude of the task seemed enormous—and there wasn't enough time to accomplish it. He was an old man, and this old man, he felt, was not much longer for this world.

Such distressful thoughts were rare, however. The success of his project was too obvious to be dissolved in melancholy chimera. Its lesson, so brilliant and so compelling, was clear. Ferney was a model town. Its people dwelt in comfortable homes which they owned themselves; they were employed and lived as contentedly as men can live. Above all they were free from the shadows of the Infamous Thing; for here Catholics and Protestants worked side by side. "When a Catholic is sick," the old man exclaimed delightedly, "Protestants go to take care of him, and in their turn receive from him the same assistance." And what benefits the lords might bring to their provinces if they would only make a serious effort! "Not only would the possessors of great domains through their generosity bring aid to those who suffer, but . . . they would help those whom they would put to work."

Two words summarize Voltaire's doctrines: freedom and justice. Not the freedom of the privileged that came through the accident of being born noble, or the freedom that came through political favor, but the freedom that was the right of every man—freedom of conscience, of worship, of speech and of the press, of assembly and petition: in a word the right to be free in one's mind and free to shape one's own destiny. The spectacle of cruelty and injustice tortured Voltaire. "I always have a fever on the twenty-fourth of August," he wrote to Count de Schomberg, the date of the massacre of St. Bartholomew. Oppressed innocence melted his heart; while persecution made him wildly angry and indignant.

The humanitarianism which flared from the depth of Voltaire's spirit was not nurtured by any naive faith in economic equality or complete democracy. Inequality of wealth was to him the handmaiden of the inequality of talent. They were inevitable and omnipresent, now and forever. "Every man," he declared, "is born with a rather violent propensity for domination, wealth and pleasure, and a strong taste for idleness; consequently every man would like to have the wives or daughters of other men, to be their master, to subject them to his every caprice, and to do nothing, or at least nothing but what is most agreeable. It is easily seen that with these handsome propensities it is as impossible for men to be equal as it is impossible for two preachers or two professors of theology not to be jealous of each other. Equality is therefore at the same time most natural and most chimerical." The great problem, as Voltaire saw it, was not to distribute wealth equitably, but to uproot tyranny and injustice, and to destroy the superstitious bigotry from which these evils sprang.

By temperament Voltaire was an aristocrat. Though born a bourgeois, he had slipped out of his bourgeois antecedents as easily as he had changed his bourgeois name. He spent nearly all his life among the upper classes, and nearly all his intimates were of the aristocracy—Richelieu, the brothers d'Argental, Frederick and the unforgettable Emilie du Chatelet. To such a man pure democracy seemed illogical and unnatural. Men, he declared, were incompetent and greedy, and to expect them to live side by side in an egalitarian republic seemed absurd and impossible. For a while such a government might function, until "there comes a voracious and vigorous man who takes everything for himself and leaves the people the crumbs."

Yet Voltaire's aristocratic tastes were tempered by his humanitarian impulses. "The lower classes," he wrote to his friend Damilaville, "will certainly be more worthy when the principal citizens cultivate virtue; they will be be restrained by example, which is the strongest and best of teachers." He went on to say that "pilgrimages, miracles, superstitious ceremonies would never make gentlemen. "Reason is making great progress, but only among a small number of people. . . . Let us be consoled that the number is growing every day. . . ." As the years went by the old philosopher's faith in education grew. Where once he had grave doubts over the ability of the people to profit by an education, his experience at Ferney caused him to change his mind. "No, sir," he declared, "all is not lost when the people are taught that they have minds. All is lost, on the contrary, when they are treated like a herd of bulls, for sooner or later they will gore you with their horns."

The basis of freedom and justice Voltaire believed was tolerance. A shaking fury entered his old, frail body when he spoke of Jean Calas and the fanatics who had killed him.

Shall a reed, he asked, crushed in the mud by the wind, say to another reed in the same tragic position, "Crawl as I crawl, or I shall petition that you be torn up by the roots and be burned?" "The individual who persecutes a man, his brother, because he is not of the same opinion is a monster." At Ferney there were no such monsters. Here Catholics and Protestants lived together in peace—indeed, from outward appearances one would never have imagined that in this village there were two different religions. Protestants took part in the procession commemorating the feast of the holy sacrament, and the curate thanked them publicly in his sermon. "Is not this better than St. Bartholomew," asked Voltaire. "I shall never cease to preach tolerance from the housetops," he wrote to a friend, "despite the groans of your priests and the outcries of ours —until persecution is no more."

In spite of the tranquility which hovered over Ferney, like warm and soothing sunshine, there were occasional tempests. For the advocate of reason and tolerance was formed, like all mortals, "of frailty and error." Time had not extinguished the roguishness in his character; trickery and perversity still lingered within its folds. Soon after settling at Ferney, the poet quarreled with one Ancian, the curé of Moens, a neighboring parish. The dispute was over a tithe of which the priest allegedly had deprived the poor. The owner of Ferney struck at the priest with character- istic frenzy. Ancian was, he said, "as brutal as a horse, cross-grained as a mule, and as cunning as a fox." The af- front was not easily overlooked, and since other insults followed in a steady stream, the relationship between the two men grew more and more hostile. Quarrel followed quarrel, and from them Voltaire always managed to emerge victorious. The feud came to a sudden climax when Voltaire announced that he intended to demolish Ferney's dilapidated church and replace it with a new one. He had obtained the bishop's feeble and grudging consent, and though the priest of Ferney appeared only mildly in favor of the project, Voltaire proceeded with his customary alacrity. He had not reckoned, however, with his old foe, Father Ancian. Quick to perceive his opportunity for revenge, the priest came to Ferney where he spread the report among the villagers that the atheistic Voltaire had profaned their church; not only had he removed its cross without the customary ritual, but he had even dared to heave blasphemy upon it. To give strength to his accusations, the indignant Ancian went to the ecclesiastic judge at Gex, where he charged Voltaire with the crimes of sacrilege and impiety and brought suit against him.

The priest's crafty move put a sudden stop to Voltaire's building operations. The workmen, threatened by a formal interdict, fled to their homes in fear and alarm. Meanwhile Voltaire was apparently helpless. Yet the man who had scoffed at Frederick and sent Maupertuis into oblivion, who from early youth had remorselessly castigated every enemy, that man certainly did not intend to let himself be brought to his knees by a country curate. The owner of Ferney turned to the ecclesiastic law-books, and as his eyes scanned their erudite pages, he found what he desired: a royal ordinance of 1627, long since forgotten but still valid, which prohibited a priest to serve either as a prosecutor or as a judge in such cases. Buoyed up by his findings, Voltaire turned upon his accusers. They had violated the law, he told them; and for the anguish and distress they had caused him he would sue them for damages. Then he bombarded them with ancient decrees and ordinances, with precedents and rulings that confounded and terrified them. In the end the harassed holy men were glad to drop their suit. "Bishop, judge, prosecutor, Jesuit," their relentless adversary exclaimed, "I have beaten them all. I am building my church as I wish, and not as they wished." To seal his triumph, utterly and forever, Voltaire applied to the Pope for a bull granting him absolute power over the churchyard, and permission for his laborers to work on feast days, "instead of getting drunk in honor of the saints." His Holiness granted the requests and also sent the petitioner some sacred relics to place in the church. When it was finished, it bore the inscription DEO EREXIT VOLTAIRE, which in the opinion of its builder made it the only church in the world dedicated to God alone and not to a saint.

The newly built church was not always the scene of quiet dignity. There were times, indeed, when even a kindly Providence must have wondered at the incredible antics of the advocate of reason. He resolved in 1768 to take Easter Communion. To prepare himself, he received absolution from a monk whom he had invited to dinner. "I have a mind," he confided to his secretary, Wagnière, "to preach a little to those rascals who persist in stealing." Attired in his fancy waistcoat, the aged man walked to the church in the company of two armed game wardens. After receiving the sacrament, instead of saying his prayers and returning humbly to his seat, he suddenly turned to face the amazed congregation, and without further ado he burst into an address. "Natural law is the most ancient," he began, and proceeded to denounce pilfering. He concluded his discourse with a few flattering compliments addressed to the bewildered priest, and having apparently accomplished his purpose, he returned to his pew.

Voltaire's impiety evoked a prompt rebuke from the Bishop of Annecy. "They tell me, Sir, that you received the Easter Communion. Many persons have been little edified by this, because they imagine it is only one more comedy for the public, in which you would again make sport of what is most sacred in our religion. As for me, Sir, I think more charitably; I cannot persuade myself that M. de Voltaire, the great man of our age, who, by the force of pure reason and the principles of a sublime philosophy, has declared himself above all mere pride, all the weaknesses and prejudices of humanity, could have been capable of betraying and dissembling his sentiments by an act of hypocrisy which in itself would suffice to tarnish all his renown, and to debase him in the sight of all thinking men. I must believe that your actions are marked by sincerity." The Bishop then reminded Voltaire that "the quality of the tree will be judged by the fruits"; and that the seventy-five-year-old poet should ever remember that "a wearied body, already bowed beneath the weight of years, warns you that you approach the term which all the famous men who have preceded you have reached at last— men who are now almost forgotten."

"How can you reproach me," Voltaire asked with feigned surprise and imagined injury, "for having fulfilled the duties of which every master should give the example upon his own territory, which no Christian should dispense with, and which I have fulfilled so often?"

A lively interchange of letters followed in which the Bishop apparently had the last word. "You know the works which are attributed to you; you know what is thought of you in every part of Europe; you know that nearly all the unbelievers of our age boast of having you for their Chief, and of having derived from your books the principles of their irreligion. . . . If these are calumnies, as you pretend, you must vindicate yourself, undeceive the public which now believes them." The prelate added that this was not difficult for one who is a true Christian at heart and spirit. "I will leave you, Sir," he concluded, "to judge what is proper for you to do."

The Bishop of Annecy not only had the last word; he also sent a copy of the correspondence to Versailles. Louis' reply warmed the Bishop's heart: He had been right, utterly right, both in theory and in practice, and Monsieur de Voltaire would be duly informed by the Court that he had behaved disgracefully. Encouraged by such an edifying response, the emboldened cleric published the text of the letters together with the Crown's reply. What the Bishop hoped to achieve by his act is not clear. Could it be that, in his exuberant confidence, he overestimated his own prowess? that he imagined that a show of the episcopal might would intimidate the aged philosopher? Or was the Bishop of Annecy simply a prudent man who, believing in candor, desired the whole world to know his story? Whatever the Bishop's motives may have been, the publication of the letters could produce but one result. Instead of undeceiving the public about the nature of his books, as the prelate had suggested, Voltaire burst into a wild rage. He hurled his choicest epithets at the holy man—the Bishop was "a fanatical idiot"; he was the "son of a miserable mason"; he was "a fool," "a monster" and "an ambitious rogue," one "who swears like a devil that he will have me burned in this world and in the other." The Bishop of

Annecy replied by forbidding the priesthood to allow Voltaire to confess or communicate.

Yet this was not the end. About a year later Voltaire had perfected a plan for his revenge. He summoned a Capuchin monk to his bedside and, pressing a coin into the hands of the astonished man, he asked him for absolution. Mindful of the bishop's order, the friar was evasive; he had no time, he said; too many people were waiting for him in church. Then, with a promise that he would return in three days, the Capuchin made a hasty exit.

When the monk failed to come back, Voltaire sent word that he was ill: his condition was deplorable—he was once more at the point of dying. Yet the friar, not deceived, took no step to succor the "dying" man, who now "with regret" found himself constrained to invoke the help of the law. Should the holy man persist in his obstinacy, then Voltaire would have him indicted by the Parliament for refusing to administer the sacraments to a dying Christian. The threat was too much for the distressed friar, and on the next day, timorously and reluctantly, and in the presence of a lawyer whom the poet had summoned to record the proceedings, the Capuchin gave Voltaire the desired absolution. No sooner had the friar and the lawyer departed than the dying man leaped from his bed, and went for a stroll in his garden. On the following Sunday, which happened to be Easter, he took communion.

When the news of Voltaire's conversion reached the *Philosophes* they were astounded. It seemed inconceivable to them that the most intransigent, the most vitriolic enemy of the Infamous should suddenly hurl away his flag and join the common foe. Yet their fears were quickly dispelled, for their comrade made no mystery of the affair.

"I am situated," he wrote to d'Argental, his "guardian angel," "between two bishops who date from the fourteenth century, and I must howl with these holy wolves. I must be on good terms with my curate, were he an imbecile or a rascal, and there is no precaution I should not take. . . ." He went on to explain that it was not the same with a poor farmer as with the Parisian nobles, "who can escape with a noon-day walk in the Tuileries." "I have to render the blessed bread in person in my parish; I am alone of my band against two hundred and fifty timorous consciences; and when it costs no more than a ceremony prescribed by law to edify them, there is no use making two hundred and fifty enemies." He concluded that since he made no pretense no one could reproach him for hypocrisy.

Yet reproached he was. In spite of everything he could say, his act was recognized for the hypocrisy it really was. It was vehemently denounced on all sides, even by some of his friends. A few fanatics called for the stake and the fagot; but as for the authorities, they were apparently willing to let the matter drop. As long as he remained within the letter of the law, took the sacrament, and denied the authorship of his evil books, they were willing to avert any further unpleasantness. As for Voltaire, for once he, too, was willing to cooperate.

In spite of his many activities as landlord, farmer, manufacturer and colonizer, in spite of his incessant quarreling and conniving, Voltaire in some mysterious and inscrutable way still found time enough to write. His more than three score years and ten had apparently not diminished his literary ardor. He now wrote with a greater energy than ever, as if in the realization that his pen was racing against time. In two years alone, 1767 and 1768, he composed more than fifty pieces. Dramas and romances poured from him. Yet his main literary effort was still in the interest of reform. The Encyclopedia, he remarked, with its "twenty volumes folio will never make a revolution —it is the little pocket pamphlets that are to be feared." And it was in the little pocket pamphlets that he specialized. For this type of literature, so light yet so deeply serious, Voltaire perfected two forms—the dialogue and the short essay. Either form gave him a magnificent vehicle to bear down on his pet aversions. None of these compositions was very long; yet all of them bristled with wit and mockery, and all of them shouted for some reform. He called for better education of women, and laughed at the idea of women being taught by nuns in convents to fit them to be the wives and mothers of the world. Suddenly he would become statistical. There were, he said, 9,468,800 victims, hanged, drowned, broken on the wheel, burned for the love of God, from the time of Constantine. Eighty-two holidays, he announced, had been set apart by the Church, "on which it was criminal to work, but not to be drunk." He warned his readers on the "horrible dangers of reading." "Our French people want to learn without studying," was his sarcastic remark. His faith in the progress of enlightenment was boundless. "The revolution," he said, as he wrote one pamphlet after another, "the revolution works in all minds," and "reason penetrates into the merchants' shops as into the nobles' palaces."

The busy years sped by. At eighty, Voltaire had become feeble. The energy which he once possessed so superabundantly had been almost entirely consumed. His puny body, which had begun life so precariously, had served him far beyond his fondest hopes. Yet now it plainly showed the traces of the years. The thin and spindly form, the skull-like countenance, with its covering of wrinkled parchment, the cheeks, hollow and emaciated, the sunken eyes, still glittering in defiance, and the mouth twisted into a ghostly, malicious grin—such had become the features of the world's most famous man.

Yet, though Voltaire's body had felt the touch of time, his spirit decidedly had not; though he moved with cautious, measured steps, his mind, oblivious to the passage of the years, was apparently as quick and nimble as ever. In its hidden chambers Voltaire still compounded the crisp and scintillating pieces, to the delight of his admiring contemporaries. Of all his writings, only his dramas showed a perceptible lapse, and of this even he seemed to be aware. But his romances, his tracts and pamphlets, still sparkled, as did his letters to his many friends.

The tragic lot which so often befalls the aged, that they end their days in loneliness, was fortunately not Voltaire's. Not only was he surrounded by multitudes of devoted colonists, but time had spared even his most intimate friends. Richelieu, the brothers d'Argental, Hénault, who long ago had pulled the manuscript of the *Henriade* out of the flames, and Madame du Deffand—all had been Voltaire's friends when he was a youth.

Voltaire had been as unshakable in his friendships as in his opinions, and in his ebbing years he found his friendships a supreme consolation. "I find that old age makes friendship necessary," he wrote to Madame du Deffand. "It is the consolation of our woes and the support of our weakness even more than is philosophy." He wrote constantly to all his friends, addressing them in the most affectionate tone, revealing to them his inmost feelings, consoling them in their bereavements, cheering them with his irrepressible humor.

The letters he wrote to Madame du Deffand were among his best; and certainly they were among his most touching. The aged woman, blind, unloved, forlorn, living in the shadow of despair, was herself a gifted correspondent, and under the caress of Voltaire she was enchanted. To dispel her morbid pessimism, Voltaire wrote her indefatigably. The news of her blindness stirred him profoundly. "I assure you," he wrote, "that my eyes were a bit moist when I heard what has happened to yours. I had judged . . . that you were in twilight, not entirely in the night. I thought you were in somewhat the same condition as Madame de Staal, but having the added advantage of being free, of living at home . . . of having friends who think and talk freely with you. . . . I agree with you that life is not good for much; we endure it through the force of an almost invincible instinct that mother nature has given us; and she added to this the instinct at the bottom of Pandora's box, hope. . . ."

As the years moved on Madame du Deffand's cup of sorrow overflowed. In her most dreadful moments she contemplated suicide. When Voltaire became aware of the abysmal depth of her despair, he tried to divert her. "I would not commit suicide," he said, "because I am receiving life annuities from two sovereigns and I would be inconsolable if my death enriched two crowned heads."

More seriously, however, he felt that "upon reflection I think we should never think of death; the thought is good for nothing but to poison life. The real business of life is not to suffer, for, as for death, that moment is as insensible as the moment of sleep. People who announce it ceremoniously are the enemies of the human race; we must keep them from ever approaching us. Death is nothing at all; the idea alone is sad. So let's never think of it, and live from day to day. Let us get up in the morning saying: What can I do today for my health and amusement? That's the final answer for people of our age."

Return To Paris

IN MAY, 1774, Louis XV died. He had been King of France for almost sixty years, and into those years he had compressed all the vices of his age. He was bigoted and brutal. His lack of personal morality, his indolence and utter indifference to the welfare of his subjects almost defy the imagination. "A man without love, without spirit," one of his ministers characterized him, "liking evil, the way children like to torment dumb animals, and having the faults of the vilest and most sordid." During his ignoble reign France lost India and Canada, and plunged into the deepest bankruptcy, while Louis spent a million dollars a year on fireworks, and his mistresses spent even more on themselves. Despite frequent warnings from the more able ministers that there must be governmental reforms, the king remained apathetic. "The machine will last through my life," he said with a shrug of the shoulders. He lived for himself and for his mistresses, selfish, profligate, debauched, until, racked by disease and dreading the approaching end, he confessed and received absolution.

The king's death drew Voltaire's eyes toward Paris, for it had been Louis who had stood in the way of the poet's return. True, the order for Voltaire's exile, which Louis had signed at the request of his daughters, had never been formally executed. Yet, though it lacked the force of an actual order, its effect had been the same. During Louis' lifetime Voltaire was not safe in Paris, and to return would have meant immediate imprisonment. With the monarch's death Voltaire's situation changed. He was assured by friends that, should he desire to return to the capital, he would be unmolested; and even though the new king, Louis XVI, would in all likelihood not give his personal approval to Voltaire's return, at least he need have no fear of persecution.

Voltaire hesitated. He was too feeble to undertake the long journey over rough and hazardous roads; his wretched health would never stand the strain. Besides, his villagers needed him—"my colony needs my actual presence," he wrote to d'Argental. Furthermore, in spite of the assurance that he would be safe, the old man felt skeptical. "There are in Paris," he said, "forty thousand fanatics who, while blessing Heaven, would carry forty thousand fagots to make a fire to burn me. That would be *my* bed of honor."

Nevertheless, the lure of Paris was enormous. Voltaire had not seen his native city for almost thirty years. He had pretended at times that he disliked it immensely; but in the depth of his heart Paris, with all its tumult and frivolity, with all its bickering and fanaticism, was still supreme. All his friends were there, all the attachments, all the associations which made a hard life tolerable. He had longed for

Courtesy of New York Public Library

A drawing of Voltaire

them many a time. His own life, he realized, was hastening away. Soon it would be too late.

While Voltaire was trying to make up his mind, torn between his common sense and the natural nostalgia of an old man to revisit the scenes of his earlier life, an event occurred which drew him irresistibly away from Ferney. The poet had written a play, *Irène,* which had been accepted by the *Comédie* and in which, as usual, he had tremendous confidence. Unfortunately, at the last moment Lekain, for whom the lead had been written, refused to accept the part. Voltaire tried to persuade his old friend to reconsider his action, but in vain. The actor's decision was in itself without significance; yet in its effect its weight was considerable. It was, indeed, the factor which more than any other made Voltaire decide that he must return to Paris.

On the 6th of February, 1778, accompanied by his valet and a servant, Voltaire left Ferney. He had promised the villagers that he would be back within a few weeks. In spite of his reassurance, the thought of his departure saddened them, and as they lined the road to say farewell their eyes were dimmed with tears.

The trip soon turned into a triumphal tour. The vainglory of fame, which Voltaire had so often pretended to despise, was abundantly his. Everywhere the great man appeared, tumultuous crowds pressed upon him. To be near him some of his adorers disguised themselves as waiters; others serenaded him at night; while others kissed his horses.

On the sixth day Voltaire reached the gates of Paris.

"Do you have anything to be declared?" one of the customs officials asked.

"Upon my faith, gentlemen," a high-pitched voice from within the coach gayly retorted, "I think the only contraband here is myself."

Puzzled, the guard peered into the carriage to have a closer look at who was inside it.

"Good heavens!" he exclaimed, "it's Monsieur de Voltaire!"

Late in the afternoon Voltaire's carriage rattled into the busy, cobbled streets of the capital. By a strange coincidence, he was on his way to the *Rue de Beaune,* to the house he had occupied as a young man, when it belonged to Madame de Bernières, and where he had composed part of the *Henriade.*

Apparently the trip had not affected him adversely. He was in rare spirits, and talked incessantly, bantering and laughing, and gesticulating as furiously as ever. He rested for only a few moments, after which he hurried off to visit his "guardian angel" d'Argental. The reunion of these lifelong friends, separated so many years, spurred their Gallic emotions. They wept and laughed and talked, seemingly all at once.

The news of Voltaire's presence electrified Paris. "The appearance of a phantom, a ghost, a prophet, or an apostle," a baron wrote in his diary, "could not have excited more surprise or admiration." Versailles alone remained unmoved by what had happened. "Monsieur de Voltaire?" remarked the sixteenth Louis when told of the poet's arrival. "Ah, yes!—he is in Paris, I believe; though not with my approval."

The days following his arrival Voltaire spent in his rooms, while visitors poured upon him without end. The first day some three hundred persons journeyed to the *Rue de Beaune.* He was overwhelmed with love and adulation. There were interviews with Diderot and d'Alembert. The French Academy sent a special delegation; so did the *Comédie Française.* Richelieu came to pay his respects, as did Gluck, Madame Dubarry, and the British ambassador. "All Parnassus was there," said Madame du Deffand, "from the mire to the summit." All day long the tireless old man displayed himself in night cap and flowing dressing gown. His lustre had not been dimmed by the years, and as the admirers thronged about him, he shone upon all of them with that graceful affability of which he was the master. It was easy to see that he was happy.

Among those who came to *Rue de Beaune* was Benjamin Franklin, then in Paris to seek the help of France in America's struggle for independence. Though the room was filled with Frenchmen, Voltaire addressed the American in English, only to be reminded by one of the guests that Franklin spoke excellent French. "I beg your pardon," Voltaire apologized. "I yielded for a moment to the vanity of showing that I can speak in the language of Franklin." Fully aware that all eyes were upon them, the two men played their parts, slowly and deliberately, like experienced actors in a drama. "If I were only forty years old," Voltaire exclaimed, "I should go and settle in your happy country." Whereupon Franklin presented his grandson, a youth of seventeen, for whom he asked the poet's blessing. With his ever-ready eye for the theatrical, Voltaire made the most of his opportunity. He placed his hand upon the boy's head, and with great solemnity he slowly uttered these words: "For God and Liberty."

It became evident before very long that Voltaire was wearing himself out. The constant excitement in which he found himself was too much for his frail physique. He was easily fatigued and upset. He was living, Doctor Tronchin cautioned him, on the capital of his strength instead of on the income—and he ordered the ailing man to bed.

No doubt Voltaire was in bad health. Yet within a few days he was miraculously well once more—well enough at any rate to give his attentions to *Irène*. Not only was he rewriting the drama, but he summoned the actors to his rooms, assigned them their parts, and began to rehearse them.

He received on the same day a letter from an Abbé Gaultier. The Abbé wrote that there were many persons who admired Voltaire, and that if the poet consented, he too desired that privilege. "Although," he continued, "I am the most unworthy of all ministers, I will say nothing unworthy of my ministry and nothing which could be unpleasant to you." He went on to say that if he dared not flatter himself that Voltaire would bestow such happiness on him, he would nonetheless remember him in the Holy Sacrifice of the Mass. "I shall pray the just and merciful God, with all the fervor of which I am capable, for the welfare of your immortal soul, which is perhaps soon to be judged for all its actions." It was, he concluded, his intention to render Voltaire the greatest of all services. "I may do so with the help of Him who chooses the weakest to confound those who are most mighty."

Voltaire replied graciously enough. "Your letter," he wrote, "appears to me that of an honest man. . . . I am eighty-four years old; I must soon appear before God, Maker of all the Worlds. If you have something to tell me, I shall think it a duty and an honor to receive your visit."

Not long afterward the Abbé came. He was cordially received. Had he come of his own accord, Voltaire desired to know, or had he perhaps been sent by the Archbishop? The Abbé assured the old philosopher that he had come wholly on his own initiative; that he had come, indeed, to offer himself as Voltaire's confessor. Somewhat astonished, Voltaire replied that he loved God; whereupon the priest retorted that it would be necessary for him to give proof of that love.

"What do you think of the Abbé, sir?" Wagnière asked his master after Gaultier had left.

"He is a good-natured old imbecile," the grinning Voltaire replied.

A few days later Voltaire's health collapsed completely. His legs had swollen enormously; and he was seized by frequent coughing spasms, accompanied by much spitting of blood. When Doctor Tronchin came, he promptly ordered Voltaire to bed, and to make sure that the irrepressible old man would stay there, he hired a nurse to watch him.

Voltaire's illness was obviously very serious—so serious, indeed, that he began to prepare himself for the approaching end. He had no fear of death. There was no pain to death; it was just like falling asleep—of that he felt certain. Nor did the thought of annihilation disturb him. What he dreaded was not death, but the paraphernalia of death—"the barbarity of extreme unction and the cruelty of people in warning us that it is all over." On the other hand, he was haunted by the horror that he might suffer the fate of Adrienne Lecouvreur, that at the very end the Church might yet achieve a ghastly triumph, and cast his mortal remains in some obscure spot. He wanted to die "like a philosopher"; yet he also desired "to leave in good taste," at least in the form of the religion of his birth.

Shortly after being stricken Voltaire wrote a statement which he gave to Gaultier and which said that he wished to "die in the Catholic religion in which he was born, hoping that God would design to pardon all his faults, and that if he had ever offended the Church and God, he asked its pardon." Soon afterward he made another declaration which he gave to Wagnière, and which read: "I die admiring God, loving my friends, not hating my enemies, and detesting superstition."

Neither declaration was immediately necessary. For as the days went by the ailing man showed a decided improvement. Before long his iron determination triumphed over the infirmities of his body; and soon he was sitting up in bed, working on *Irène* and dictating to Wagnière as usual. As for the statement he had signed for Abbé Gaultier, the poet assured his secretary that it was nothing. It was merely a declaration of principle; it was not an orthodox confession. "It is necessary," he said, "for a man to die in the religion of his fathers. If I lived upon the banks of the Ganges, I should wish to die with a cow's tail in my hand." For the time being, Voltaire appeared to be out of danger; yet on one point Doctor Tronchin was insistent: the poet was not, under any circumstances, to attend the first performance of *Irène*.

The premiere of *Irène* was on the 14th of March. The play itself was insignificant. Set in the ancient palace of Constantine in the reign of the Emperor Nicephore, it concerned itself with a conspiracy to destroy the ruler. His wife Irène was in love with Prince Alexis, who had been away waging a brilliant campaign against the enemy.

On his return the conquering prince staged a *coup d'état* in which the Emperor was murdered. Upon ascending the throne Alexis proposed marriage to the slain man's widow. Horrified by the thought of marrying the blood-stained Alexis, Irène fled to her father, the pontiff of the country. After five acts in which the unfortunate woman found herself torn between love and conscience, she ended her agony by committing suicide.

That the play was one of Voltaire's worst apparently made little difference to the audience. It had come determined to applaud—and applaud it did. Voltaire had made arrangements to be kept informed of the play's progress. Accordingly, after each act a messenger hurried to the *Rue de Beaune* to report that all was well. When the performance was over, the poet's friends rushed to his bedside to tell him that the play had been a tremendous, a magnificent success; that not a single eye was dry; that Marie Antoinette had been there—but not her husband—and that the queen had been observed writing down the lines that pleased her. "What you say consoles me," the invalid remarked, "but does not cure me."

Nevertheless, *Irène's* success was an excellent tonic, and before long the poet left his bed. "His recent indisposition," the *Journal de Paris* reported, "has left no after-effects." Apparently it had not, for within a week of *Irène's* triumph, the poet felt well enough to go visiting.

Sitting in his carriage Voltaire cut a conspicuous figure. Fashions had changed greatly since he had left Paris, and he had made no effort to keep abreast of the latest styles. A huge wig towered over him like an immense bird's nest, while on top of it was perched, precariously balanced, a square red cap. His face, barely visible underneath the cascading curls, peered forth pallidly, like a waxen mask. He wore a red coat, and though it was lined with sable, he shivered with cold. In his hand he held a cane whose head was embellished by a genuine crow's beak, and which Voltaire had always deemed the height of sartorial refinement.

It was only natural, now that his health was better, that Voltaire should long to see *Irène*. Doctor Tronchin had been severe in this matter, for he feared that the excitement of attending a play would be too much for the patient. To soften the physician's hard resistance, Voltaire had employed all his wiles. He had used the most hyperbolic compliments; he had been fiercely remonstant; yet in the end Doctor Tronchin was unmoved. Then one day the physician announced that the danger was past and that Voltaire might safely venture to the theatre.

He made up his mind to see *Irène* the following Monday, the 30th of March. In the afternoon he planned to attend a special meeting of the Academy, after which he would proceed leisurely to the *Comédie*. When he stepped forth from his house into the *Rue de Beaune*, the street was filled with a crowd of cheering people, who, having recognized his carriage of brilliant blue and silver stars drawn up at the curb, had waited for the great man to appear. The news that Voltaire was to be about had spread swiftly, and as his carriage moved through the streets, the multitudes gathered on both sides to acclaim him. As he entered the courtyard of the Louvre, where the Academy held its sessions, some two thousand persons hailed him, shouting, "Vive Voltaire! Vive Monsieur de Voltaire!" and clapping their hands.

The cheers that echoed and reechoed through the streets

of Paris were all for the same man—Voltaire. But that man was not just one man: he was several men in one. Some cheered him as France's greatest living dramatist and the author of the *Henriade;* others shouted because he was France's greatest wit, the creator of rollicking romances and the unforgettable *Candide;* but to nearly everyone he was the man of justice, the militant, indefatigable, irrepressible defender of Calas, Sirven, and others.

The Academy greeted him in the great hall, an honor never accorded to anyone. The clerical members had stayed away—the last flicker of an expiring cause. Voltaire was conducted to the President's Chair and there he was unanimously elected to that office. D'Alembert then proceeded to read a discourse on the poet Boileau, but which was more in the nature of a eulogium of Voltaire. "The poetry of Boileau," declared the speaker, "was like the statue of the Gladiator, correct, strong, nervous; while that of Voltaire was like Apollo Belvedere, easy, graceful, and always noble." In the tumult of his delight, it was not easy for the poet to remain calm, and his eyes filled with tears. When he rose, his fellow members rose as a body, and accompanied him to the great hall where they had received him.

Meanwhile the crowd in the streets had become even denser. People were leaning out of windows; they had climbed upon step ladders and scaffolds; they were standing on roof tops, peering perilously over the edge into the streets below, and as Voltaire passed they cheered frantically.

At the theatre the awaiting throng had become a seething mob. When the carriage came to a stop, excited people swarmed over it, climbing on the wheels, standing on any part that offered a foothold, thrusting their hands through the windows in the hope that they might touch their idol. People had to clear a path for the aged man as he entered the theatre.

Once inside, he sought refuge in one of the boxes. But the spectators soon caught sight of him, and at once the place was in turmoil. "To the front!" came the cry. "Come to the front!" There was no use in trying to hide—the crowd was too insistent. When Voltaire showed himself at the front of the box, the outburst was tremendous. "The crown!" someone shouted, "the crown!" An actor, Brizard, now stepped toward Voltaire and placed a laurel wreath upon his head. "Ah," the old man cried, "would you have me die with all this glory?" Then, taking the wreath from his head, he placed it upon the young Marquise de Villette, who was standing beside him. To this the house objected. Yet, when the Marquise sought to return the laurel, Voltaire resisted. Whereupon the Prince of Beauvais stepped forward and, with a manner that denoted that he meant to be obeyed, he put the wreath back on Voltaire.

When the play finally began, no one paid much attention to it. People were too intent upon watching the newly crowned king to give any heed to what was happening to *Irène*. No one seemed to listen; yet seldom was a play more furiously applauded. When the curtain descended at the end of the last act there was a tremendous outburst. The spectators rose and, facing the aged author, they stood for several minutes while they applauded him.

Meanwhile the curtain had risen once more, and on the stage there was a scene such as the French theatre had never witnessed. In the center of the stage stood a pedestal bearing the bust of Voltaire. Around it in a semi-circle the entire cast had ranged itself, bearing palms and garlands of laurel; while behind them stood the carpenters and stage-hands, the property man and the prompter—indeed, everyone who had had a hand in the production. Brizard, still in the monk's robes in which he had played his part, stepped forward and, to the sound of drums and trumpets, he placed his laurel garland upon the bust, after which the others followed his example. When there was no more room for all the garlands, they were slung over the bayonets of the stage guards, who formed an improvised triumphal arch.

Voltaire was deeply stirred. For a moment he sought to escape, but the Marquise de Villette drew him to the front of the box. There he stood, in silent awe and wonder, a witness to the greatest triumph of his long life, a glory which, even in his wildest fancies, he could never have imagined. As he stood there, dazed by the incredible grandeur of his acclamation, Madame Vestrix, who had played *Irène*, came forward and, in a voice renowned for its loveliness, she read an ode addressed to Voltaire. The curtain fell, and rose again for a performance of one of Voltaire's comedies.

The diary-keeper, Grimm, who had been present at the scene of Voltaire's triumph, was careful to record his impressions. "The moment," he wrote, "when M. de Voltaire left the theatre seemed even more touching than that of his arrival. . . . All the women stood waiting for him, both in the corridors and upon the staircase; they bore him along, as it were, in their arms, and it is thus he arrived at the steps of his coach. He was kept back, as long as possible, at the doors of the *Comédie*. The people cried out: 'Torches, torches! Let us have a good look at him!' Once he was in his coach, the crowd pressed all around him; people got on the step and clung to the doors of the coach in order to kiss his hands. Some of the common people began to shout: 'He is the one who wrote *Oedipus, Mérope, Zaire;* he is the one who has sung of our king,' etc. They begged the coachman to walk his horses, so that they might follow him, and a great number of persons accompanied him thus, crying out, 'Vive Voltaire!' as far as the Port-Royal."

Back in the *Rue de Beaune,* the author of *Irène* burst into tears. It had been too much. "If I had only known the people would commit such follies," he cried, "I would never have gone to the *Comédie.*" The people meant well, but their kindness was too much; they would stifle him under roses, he told Wagnière. "You do not know the French," he added. "They would have done the same for Jean-Jacques." "The Parisians," he observed, "pass their time in hissing and clapping—in putting up statues and pulling them down again."

As the days slipped by, Voltaire's thoughts turned more and more to Ferney. Now that he had gratified all the desires which had lured him to Paris, he was anxious to return to his colonists and his beloved retreat in the shadow of the Alps. But when he broached the subject to Madame Denis, she objected. She had no wish to leave the gay capital; and certainly she did not care to return to the rustic solitude of Ferney. What was more, she felt certain, she told her uncle, that his delicate health would never stand the strain of the long journey.

It was evident, however, that Paris was no place for Voltaire. "You have too much intelligence," Doctor Tronchin told him, "not to realize that a tree eighty-four years old is not transplanted unless it is desired to kill it." The physician urged the old man to return to Ferney before it might be too late. "I would give a hundred louis to see you back at Ferney. Go in a week."

"Am I able to travel?" asked the anxious Voltaire.

"I will stake my head on it," Tronchin reassured him.

Nevertheless, the physician's warning failed to impress Madame Denis. Though she professed to love her uncle—and perhaps in her selfish way she did—she could not bring herself to the point of leaving Paris. By way of compromise, she tried to persuade her uncle to purchase a house in the city's outskirts, where he might have his cherished garden, and yet be close to the capital. When this scheme fell through, she finally talked him into buying a house that was being built in the *Rue de Richelieu*. "Ah, my friend," he said disconsolately to his secretary, "I have just bought a house, and I have acquired only my tomb!"

Meanwhile, he resumed what had become a detested routine. He was overwhelmed by visitors and invitations. Wherever he went people gathered to acclaim him. Yet the glitter of fame no longer seemed attractive; he was surfeited with praise and acclamation; he was old; and he was weary. All his feelings were concentrated in one supreme desire: he must return to Ferney.

"It is absolutely necessary that I return," he insisted.

"Why do you have to return?" Madame Denis asked.

"Because I love the country," he burst out. "Because it keeps me alive—you stay here and amuse yourself, you who hate the country. But let me go."

Madame Denis glanced at her uncle. "What makes you think I hate the country, uncle?" she continued.

"My experience," he retorted, and would say no more.

Against the obstinacy of his niece Voltaire could do little. For a time he sought solace, as he had always done before, in work. He began a tragedy; he wrote letters; and he made plans for the compilation of an immense, up-to-date dictionary of the French language, to be edited and written by members of the Academy, and to which he himself would contribute the letter A.

In May he was suddenly stricken by a fainting spell, followed by nausea and intense pains. The illness seemed to be similar to the previous one. When the suffering grew worse, he took an opium preparation which Richelieu had recommended. The drug brought relief and he resumed his work—only to be stricken again. Finally, as his suffering became acute, he summoned Doctor Tronchin. "The patient of the *Rue de Beaune*," he wrote, "has suffered all night, and still suffers, from a violent convulsive cough. He has spat blood three times. He begs pardon for giving so much trouble over a mere carcass."

There was little the doctor could do. One look at the ailing man sufficed—the capital of his health was almost spent. During the days that followed all Paris kept its eyes on the *Rue de Beaune*. Could it be, people wondered, could it really be that Voltaire would die?

The debilitating effect of the opium passed, but it left the patient with a repugnance for food. He would not even take broth; and thus his feebleness increased, while death slowly approached.

The Abbé Gaultier had not forgotten his promise to Voltaire that he would "render him the greatest of all services." He appeared daily at the stricken man's bedside, beseeching him to recant and confess—but in vain. When it became evident that death was imminent, the Abbé brought de Terse, the curate of Voltaire's parish, St. Sulpice. "Monsieur de Voltaire," de Terse said, as he leaned over the dying man, "you have reached the end of your life. Do you acknowledge the divinity of Jesus Christ?" At this Voltaire wearily turned his back. "Let me die in peace," he whispered faintly. Exasperated, de Terse shook his head. Then, turning to the hushed people standing about him, "You see, he has lost his senses!" And the two priests departed.

Death came within a few hours. When it came it came mercifully, just as he had always said it would, without pain, without remorse, without fear. He died at eleven o'clock at night on the 30th of May, 1778.

Yet even though he was dead the poor man's struggle against his foes was not ended. The Archbishop of Paris refused burial in consecrated ground. The refusal was no surprise. It had haunted the poet throughout his life. His friends had anticipated it too. Accordingly they acted with promptitude. Almost immediately after Voltaire's death, his body was hastily embalmed and taken to the Abbey of Scellières in the parish of the Abbé Mignot, a relative of Voltaire. Here in the parish churchyard Voltaire was buried. The Archbishop's order had come too late.

Eleven years after Voltaire's death the people of France revolted against their rulers. The seeds which Voltaire had planted—liberty, justice, tolerance—had borne fruit. To advance the noble cause many others had helped; yet for the last twenty years of his life Voltaire had been the acknowledged leader. The Old Regime which he had attacked so remorselessly in the "English Letters" and in his tracts and pamphlets, which he had castigated with bril-

liant ridicule in *Candide* and "The Philosophical Dictionary," and hosts of dialogues and romances—that regime was
tottering at last. The example he had set in his long
struggle to obtain justice for the innocent Calas was not
in vain; nor were the ideals which had inspired the humanitarianism and philanthropy at Ferney. He understood
his countrymen perhaps better than they understood themselves. "They are nearly always too late in achieving their
aim," he once had said, "but still they do it in the end."

In 1791, in the midst of the French Revolution, the
body of Voltaire was brought to the Pantheon. Behind his
coffin marched one hundred thousand men and women in
solemn procession. His sarcophagus contained the epitaph:

"He avenged Calas, La Barre, Sirvens, and Montbailli.
Poet, philosopher, historian, he gave great impetus to the
human mind: he prepared us to become free."

BIBLIOGRAPHY

In this bibliography the author has relied largely on primary sources for his information. Among the newer materials referred to were the "Boswell Papers," published under the auspices of Colonel Isham, and Voltaire's "English Notebook." The letters quoted throughout the book are translations from the original letters of Voltaire available in Paris. A great deal of information was derived from numerous private letters and documents to which the author had access in Geneva, Versaoix and Ferney. These were of significance for the light they threw on Voltaire's political, economic and social views in relation to his activity at Ferney.

Oeuvres de Voltaire. Ed. Moland, 1883. 52 Vols.

Voltaire's Works. Ed. Saint Hubert Guild. New York. 1903

G. *Desnoiresterres.* Voltaire et la Societe Francaise. Paris. 1867-76.

Longchamp et Wagnière. Memoires sur Voltaire. Paris, 1825.

Lettres de Mme. du Chatelet. Paris, 1882.

M. J. A. N. C. *de Condorcet.* Vie de Voltaire. Kehl, 1789.

Frederick the Great. Works. Berlin, 1846-57.

G. *Lanson. Voltaire.* Paris, 4th edition, 1922.

E. *Faguet. Le XVIII Siècle.* Paris, 1890.

R. *Aldington. Voltaire.* London, 1925.

G. *Brandes. Francois de Voltaire.* Copenhagen, 1916-17.

T. *Carlyle. Voltaire* (essay).

T. *Carlyle. Frederick-the-Great.* 1855-1865.

J. *Morley. Voltaire.* London, 1872.

J. *Parton. Life of Voltaire.* New York, 1885.

J. M. *Robertson. Voltaire.* London, 1922.

S. G. *Tallentyre. Voltaire.* London, 1903.

INDEX